Good design
for ease of revision

Subheads break the content into manageable units

Content informs you about the structure and composition of the English language

Key facts for the exam are given

Worked examples:
- help you interpret questions
- show you the answers the examiners expect
- teach you correct conventions

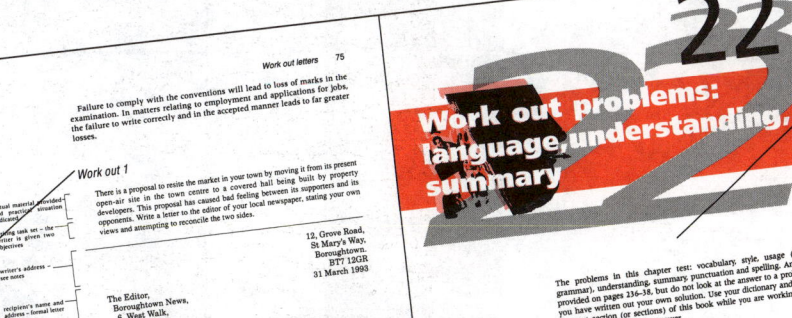

20 problems allow you to:
- *test* the knowledge you have gained
- *check* your solutions against the answers at the end of the book

Good design
for effective revision

1. Examinations and changes

Syllabus analysis Ensures you only do the topics you need – no more, no less

Start and completion column Keeps tabs on your progress – see at a glance which areas still need to be worked through

Self assessment For you to note how well you've done or areas which need to be revised again

Chapter breakdown Shows you in detail what is covered in the chapters

LEAG	MEG	SEG	NEAB	WJEC	NICCEA	Topic	Date attempted	Date completed	Self Assessment
✓	✓	✓	✓	✓	✓	Examinations and changes			
✓	✓	✓	✓	✓	✓	Coursework			
✓	✓	✓	✓	✓	✓	'Differentiation'			
✓	✓	✓	✓	✓	✓	An approach to the subject			
✓	✓	✓	✓	✓	✓	Speaking and listening			
✓	✓	✓	✓	✓	✓	Reading			
✓	✓	✓	✓	✓	✓	Ways and means			
✓	✓	✓	✓	✓	✓	Writing			
✓	✓	✓	✓	✓	✓	Practical writing			

Contents

Topic	
Introduction	xi
1 Examinations and changes	1
2 Coursework	6
3 Attainment targets	10
4 'Differentiation'	16
5 An approach to the subject	20
6 Speaking and listening	24
7 Reading	32
8 Ways and means	48
9 Writing	77
10 Practical writing	83
11 Editing, summary and redrafting	99
12 Directed writing	120
13 Expression	130
14 Personal writing	165
15 Using words	168
16 Misusing words	176
17 Correct grammar	184
18 Punctuation	202
19 Spelling	211
20 Presentation and handwriting	219
21 Reference material	225
22 Work out problems: language, understanding, summary	227
Answers	236
Index	239

Acknowledgements

The authors and publishers wish to thank the following for permission to use copyright material: Margaret Coles for 'How to face a live audience'. *Sunday Telegraph*, 10.5.92; The Economist for material from *The Economist*, 8.8.92; Elaine Greene Ltd on behalf of the author for an extract from *Death of a Salesman* by Arthur Miller, Penguin Books Ltd. Copyright © 1949 by Arthur Miller; David Higham Associates Ltd on behalf of the author for 'I Spy' from *The Short Stories* by Graham Greene, Heinemann; The Observer Ltd for 'Back to the lonely sea and the sky' by Frank Page, *BBC World Magazine*, July 1992, and 'An inventor making waves' by Bill Carter, *BBC World Magazine*, August 1992; Oxford University Press for 'My Wicked Uncle' from *Poems 1962–1978* by Derek Mahon, 1979. Copyright © Derek Mahon 1979; Solo Syndication Ltd for 'Why can't we sit still any more?' by Mary Killen, *Evening Standard*, 29.5.92; The Spectator for 'My century has a cleaner bottom' by Hardy Amies and picture by Jeffrey Morgan, *The Spectator*, 18.7.92; Times Newspapers Ltd for 'Death of the lad of letters' by Bernard Levin, *The Times*, 29.6.92. and '...moreover' by Philip Howard, *The Times*, 4.7.92.

Every effort has been made to trace all the copyright holders, but if any have been inadvertently overlooked the publishers will be pleased to make the necessary arrangement at the first opportunity.

First and second editions © S. H. Burton 1986, 1987
Third edition © S. H. Burton & J. A. Humphries 1993

All rights reserved. No reproduction, copy or transmission of this publication may be made without written permission.

No paragraph of this publication may be reproduced, copied or transmitted save with written permission or in accordance with the provisions of the Copyright, Designs and Patents Act 1988, or under the terms of any licence permitting limited copying issued by the Copyright Licensing Agency, 90 Tottenham Court Road, London W1P 9HE.

Any person who does any unauthorised act in relation to this publication may be liable to criminal prosecution and civil claims for damages.

First edition 1986
Second edition 1987
Third edition 1993

Published by
MACMILLAN PRESS LTD
Houndmills, Basingstoke, Hampshire RG21 6XS
and London
Companies and representatives
throughout the world

ISBN 0–333–64358–5

A catalogue record for this book is available from the British Library.

Printed in Hong Kong

10 9 8 7 6 5 4
04 03 02 01 00 99 98 97 96

S. H. Burton & J. A. Humphries

English GCSE Key Stage 4

MACMILLAN

What the exam boards want

Topic		LEAG	MEG	SEG	NEAB	WJEC	NICCEA
Speaking and listening							
6	Recount personal experiences	✓	✓	✓	✓	✓	✓
6	Discuss and exchange ideas	✓	✓	✓	✓	✓	✓
6	Inform and explain	✓	✓	✓	✓	✓	✓
6	Plan and present topics	✓	✓	✓	✓	✓	✓
6	Know how spoken communication varies	✓	✓	✓	✓	✓	✓
6	Complement reading and writing	✓	✓	✓	✓	✓	✓
Reading							
8	Read a range of literary texts	✓	✓	✓	✓	✓	✓
8	Read a range of non-literary texts	✓	✓	✓	✓	✓	✓
7,8	Show and explain preferences	✓	✓	✓	✓	✓	✓
7,8	Give an informed response	✓	✓	✓	✓	✓	✓
8,15	Show an awareness of devices used by writers	✓	✓	✓	✓	✓	✓
11	Demonstrate the ability to draw conclusions	✓	✓	✓	✓	✓	✓
21	Show ability to select and combine information	✓	✓	✓	✓	✓	✓
8	Read 20th and pre-20th century material	✓	✓	✓	✓	✓	✓
8	Read and appreciate some of Shakespeare's work	✓	✓	✓	✓	✓	✓
5	Note some of the changes as language has evolved	✓	✓	✓	✓	✓	✓
7	Keep a reading log or diary	✓	✓	✓	✓	✓	✓

Topic

		LEAG	MEG	SEG	NEAB	WJEC	NICCEA
Writing							
10,14	Convey experiences and impressions	✓	✓	✓	✓	✓	✓
11,12	Understand the order and presentation of facts	✓	✓	✓	✓	✓	✓
12,13,15,16	Show a sense of audience and the awareness of style	✓	✓	✓	✓	✓	✓
12,13,15,17	Appreciate how language is used in writing	✓	✓	✓	✓	✓	✓
15,16,17	Correct, edit, redraft and revise	✓	✓	✓	✓	✓	✓
12,13,14	Make use of different forms of writing – stories, reports, advertisements, letters, etc.	✓	✓	✓	✓	✓	✓
21	Research and information-retrieving	✓	✓	✓	✓	✓	✓
Presentation							
19	Spell correctly	✓	✓	✓	✓	✓	✓
19	Check and correct misspellings and other weaknesses	✓	✓	✓	✓	✓	✓
20	Write fluently and legibly	✓	✓	✓	✓	✓	✓
20	Present clear and attractively finished work	✓	✓	✓	✓	✓	✓

Revision
hints for passing

1. It's up to you. When it comes to passing examinations, your destiny is governed mainly by your own application to the tasks in hand. Obtain your syllabus and recent examination papers from your teacher or lecturer. Before you start, check the right way to get to your destination.

2. Panic is the quickest way to failure. If you can keep calm under pressure, then you are fulfilling one of the main examination requirements.

3. Controlled breathing aids concentration. Breathe slowly up the left nostril to the count of eight, hold for eight, breathe out through the right nostril counting eight. Then repeat the process in the other direction. Oxygen is released into the brain, a sense of calmness follows and revision – or examination performance – is improved.

4. Always read the instructions. It is as important to know the number of questions that you have to answer as it is to know at what time the examination is over.

5. Think before writing. Always have in mind both the ultimate matter concerning examination questions – 'What am I required to do?' – and the all-important response – 'To *answer* the question!'

6. Legibility of handwriting matters. Elegance, perfect lettering and neatness, of course, help. Clarity is vital.

7. Timing is also vital. Work out a 'budget' that involves the minutes that you intend to give each section of the examination paper. Remember that the first ten minutes that you spend on a question probably earn far more marks than the final ten.

8. 'Compulsion to closure' is a phrase used by salespeople who hope to complete a deal and make money. Have the same urgency of mind in wanting to complete your answer in an effective, tidy way.

9. Anonymity is an advantage. You are unknown to the examiner and he or she is not aware of how much or how little preparation you have done. You are known by what you write: you have a limited number of minutes to become recognised and to make an impression.

10. Try, above all, to *take pleasure* in completing a good examination paper and you will *give pleasure* to the person marking it. Those involved in marking often have to undertake their work when others are relaxing – on long summer evenings, for example. If you can provide the 'treat' of a clear, accurate and thoughtful examination script, then you, in turn, will be treated very well.

Exam Board Addresses

For syllabuses and past papers contact the Publications office at the following addresses:

Midland Examining Group (MEG)
c/o University of Cambridge Local Examinations Syndicate
1 Hills Road
CAMBRIDGE
CB1 2EU
Tel. 01223 553311

Southern Examining Group (SEG)
Publications Department
Stag Hill House
GUILDFORD
Surrey
GU2 5XJ
Tel. 01483 302302 (Direct line)

Northern Examinations and Assessment Board (NEAB)
12 Harter Street
MANCHESTER
M1 6HL
Tel. 0161 953 1170
(Also shop at the above address)

University of London Examinations and Assessment Council (ULEAC)
Stewart House
32 Russell Square
LONDON
WC1B 5DN
Tel. 0171 331 4000

Northern Ireland Council for the Curriculum, Examinations and Assessment (NICCEA)
Beechill House
42 Beechill Road
BELFAST
BT8 4RS
Tel. 01232 704666

Welsh Joint Education Committee (WJEC)
245 Western Avenue
Llandaff
CARDIFF
CF5 2YX

Scottish Examination Board (SEB) for full syllabuses
Ironmills Road
Dalkeith
Midlothian EH22 1LE
Tel. 0131 663 6601

or recent papers from the SEB's agent
Robert Gibson & Sons Ltd
17 Fitzroy Place
Glasgow G3 7SF
Tel. 0141 248 5674

Remember to check your syllabus number with your teacher!

How you will be graded

Your GCSE grades will be given on a scale from U (for Unclassified) through G – F – E – D – C – B – A to A* at the highest. For many purposes, such as further education requirements, job applications and advice about Advanced Level opportunities, the grades of C and above will be taken as indicating a degree of success in the subject.

The assessment will be based on your abilities in:

- speaking and listening
- reading
- writing
- presentation

The way in which your grades are calculated is quite complicated and depends on the assessing of the so-called 'levels' that you attain on the National Curriculum ten-level scale. It may help you to think of your attainment levels in terms of the initial letters of the grades that you are finally awarded, together with an appropriate word that sums up your achievement (or lack of it).

- Levels 1 & 2: U for Unable to cope with the demands of language
- Levels 3 & 4: G for Grasp of basics
- Level 5: F for Feeling for some features of language
- Level 6: E for Exercising a limited number of skills
- Level 7: D for Development of... C for Competence in many areas
- Level 8: B for Bonus of a full range of skills
- Level 9: A for Achievement of expertise
- Level 10: A* for Attainment of the exceptional brilliance of a star!

Introduction

The purpose of most books is to enable readers to learn more and to see aspects of life in different ways. Authors explore a subject and then invite an audience to share their thoughts. If pleasure is a by-product of this process, then that is a bonus for all concerned – reader, writer and publisher.

Work Out English attempts to do four things. Its primary function is to *inform* you about the structure and composition of the English language in general, and the demands of the authorities responsible for the GCSE Key Stage 4 examinations in particular.

Its second purpose is to *advise* you on how to approach examinations, and on the skills demanded in the composition of clear, effective writing. This book attempts to improve the ways in which you speak, listen and read as well as write, and to encourage an enlightened attitude towards the challenging matters involved in taking examinations.

Thirdly, this text *shows* you how to answer specific questions, read selected passages, and compose the sort of written material demanded by those who set examinations and who moderate coursework.

Finally, *Work Out English* endeavours to *promote success.* You are invited to take part in a series of activities that will strengthen your command of the language, give you confidence to approach the tasks of communication, and help you strive towards success in those areas of life where accuracy and the inventive use of words matter.

We hope that with this book you will be able to *work out* what hitherto may have puzzled you about the seemingly elaborate details of language and of examination requirements. We hope also that you will *work out* – in the sense of 'exercise' – your mind, using some of the techniques explained here. May the thoughts and actions that derive from your work with this book ensure that your own speaking and listening, and reading and writing, all *work out* with increasing success.

S. H. Burton and J. A. Humphries

Examinations and changes

LEAG	MEG	SEG	NEAB	WJEC	NICCEA	Topic	Date attempted	Date completed	Self Assessment
✓	✓	✓	✓	✓	✓	**Examinations and changes**			
✓	✓	✓	✓	✓	✓	**Coursework**			
✓	✓	✓	✓	✓	✓	**'Differentiation'**			
✓	✓	✓	✓	✓	✓	**An approach to the subject**			
✓	✓	✓	✓	✓	✓	**Speaking and listening**			
✓	✓	✓	✓	✓	✓	**Reading**			
✓	✓	✓	✓	✓	✓	**Ways and means**			
✓	✓	✓	✓	✓	✓	**Writing**			
✓	✓	✓	✓	✓	✓	**Practical writing**			

1.1 The growth of the 'examinations industry'

There have been more changes in the 20th century than in all the previous centuries put together. Men and women have explored the most distant reaches of the Earth; inventions have harnessed natural forces to enable people to move quickly and efficiently by land, sea and air; innovations have helped create conditions for longer life; communications have improved so that people are kept in instant contact with one another by television, radio and electronic devices of many sorts. Despite two world wars, countless conflicts and much misuse of resources, at least the *potential* for the successful management of energy and its applications is being realised.

Among the transformations that have taken place is the growth of educational facilities. At the beginning of this century, most children left school as their teenage years were starting. Now the pattern involves many more years of schooling and attendance at colleges. If the American pattern is followed, then soon few people will be in full-time employment before their early 20s. That is a ten-year difference that has come about within one hundred years.

Each new generation is being taught for a little longer and by more individuals than ever before. The authorities have felt the need to check on the progress that is being made and, consequently, many types and series of tests and examinations have been introduced in order to monitor the work, to assess the skills of students and teachers, and to gauge the quality of ideas that are being received and generated. A whole 'examinations industry' has grown up. Depressions and recessions come and go, but here is an industry that seems to weather economic storms and continue to expand.

At one time, in the 19th century, school inspectors would test the reading skills of pupils and then calculate the pay of the teachers accordingly. This scheme was called 'payment by results', but it ran into some difficulties. So much was at stake for teachers that their horizons became somewhat restricted. The classroom became a place where the protection of salaries sometimes mattered more than intellectual stimulus and advancement.

Older generations recall the School Leaving Certificates and Matriculation. Failure in one key subject meant that *everything* had to be repeated. The passing of individual subjects to fulfil specific requirements became the accepted pattern with the General Certificate of Education and the Certificate of Secondary Education. These were replaced in the late 1980s by the General Certificate of Secondary Education in which candidates' coursework became a more important element. As far as English language was concerned it became in many cases the all-important element, for a considerable number of schools adopted assessment by 100 per cent coursework.

1.2 The National Curriculum and Key Stage 4

The demands of the National Curriculum meant another significant change. Certain specific attainments in communicating skills were set and the so-called Key Stage 4, the final section of the Curriculum, was grafted onto the GCSE examinations. The requirements for English have to be tested by a series of examinations taken at the end of the course, usually at the end of the fifth year in secondary schools, or at any time for mature students.

So there has been a marked alteration in the ways in which the speaking and writing of the English language are to be assessed. Further methods of testing will undoubtedly evolve, because it is the nature of this process to observe, experiment, consider, select and amend the ways and means of judging. However, the year 1994 may become one of those dates that lingers in people's minds as marking a 'turning point'. The introduction of the GCSE Key Stage 4 may have heralded a long period of examination stability.

1.3 'Only connect ...'

It is interesting to note how certain years have particular implications, and are therefore remembered: 1944 for the last major Education Act, for example; 1945 for the end of the Second World War; '47 for a bitterly cold British winter and '76 for remarkably hot summer; '53 for the beginning of a long reign by the monarch and '79 for an incoming government that won successive General Election victories; '87 for the simultaneous crash of the Stock Market and damage caused by a hurricane; and '92 as the year in which, with the introduction of the European single market, we edged closer to the countries of continental Europe. All in all we live in changing times; only gradually do we become aware of the constants as well as those features in a state of flux.

The famous English author, E. M. Forster, wrote on the title page of his novel, *Howard's End*, the words 'Only connect ... . It is the purpose of this book to help you make connections between your ideas and the ways in which you use words. It should help you to come to terms with the steadying factors in the shifting movements of expression, meanings and style. If you can see how ideas can be brought to life and then presented effectively, then you will have succeeded in overcoming one of the great obstacles to understanding – the lack of perception or insight.

The system by which a candidate's performance could be judged totally on 100 per cent coursework set within the school has ended. This approach had many similarities with the American methods whereby individual schools have the power to 'graduate' their pupils. Although the performances of students in the United States are monitored, local inconsistencies can and have occurred. Two New Jersey parents once took the local Board of Education to court because they claimed that their

16-year-old son had been passed as proficient in English by his school, but was allegedly unable to read his own graduation certificate!

So now all candidates in the United Kingdom will have to take an external examination and sit two test papers that will count for 60 per cent of the marks awarded. It has been arranged by the various examination boards that these papers be set on the same days. Consequently the hundreds and thousands of candidates are taking part in the same type of mass-response that occurs when a popular event is shown on the television – the vast, simultaneous reaction to a shared stimulus. It may not arouse the same interest as a Royal Wedding or the excitement of a World Cup match or Olympic race, but there is certainly the similar involvement of many people in all parts of the country.

1.4 Examinations test more than knowledge

Examinations are a part of our way of life. In their academic form they feature for anything up to twenty years of our 'growing up' period – from the first National Curriculum tests for 7-year-olds to the last professional examinations taken by people well into the early stages of their careers. They measure the things that we know, of course, as well as our abilities to survive the pressures of being tested. Consider for a moment how we have to react to the various stimuli of the examination papers:

- to think spontaneously – or, as we say idiomatically, 'on our feet';
- to think under controlled conditions at a desk and table (on our seat!);
- to get our timing right;
- to be prepared for a variety of topics;
- to generate, plan and organise relevant ideas;
- to write efficiently;
- to check in order to edit – to amend or correct;
- to strive to finish the tasks that are set.

'Terminal' can be an ominous word suggesting the end of something, perhaps with a painful association. Likewise, the word 'examination' may not conjure up something mentally or physically pleasurable. The combination of the two – 'terminal examination' – is enough to cause gloom in the sunniest of dispositions. However, try to think of it as being linked with the word 'terminus', which often marks the end of a journey or an important junction during travelling. The successful passage through a terminus brings the traveller into a new environment and provides different opportunities. The same can be applied to the successful passing of an examination.

Much that is done in preparation for an examination or during the actual time of testing depends upon having a certain attitude of mind. Being in the right frame of mind helps. Indeed, being able to structure ideas in a particular way to act to your advantage is a great asset. This has been termed the knack of being able 'to re-frame the picture'.

1.5 'Re-framing the picture'

It may be helpful to re-frame your picture of examinations in the following way. We are all required both to examine and to be examined as a part of everyday life. This may be no more than observing things, eyeing a situation, watching other people. It may be a little more structured, as with the art of shopping for goods by comparing qualities and prices before purchase. On occasions it may involve the written word, as when being formally questioned as part of an investigation or survey. At times it may mean scrutinising something – a piece of work, an example of craftsmanship, a car or maybe a house. Then there are the very formal occasions: the medical test when we are the object of attention, or the driving test when the behaviour of the vehicle reflects our own skills – or the lack of them! Within this framework of constant surveillance comes the academic or professional examination. It's just part of the process that human societies have developed to ensure and then maintain standards.

Whether we approve or not, the societies in which most of us live expect certain standards from the majority of people. Achievements in literacy, for example, are expected, although not demanded as a condition of being considered as a citizen with full rights. Some standards of quality are determined by the 'marketplace' and by customers' reactions; others are covered by legal regulations. The soundness of the money in our pockets, the goods and services that we purchase, and the safety of the buildings that we inhabit are all examined by somebody with important technical qualifications. Examinations at school, college and workplace introduce us to being part of an advanced human civilisation, which has its faults, but which strives to render some constant standards in a changing world.

Coursework 2

LEAG	MEG	SEG	NEAB	WJEC	NICCEA	Topic	Date attempted	Date completed	Self Assessment
✓	✓	✓	✓	✓	✓	Examinations and changes			
✓	✓	✓	✓	✓	✓	Coursework			
✓	✓	✓	✓	✓	✓	'Differentiation'			
✓	✓	✓	✓	✓	✓	An approach to the subject			
✓	✓	✓	✓	✓	✓	Speaking and listening			
✓	✓	✓	✓	✓	✓	Reading			
✓	✓	✓	✓	✓	✓	Ways and means			
✓	✓	✓	✓	✓	✓	Writing			
✓	✓	✓	✓	✓	✓	Practical writing			

2.1 Individual responses

Most of the marks awarded for the English Language examination depend upon performance in the terminal examinations. Yet there remains a significant role played by **coursework** assessment, in which a 40 per cent allocation of marks can be given. So it is well worth putting considerable efforts into this part of the activity.

Coursework is the element of the subject that puts strong emphasis on the candidate's individual responses, application to work, and abilities to complete a number of topics. By now individual schools will have developed their own programmes and methods and the examination boards continue to produce suggested material. This section of the GCSE examination gives the opportunity for candidates to develop a style and approach of their own that is not subject to two of the inhibiting factors of normal examining. One concerns time; the other preparation.

Normally in examinations the relentless passage of time is even more obvious than in the rest of life. There is little time for reflection and less for developing an interesting theme. Questions have to be answered; the examiner has to be satisfied. With coursework it is possible to devote considerable periods of time to a topic and to be able to dwell on aspects of the work. The pressures are not so stark.

A weakness of most examination systems is that much time is spent by candidates preparing for topics that are not tested in the actual papers. This may be inevitable, but there is something inherently wasteful in days of preparation leading either to limited or to no opportunities for expression. With coursework the research that is done has the advantage of being relevant. Resourcefulness in finding out about various features has a direct reward, not just a possible advantage.

2.2 The requirements

There are some variations within the examination boards' approaches, but the framework has been set by the National Curriculum's so-called **attainment targets**, which are considered in the next section. Candidates are asked to respond to a series of guidelines and the centres at which they study are expected to devise tasks that will fully integrate reading and writing with speaking and listening.

The instructions given to the centres and schools where candidates are prepared for the examination usually stress that towards the end of the course a selection of work should have been gathered into the 'written coursework folder' and be ready for the moderator to consider. The emphasis of the material included could profitably be on the following:

1 *Personal writing* This may be in the form of imaginative fiction, perhaps including description or narration, or drawn from actual experience in the form of biography or autobiography.

2 *Response to literature* This may cover more than one period and should refer to complete works of literature. Candidates for the higher levels should study some pre-20th century material, including the writing of Shakespeare and Dickens.

Within these categories is an enormous range of possibilities. The aim of the best written coursework should be to display a personal commitment to the writing and a response to the literature read. It's these qualities that are less likely to be fully demonstrated in a written examination.

In addition the coursework selection should reveal the following skills, which are difficult to assess fully within the routines of examinations:

3 *Research and information-retrieval skills* These are the skills of using a range of literary, non-literary and information texts. The coursework should involve finding and using relevant reference material from a number of sources.

4 *Drafting, redrafting, revising and proof-reading skills* (on paper, word-processor or computer screen) Here the aim is to show that the search for accurate meaning and clarity exploits the ability to make constructive criticism and consequent amendments.

5 *Knowledge about language* This should be displayed as part of the work on the literary texts, although there could be scope for an additional topic that considers such features as the relationship between spoken and written English, bilingual matters, or the historical development of language (including local place- and family-names).

Some assessment of reading skills should be made through speaking and listening activities as well as by written work. Teachers and tutors will have to keep records of the types of activity undertaken and of performances noted.

2.3 What counts in coursework

The variety of approaches to coursework is limitless, but it could be useful to note that within the many permutations are certain common factors. These are:

1 Application of time, energy and imagination is required ... and is immediately recognised by those assessing the coursework.

2 Like it or not, you will become personally involved with the work expected of you.

3 Craftsmanship is the end-product; accuracy, relevance and style are the features that will be noted.

4 The various topics will have to be completed and so the business involving 'compulsion to closure' (see page ii) will play its part.

5 You are not anonymous, but known about by your teachers and tutors.

6 The coursework will reflect the relationship that you have with your

school or college as well as indicate something of the sort of person that you are. The spirit of endeavour can be detected quickly and will be well received.

7 'Self-improvement' was a favourite concept of Victorian times. It helped many people realise their opportunities and make a conscious decision to try to improve their natural talents. The French psychologist, Émile Coué, attempted to create a formula to encourage striving towards an improved state of skill and awareness – 'Every day, in every way, I am getting better and better.' His words could well apply to the driving motives that we need to perfect our application to coursework.

8 Above all, the time and opportunities offered by the range and flexibility of coursework allow us to master situations – in this case, a substantial minority of the marks available in the English Language paper.

Attainment targets 3

LEAG	MEG	SEG	NEAB	WJEC	NICCEA	Topic	Date attempted	Date completed	Self Assessment
✓	✓	✓	✓	✓	✓	**Examinations and changes**			
✓	✓	✓	✓	✓	✓	**Coursework**			
✓	✓	✓	✓	✓	✓	**'Differentiation'**			
✓	✓	✓	✓	✓	✓	**An approach to the subject**			
✓	✓	✓	✓	✓	✓	**Speaking and listening**			
✓	✓	✓	✓	✓	✓	**Reading**			
✓	✓	✓	✓	✓	✓	**Ways and means**			
✓	✓	✓	✓	✓	✓	**Writing**			
✓	✓	✓	✓	✓	✓	**Practical writing**			

The Education Reform Act 1988 provided for the establishment of a National Curriculum for core and other foundation subjects. English, of course, is a core subject on which a great deal depends. Its significance is so vital that, in many ways, it goes without saying! This expression – 'it goes without saying' – is in this case a paradox, because so much of the importance of the language depends precisely upon being able 'to say': to express yourself in words, whether spoken or written. Those who have drawn up the Curriculum have placed great emphasis on the attributes of speaking and listening, reading and writing. Their aim is to persuade and encourage us to set high standards in which full communication takes place and in which standards of presentation, handwriting and spelling assume important roles.

3.1 Speaking and listening

The first action performed by human beings when born is to cry out. The intake of breath starts a process that, all being well, will continue for scores of years. Sounds are then made continually. As we breathe we create noises, however quiet they may be on occasions. Parents listen attentively to the breathing patterns of babies, begin to interpret the apparently meaningless noises made, learn to distinguish between cries of pain, frustration, hunger and anticipation. In short, **communication** takes place.

Early sounds soon become first meaningful words. Strings of words are formed into understandable patterns. Speech rhythms develop and within five years much material has been learnt. The wonder is that it does not involve hard work, but simply a subconscious learning process. 'The child,' as Caldwell Cook, an American psychologist, once observed, 'is the true amateur.' He or she responds without considering the expenditure of time, energy or other people's efforts. Most humans soon realise that their relationships depend upon reacting to one another. The functions of speech and the abilities to listen provoke a powerful interplay between people that gives rise to all manner of emotions, entertainment and information.

The National Curriculum specifies that certain targets involving speaking and listening should be attained. It is obviously worthwhile looking closely at these requirements, but it should borne in mind that these are everyday activities that millions of people undertake without 'special' training. Candidates must demonstrate in conversation, discussion and writing that they can:

- recount personal experiences, views and feelings;
- share and exchange views and ideas;
- use language to inform and explain;
- plan and take part in group presentations;
- show an awareness of how spoken communication varies according to situation, purpose and audience.

Think for a moment about the nature of speech between people. It takes place everyday, everywhere; in homes, streets, places of work and recreation; on buses, trains and in cars; on television and radio; and is widely reported in newspapers, magazines and books. Speaking and listening is part of the very air that we breathe. So we must not be in awe of this part of the attainment targets.

The examining boards want candidates to be given many opportunities to meet the objectives by undertaking a wide range of activities. These might include giving instructions, undertaking problem-solving activities or group presentations, and engaging in debates and argument. There should be encouragement to reflect on language in all its forms, and to discuss one's own language use and that of others in relation to particular purposes and audiences.

These certainly sound rather formal. Yet just create in your mind a scene in any busy main street. People going about their day-to-day business will be engaging, quite spontaneously, in these activities. What is being said will preoccupy those who are buying, selling, explaining, finding things out or working out the best ways of doing things, In the cafés, bars, rest areas and public parks there will be time for reflection on what has been said and done.

An area of some interest concerns the importance of spoken **Standard English** and its use in appropriate situations. Candidates are asked to discuss matters relating to these topics. This can cause uncertainty because there are so many local varieties of spoken English. It has been calculated that there are 41 distinct **dialects** (regional forms of language) and numerous **accents** (vocal qualities found in a locality) in the United Kingdom alone. **Received Pronunciation (RP)** is the way in which the language is pronounced in official circles, traditionally the pronunciation used by radio and television announcers, on formal occasions, or at church and civic events. RP is associated with London and the cultural history of the triangle of land that links the capital with Oxford and Cambridge, the traditional centres of learning: it reflects the dominant social and economic role played by south-east England in the life of the British Isles. Nowadays, though, the wealth of other accents is being explored and enjoyed in the media and elsewhere. There is no longer any pressure on educated people to speak using RP, but English Language candidates should be aware of the significance of accents and dialects.

3.2 Reading

The second part of the attainment targets involves reading. It is worth remembering that the literacy rates are very high in Britain, as they are in most countries of the West. As many as 98 per cent of the population can read and write, but here it's the *effectiveness* of the skill that counts. Some people can manage to understand basic meanings, while others are able to perceive the much wider implications that can be conveyed by a passage. Success in this area depends partly on practice, and there are many people whose lives and jobs do not demand that they read either widely or deeply. It is quite easy to forget how to read effectively, so it's just as well that English Language examinations are taken close to the time when candidates are attending school or college!

Candidates must demonstrate in conversation, discussion and writing that they can:

- read a wide range of texts (including fiction, poetry, non-fiction and drama), accurately and with confidence;
- respond to literature;
- appreciate the characteristics of non-literary and media texts and evaluate the effectiveness of their use;
- select, retrieve, evaluate and combine information from a range of reference materials and texts;
- understand how writers make use of language and how language changes.

Think again about the implications of these skills for everyday life. Although these requirements feature in classroom work, they are by no means exclusive to schools and colleges. The television and radio services provide endless material based upon literary work; newsagents have an ever-changing stock of well-produced papers and magazines; libraries contain numerous works of reference. After all, we are surrounded by a constantly changing array of words in the advertisements, newspapers and information presented to us. We know how words can arouse as well as bore us; how they can cause awareness and mystery; how they can pass by unnoticed for years on end.

Some discussion has centred on the 'difficulties' presented by the requirement that Shakespeare and other pre-20th century authors be studied as part of the course. Three things should be remembered here. One is that this is only a part of the course; another is that writers such as Shakespeare and Dickens had considerable popular appeal in their time; a third is that the dictates of the opinion-formers of one era should not discourage the young of their own and succeeding generations from studying the classics. These are books that have stood the test of time and of people's judgements for perhaps hundreds of years.

There is really no need to justify the inclusion of some of the great English writers as part of an English Language examination. Bernard Levin, the columnist in *The Times*, felt particularly strongly on this issue when the government indicated that 14-year-olds would be tested on their knowledge of the classics and opposition to the scheme appeared. His remarks here are meant to be strong and persuasive, vigorous and cutting; at times, exaggerated and sarcastic.

Death of the lad of letters

Bernard Levin asks how schools feed minds without literature

Here's a fine state of affairs. No sooner has the government decreed that children studying the English language in our schools should not do so from the more idiotic television programmes (or even the less idiotic ones), but from the English classics, than a howl of anguish has gone up from the teachers of our unique and infinite tongue. For the nature of the howl, I turn to the education correspondent of *The Sunday Times*, Charles Hymas: "Classic works by Shakespeare and Dickens and the Bible have been branded as 'too difficult' by secondary schools taking part in the first of the government's new English tests. Comprehensives across the country are withdrawing pupils from the tests because they are not ready ... the set texts, central to the back-to-basics drive ... are beyond the abilities of too many pupils ... the pilot tests for 14-years-olds, due to start next month, were in danger of collapsing in disarray ..."

The first thing we have to do is to sack, say, nine-tenths of the teachers of English in the country without redundancy payments or pension. The second is to blow up the Department of Education with the entire staff in it. The third is to sit down and weep.

Shakespeare, Dickens and the Bible; these are singled out, it seems, to illustrate what a 14-year-old cannot understand. I pluck down, first, a volume of my beautiful Nonesuch Dickens; it is *Nicholas Nickleby*. Here is Dickens's incomprehensible description of Squeers:

> He had but one eye, and the popular prejudice runs in favour of two. The eye he had was unquestionably useful, but decidedly not ornamental; being of a greenish grey, and in shape resembling the fan-light of a street door. The blank side of his face was much wrinkled and puckered up, which gave him a very sinister appearance, especially when he smiled, at which times his expression bordered closely on the villainous.

I turn now to Shakespeare, also in the Nonesuch edition (the post-war one). In case I am accused of setting the sights too high, I take a passage of prose, and I have even (it goes hard) modernised the orthography. Here is the impenetrable Shakespeare, where Henry the Fifth is wooing Katharine:

> A good leg will fall, a straight back will stoop, a black beard will turn white, a curled pate will grow bald, a fair face will wither, a full eye will wax hollow, but a good heart, Kate, is the sun and the moon; or, rather, the sun, and not the moon; for it shines bright and never changes, but keeps his course truly. If thou will have such a one, take me; and take me, take a soldier; take a soldier, take a king.

For the third test, yet again with Nonesuch, I choose the unintelligible St John, after the Last Supper:

> Let not your heart be troubled; ye believe in God, believe also in me. In my Father's house are many mansions: if it were not so, I would have told you. I go to prepare a place for you. And if I go and prepare a place for you, I will come again, and receive you unto myself; that where I am, there ye may be also. And whither I go, ye know, and the way ye know. Thomas saith unto him, Lord we know not whither thou goest; and how can we know the way? Jesus saith unto him, I am the way, the truth, and the life: no man cometh unto the Father, but by me.

Now for some rage. I am a childless bachelor, but this crime perpetrated on the young transcends in its wickedness any distinction between those with children and those without. My school was by no means a forcing-house, but by the time I was 14 I had not only read practically all Shakespeare, but committed to memory something like 2,000 lines of his. I had certainly read at least half a dozen of Dickens, *The Three Musketeers*, *Treasure Island*, most of Kipling's poetry, *Don Quixote*, most of Chesterton and Belloc, Peacock, Karel Capek, Beerbohm, heaps of Shaw, Hazlitt and Cobbett, and – as anyone who has done me the honour of reading my book *Enthusiasms* will know – *Moby-Dick*.

But I do not give that catalogue to show how precociously clever I was; the whole point is (with the exception of the memorising – I had a freak memory), *all my coevals could have said the same and many could have said more*. Who robbed this country's children of the understanding of books?

The excuses will come pouring in. Families have ceased to urge the love of reading; the children themselves have vastly more entertainments than we did, preeminently, of course, television. But we have missed the point. The terrible charge is not that children of 14 reject the reading and studying of substantial and serious books; it is that they haven't been taught to understand them.

It must be obvious that children who have reached the age of 14 without also reaching the habit of real books and their meaning are very unlikely to get the habit later on; we are not only stealing from our children one of the most precious and costly jewels we could give them, we are simultaneously breeding a race of illiterates. Look at my three excerpts. Now tell yourself that they would probably be rejected as a test of the English language, on the ground that they could not be understood by 14-year-olds. Moreover, the original intention in the testing process was not the use of Shakespeare, Dickens and the Bible; the list included *The Ancient Mariner* and *Jane Eyre*, though it seems they disappeared early on, presumably because if 14-year-olds jibbed at Dickens, it would take contestants of 28, or indeed 56, to unravel those mysteries.

We heard a good deal from the then minister of education before the election, and we have heard more from his replacement. Their theme is spelling and punctuation, and, indeed, grammar; but if 14-year-olds do not understand Dickens, Shakespeare or the Bible, a fat lot of use it will be to tell 10-year-olds the difference between dative, accusative and genitive.

I have said more than once, and not as a paradox or metaphor, that the English language is the greatest work of art the world has seen. But if it is, then what we are doing with it is the equivalent of ripping up a Leonardo, banning Beethoven and pulling down the Parthenon.

All the talk we ever have heard
Uttered by bat or beast or bird –
Hide or fin or scale or feather –
Jabber it quickly and all together!
Excellent! Wonderful! Once again!
Now we are talking just like men.
Let's pretend we are – never mind!
Brother, thy tail hangs down behind!

3.3 Writing

Candidates are asked to demonstrate in their writing that they can:

- make use of different forms of writing (including stories, scripts, letters, newspaper articles and reviews) to suit a range of purposes and contexts;
- plan, organise and paragraph using appropriate punctuation;
- choose a vocabulary which is suited to its purpose and audience and use correct grammar and Standard English where appropriate;
- correct, edit and revise their own writing;
- show an awareness of how language is used in writing.

We are well aware that these aspects of writing do not come naturally to most of us. It is a learned rather than inherited response and one which demands some hours of practice. Yet these forms of expression and the management of the words and layout that they demand are in evidence wherever we see English words in print. Newspapers, magazines and books are written by professionals who observe certain codes and whose work is then subjected to the conventions demanded by publishers. It's all part of a process of communication and the English Language examiners want to see that you know and can imitate the necessary structures and guidelines.

3.4 Presentation

This is a newly recognised area for direct examination assessment, although it has always been popular with examiners – simply because it makes their job easier. Candidates should demonstrate in their writing that they can do the following:

- spell common words;
- write legibly and present finished work clearly and attractively.

In so many ways this is little more than good manners – especially in that these features are noticed when missing! The mastering of the 100 or so most commonly misspelt words and the clear formation of the 26 letters of the alphabet does require some application of mind and hand. It should not be a daunting task, and yet it is one that can have quite dramatic results. Chapters 19 and 20 are devoted to these matters which will provide your work with the finishing touches and, perhaps, help you finish your studies a little more effectively.

'Differentiation' 4

LEAG	MEG	SEG	NEAB	WJEC	NICCEA	Topic	Date attempted	Date completed	Self Assessment
✓	✓	✓	✓	✓	✓	Examinations and changes			
✓	✓	✓	✓	✓	✓	Coursework			
✓	✓	✓	✓	✓	✓	'Differentiation'			
✓	✓	✓	✓	✓	✓	An approach to the subject			
✓	✓	✓	✓	✓	✓	Speaking and listening			
✓	✓	✓	✓	✓	✓	Reading			
✓	✓	✓	✓	✓	✓	Ways and means			
✓	✓	✓	✓	✓	✓	Writing			
✓	✓	✓	✓	✓	✓	Practical writing			

4.1 Key stages and levels

The planners of the National Curriculum have divided the time spent in school into various **key stages** and set certain targets or **levels** that should be attained by students. It's a complicated matter and one that can be overwhelming, for many pages of definition and explanation have been published. There will obviously be amendments and changes following the first years of the scheme, but what remains is that a defined structure has been set and that the work done in schools and colleges will be determined by the requirements of the National Curriculum.

Here is a chart showing the relevant years, stages and levels.

The various levels (1–10) are used to define the attainments that are considered possible at the different key stages. The work outlined in this book is designed to assist candidates of 16 years of age and above taking the GCSE examination at the end of Key Stage 4.

The following is a simple way of looking at the various levels, remembering that they relate to the expectations for people at certain ages as well as to the intellectual powers of a wide range of the population. In the documents on the National Curriculum, the areas relating to 'Speaking and listening', 'Reading' and 'Writing' are presented separately. Here we have attempted to amalgamate references to the skills and attitudes that can be attained:

- *Levels 1–3 Coping* with basic situations of communication.
- *Levels 4 & 5 Recognising* significant differences; handling more detailed matters; and using reference material.
- *Levels 6–8 Understanding* increasingly complex material; expressing oneself with effectiveness, clarity and well-structured paragraphing; contributing more fully; reading a range of literary material, including some pre-20th century work; developing ideas.
- *Levels 9 & 10 Showing skill and expertise* in organising material; writing

with assurance and an individual style; appreciating, evaluating and displaying an independent judgement; presenting ideas with confidence and flair.

The attainment targets relating to Writing also include Spelling, Handwriting and Presentation. These are assessed slightly differently.

Spelling

Levels 1–4 include the mastering of simple, common and some longer words together with an awareness of the relationships of word-families and the main patterns of English spelling.

Handwriting

Levels 1–4 include control, legibility and fluency in producing joined-up writing.

Presentation

Presentation is the combination of Spelling and Presentation at Levels 5–7 (there are no higher levels in this attainment target). Candidates are expected to be able to spell correctly, in the course of their own writing, words of increasing complexity; to check final drafts of writing for misspellings; to write fluently and legibly; and to have an increased ability to present their finished work appropriately and attractively.

The requirements for these levels have been abbreviated, but advice on how to tackle the tasks involved will be given in some of the subsequent chapters.

4.2 Differentiated papers

The Levels 1–10 partly reflect the age-range of pupils and partly their abilities. They are used as the indicator on the final examination mark that combines the Terminal Examinations and the Coursework element. The relationship between the GCSE Grades and the Levels used are, approximately, as follows:

Schools and colleges enter candidates according to the appropriate tier of assessment. In other words, there are in Key Stage 4 English Language, varying examination papers to reflect the different abilities of those taking the subject.

The six examination boards use different names for their tiers, but all use two of them to reflect basic and more advanced standards. The terms Foundation and Higher are used by LEAG and SEG; Standard and Higher by MEG; Tiers 1 & 2 by WJEC; Tiers P & Q by NEAB; and Tiers S & T by NICCEA. [The full names and addresses of the boards are to be found in the beginning of this book.]

Candidates are entered for the examination standard that suits their abilities or levels. Obviously they could perform better or worse than expected and this is taken into account. For example, with the London and East Anglian Group (LEAG) the Foundation Tier is targeted at levels 4–6, but will allow awards to be made in the range G–C. The Higher Tier is targeted at levels 6–10, yet allows awards in the full range of G–A*. This 'safety margin' allows for errors of judgement. The other boards are not quite so generous in their approach, but a good working rule is to assume that grades E–A* are covered by the higher tiers in all cases.

The tone that the examination boards adopt in expressing their aims does not stress 'differentiation' as something divisive, but as a means of helping individuals develop their skills. Remember the words of the Northern Ireland Council for the Curriculum, Examinations and Assessment (NICCEA) in its Syllabus for English at GCSE: 'The course aims to give students the opportunity to enjoy the experience of exploring the English Language and its literature through the programme of study while developing their mastery of it.'

The ten key words in this sentence – opportunity / enjoy / experience / exploring / language / literature / programme / study / developing / mastery – should be borne in mind and recalled whenever mental stimulation is required.

The chapter headings of this book incorporate the term 'Self-Assessment'. It may be helpful to devise a personal system (marks out of ten, for example) that monitors the extent to which these ten 'key words' are fulfilled by the contents of the various chapters.

5

An approach to the subject

LEAG	MEG	SEG	NEAB	WJEC	NICCEA	Topic	Date attempted	Date completed	Self Assessment
✓	✓	✓	✓	✓	✓	Examinations and changes			
✓	✓	✓	✓	✓	✓	Coursework			
✓	✓	✓	✓	✓	✓	'Differentiation'			
✓	✓	✓	✓	✓	✓	An approach to the subject			
✓	✓	✓	✓	✓	✓	Speaking and listening			
✓	✓	✓	✓	✓	✓	Reading			
✓	✓	✓	✓	✓	✓	Ways and means			
✓	✓	✓	✓	✓	✓	Writing			
✓	✓	✓	✓	✓	✓	Practical writing			

5.1 'Re-frame your picture'

You have bought or been given this book for a reason. Perhaps it's because you need to improve your skills in order to attain a higher grade? Maybe you want to know more about the mysteries of Key Stage 4? Possibly you are interested in the ways in which our language works? The point is that you have a picture in mind relating to yourself and the very language that you speak and read. You may see yourself as being weak at the subject or on the verge of improvement. What is important is that you should see yourself as being part of a rather remarkable process.

It all started in the 5th century when three expansionist Germanic tribes – the Angles, the Saxons and the Jutes – left the sand dunes of their native shores and sailed over the North Sea to the south-east beaches of Britain. They invaded, pushed the resident peoples towards the Celtic lands of the west, and settled. With time their **Low German** language developed into what became known as **Anglo-Saxon** or **Old English**.

Then about three hundred years later another land-hungry tribe, the Vikings, came from their relatively poor lands of Scandinavia and, with fire, rape and pillage, made their presence known. The battles were fierce, and yet when the conflict was over the invaders and the invaded settled down quickly. The reason was that they could understand one another – for their linguistic roots originated from the same areas of continental Europe before each had moved on prior to the 5th century.

About two centuries later, in 1066, the Normans, from northern France, attacked at the Battle of Hastings. It was the last successful invasion of the main part of this island to be conducted by warfare. However, the battle of the languages, between **Norman French** and Old English, took much longer and was won, eventually, by the latter. Various sound changes took place, grammar and word order were modified and the 'Old' English became **Middle English**. It was the language of the first great English poet, Geoffrey Chaucer.

In 1477 William Caxton's printing press produced its first publication and the 'new' technology had started. In 1525 William Tyndale translated the New Testament and had it printed in Germany. Many more versions and editions of the Bible were to follow. Then in 1564, almost five centuries after the Battle of Hastings, William Shakespeare was born: the dramatic arts as well as the language itself were never to be the same again. As the centuries passed plays and poetry, essays and novels, journals and newspapers were to appear from numerous sources. In the nineteenth century the whole process of publishing was given impetus by the invention of the steam-powered press. Books were in the hands of the people. Now the latest technology can electronically convey both the spoken and printed word around the Earth in fractions of a second.

The point is this – not only has this language a long and intricate history, but it is the language so often used for these global transactions. It has become a common currency, the trading medium, the words of international exchange. Anyone who is able to read this book is part of the network of those who can communicate in English. It is one of the greatest 'language shows' on Earth.

There are many reasons for the success of English as an international language. The spread of the British Empire and the establishment of the Commonwealth guaranteed livelihoods for generations of English-speakers in the Far East, in the Indian subcontinent, in Australasia, in eastern, western and southern Africa, and throughout North America.

The flexibility of its structure means that it can accommodate changes in a fast-moving world. Although English has been 'exported' from England to many parts of the world, it is its 're-export' by the United States that has ensured its prominence as the language of film and television programmes everywhere. As it is in the forefront of communications, its appeal increases and the queues grow for enrolment at English classes in countries everywhere. It has been estimated that in China alone there are more people who wish to learn English than there are actual English speakers in the rest of the world.

Consequently, a qualification in this subject has status and earning-power. Where expansion takes place, there is a demand for services. You may not have seen yourself as part of a worldwide, thriving culture that has a long, recorded history and what appears to be a dynamic future. 'Re-frame the picture' and see yourself able to use your talents and qualifications to enhance your life and those around you. Your words count.

5.2 Barometers not barriers

Some skills are caught; some taught. We may have inherited through our genes our abilities to perform certain tasks effectively or we may have had to practise them repeatedly in order to succeed. What we have all done is to experience growing up, during which time we have developed from making that first cry to undertaking the intricate tests posed by, for example, examinations. That process has been a remarkably complex one and yet we have been only partially aware of the multiple changes to our bodies, brains and personalities. Much has been absorbed quietly and without undue disturbance.

The years before we attend school are, perhaps, the busiest of our lives. An enormous amount is learnt as we cope with the drives of hunger, the manipulation of objects and instruments, the placing of affections, and the striving to manage meanings, words and sentence patterns. The learning curve rises steeply.

The formal skills that are learnt in school complement these formative years. Yet it's not just the reading and writing that matter as far as English, or any other language, is concerned. It's the contact with others, the development of the conversational response, the witty remark, the insight that is shared and enjoyed. Instruction matters, of course, but the vitality of being receptive to ideas, viewpoints, sounds and silences brings out that awareness.

So regard the attainment targets, and the levels that reflect them, as indicators of the complex learning process through which you are passing. See them as barometers of your own success, not as barriers to your getting on.

5.3 Think of it this way ...

Thousands of books have been written about the ways of absorbing, learning, assessing and teaching the English language. It's an industry in itself! The danger is that we can easily lose sight of essentials under the welter of words.

A simple way of seeing and remembering the things that matter in language and communication is to write down the sequence of letters *A–I–R–O* (and recall them as 'Airo' or 'Air Zero'). Then list the features for which the individual letters stand:

- A *Accuracy* – the need for precision, clear structures, correct spellings, balanced judgements and, above all, to 'get things right'.

- I *Imagination* – that power that enables us to bring images to mind so that we can move beyond the limitations of our present time and create 'an extra dimension' to our lives.

- R *Responsiveness* – that sense of willpower that allows us to engage with the task in hand, to understand why it has to be done, to bring alive the meanings of the words that we are reading or writing.

- O *Organisation* – the ability to manage writing and recording equipment, paper, books, storage and retrieving – in short, controlling our own information systems.

6
Speaking and listening

LEAG	MEG	SEG	NEAB	WJEC	NICCEA	Topic	Date attempted	Date completed	Self Assessment
✓	✓	✓	✓	✓	✓	Examinations and changes			
✓	✓	✓	✓	✓	✓	Coursework			
✓	✓	✓	✓	✓	✓	'Differentiation'			
✓	✓	✓	✓	✓	✓	An approach to the subject			
✓	✓	✓	✓	✓	✓	Speaking and listening			
✓	✓	✓	✓	✓	✓	Reading			
✓	✓	✓	✓	✓	✓	Ways and means			
✓	✓	✓	✓	✓	✓	Writing			
✓	✓	✓	✓	✓	✓	Practical writing			

6.1 Speaking and listening

The attainment targets that are referred to in Chapter 3 are specific and relate to the tasks that you may be asked to perform as part of the examination. This section looks at ways of improving your overall performance in this area, which is vital to human development and which preoccupies many people.

As the world population grows, so does the amount of sound produced. Yet it is now easier to get in touch with people, and mechanical devices allow us to speak effectively over long distances without raising our voices. When, in the past, there were fewer people around, they probably had to shout more often in order to make contact. Now equipment to amplify, transmit, record and store the human voice is available in every shopping centre and, in real terms, the prices of these goods – taking inflation into account – are falling all the time. So not only do we have to hear the noises of those around us, but we often have to take note of sounds recorded earlier in the day, month, year or century! It's good that sound only lingers for a short time.

People spend some of their time speaking and some of it listening. Think for a moment how your occupation, status and situation determine the actual proportions of time. Teachers, lecturers, doctors, telephonists, receptionists, managers and salespeople, for example, are paid to use speech effectively in explaining, informing and persuading. Students, among many others, are expected to be on the receiving end.

It is to be hoped that most people engage in speaking actively – that is, to put their minds to work and to have a definite purpose in the activity of speaking. There are 'passive' speakers around – those who talk to themselves, who engage in conversation regardless of whether they are creating interest, or who feel impelled to address the world at large.

On the other hand, active *listeners* are a rarer breed. They develop a special skill that will be dealt with later. Passive listeners are much more common: it is all too easy to allow words to 'go in one ear and out of the other'. The range of sounds that bombard us does encourage mental 'switching off'. This can save much frustration, although there is always the danger that a tendency will grow into a habit, and then produce a state of mind in which outside stimuli often fail to make an impression.

Let us remind ourselves of the speaking parts in which we consciously and subconsciously become involved in our day-to-day activities:

- *Talking to ourselves* When this is the character of a novel thinking about matters, it is sometimes called 'interior monologue'.
- *Passing remarks* The observations on health, weather and outlook that form the opening of many English conversations.
- *Chatting* Topics of a generally unimportant nature that are used to pass the time.
- *Conversation* An interaction in which ideas of some value are exchanged and a point of view is required.
- *Inquiry* When advice is needed, usually about a specific matter or direction.
- *Discussion* A more formal exchange of ideas, in which a group of people decide to agree or disagree.
- *Public speaking* An occasion when an audience is to be addressed on what is usually a prepared subject.
- *Acting* In a dramatic production that involves either learning lines or role-playing, or both.

6.2 Seven directives

Talk comes easily to many. Yet there are occasions, throughout our lives, when we are conscious of difficulties, find words hard to come by, and are nervous. This may be a problem in the examination room, although undoubtedly the 'testing' for GCSE and similar is undertaken under relatively relaxed conditions. The point is that we can be dumbstruck, stammer, 'freeze', or sweat or shake when under pressure. This is quite natural, but tends to become less frequent with age and experience. It does reveal how complications (and complexes) can arise when words have to be uttered under certain circumstances.

Be conscious of the following facets of speech.

Mechanics of speech

The **mechanics of speech** – the expelling of air from the voice box through the passages of mouth and nose, and the construction of sounds by the manipulation of throat, tongue and teeth – are second nature. Most of us have been taking them for granted for a long time. Even when we are tense, the conditioned patterns of behaviour will probably see us through. Take comfort.

Gestures

Gestures of the face, hands, legs and body become involved in the process, for the central nervous system is in action. Some people are animated when speaking; others are 'laid back'. Try to judge your own responses and be aware that you can probably control certain exaggerated gestures *once* you know that you are displaying them. Watch yourself.

Voice projection

Voice projection is determined by the way in which we pitch the tones used. You can test the response of others by watching them carefully as you speak to see whether your words are apparently registering. The eyes of your listeners are good indicators of their attentiveness. Speak up and out.

Emotions

Emotions can feature and there are times when we would prefer them not to. Cheerfulness of nature is reflected in buoyant sounds; sadness can cause dull tones. In order to overcome the display of unwanted feelings, try to breathe deeply (in through the nose and out through the mouth) and inject liveliness into the voice. It may project something deceptive, but nobody is impressed by misery. Just hold on.

The listener

Our listeners matter. It is vital to have a sense of **audience** – in other words, to know to whom we are talking. There are times when mistakes are made and we speak too loudly, too quickly, too casually or too politely, or make patronising remarks. It is usually a matter of excess and adjustments are quickly made. An audience, even if it consists of only one person, soon makes its feelings known. Be responsive.

Being yourself

Examinations of one sort or another are taking place all the time. Our motives, sincerity, clarity, quality of information, relevance, humour and attractiveness of tone are being constantly judged by our listeners. Examination rooms are only extensions of everyday life. Be yourself.

Having fun

Much pleasure is given and received by talking. The urge to express and be kept involved, informed and wanted is shown in the billions of conversations that take place continually throughout the day, throughout the world. Don't hesitate, join in.

6.3 Self-assessment and checklist

The simplest way of assessing yourself or anyone else's speaking abilities is to write down the four letters – *M-A-L-C* – and list the appropriate requirements and questions:

M   *Material* – is it relevant and interesting?

A   *Audience* – is their attention being held?

L   *Language* – is it suitable for the topic?

C   *Clarify* – is what is being said readily understood?

Give marks out of ten for each of the qualities. Assess your performance against those of others. Watch the professional performers on television and note how they fulfil each requirement.

Another way of trying to monitor performance is to note the following checklist of abilities. How does the subject of your inquiry carry out these actions?

- talk clearly and confidently;
- handle one-to-one conversations;
- contribute to group discussions;
- participate in classroom/public discussions;

- present relevant ideas;
- use a wide vocabulary;
- have a sound general knowledge;
- understand verbal instructions;
- show an ability to use language appropriate to a given situation;
- convey humour;
- display imagination;
- be informative;
- know how to question;
- give instructions;
- make suggestions.

6.4 Listen with care

It pays to listen. How many accidents, errors and misjudgements could have been avoided had the listener paid more attention? So often we are only partly conscious of a sound or hear something 'without taking it in'. In order to appear as though we are doing what we should, we train ourselves to look attentive while actually concentrating on some other activity that is, at least inwardly, more rewarding. Deception is widely practised.

Good listening depends upon an attitude of mind and a number of skills. First you have to *want* to listen – there must be **motivation**. Secondly, if that motivation is not strong, you may have to develop the **willpower** to overcome the lack of attractive stimuli. Thirdly, you must *know* what you have to do in order to be successful.

It is a good idea to see yourself having a definite **role** in the business of listening. Consider yourself to be part of a *network*, in which you are linked to the speaker or speakers. Then try to develop a sense of *focus*, in which your powers of concentration are directed onto the ideas that are being conveyed. As the ideas flow try to store them (obviously by taking notes if it's appropriate), by mentally *reviewing* what has been said, or by making a remark that will encourage the speaker to repeat a specific point that you think should be emphasised. Try to anticipate what is going to be said by *previewing* matters in your mind, but be prepared to be wrong. Finally, if it is in the right context, use speech to *confirm* what has been said. A passing remark, a helpful interjection, even a nod of the head, can reassure the speaker that successful communication has taken place.

Above all, keep an *open mind*. It is so easy to close our minds, believing that we've heard it all before. Here's the paradox. The variety of ideas in life is infinite. There is an inexhaustible supply of new material for mental stimulus, relaxation and restoration. Yet it has been calculated that 98 per cent of the ideas that we have in mind today are the very ones that we thought about yesterday! Our minds tend to deal with recycled material. Listening and retaining what we have heard enable us to break out of those circuits of thoughts which can become repetitive, boring and, sometimes, overwhelming.

6.5 Signs of listening skills

The Samaritans is an organisation that provides a 24-hours-a-day listening service for people wanting to talk. Its aims are to relieve suffering, to prevent suicides and to provide comfort for anyone in distress and in need of a sympathetic ear. Although their services are staffed by volunteers, they endeavour to provide a professional service.

Much of their work is performed over the telephone, where anonymity is encouraged. Some of their help is given in the form of counselling where direct contact is made between the listener and the client. What follows is partly based upon the Samaritans' advice; it is intended to promote greater awareness of how listening skills need to be thought about, encouraged and practised.

Listening involves many aspects of personality – attitudes, gestures and responses – as well as the usual variety of replies using words. To be a **good listener** you should offer certain non-verbal attributes:

- a personal quietness;
- non-threatening body posture;
- a position in which the speaker can be faced;
- the ability to make eye contact.

You should also show certain verbal attributes:

- an interest that leads to relevant questions;
- the wish to clarify points of conversation;
- non-critical responses;
- the acceptance of negative attitudes;
- a willingness to show agreement if it's genuinely felt;
- the restating of points made;
- a refusal to react to sarcasm.

A **poor listener** will probably engage in contrasting non-verbal features:

- looking away;
- fidgeting;
- nose-blowing;
- being 'glassy-eyed'.

She or he may display certain verbal habits, as well:

- taking over the conversation;
- being critical;
- diverting the talk against the speaker's wishes;
- challenging knowledge;
- imposing her or his own agenda and needs;
- disagreeing for the sake of argument;
- one-upmanship;
- trying to better the previous story.

6.6 Good intentions – poor listening

Here are a number of 'danger areas' where, often with the best of intentions, errors are made and listening becomes little more than a self-centred activity.

Placating

You want to be pleasant and supportive. You want people to like you and so agree with everything they say. You half-listen, but you're not really involved.

Comparing

You are always trying to assess who is cleverer, more competent, more emotionally healthy – you or the speaker? This makes it hard to listen.

Identifying

You refer everything that you are told to your own experience. Everything you hear reminds you of something *you* have felt, done or suffered. There is no time really to hear the other person or to get to know her or him.

Advising

You see yourself as the great problem-solver, ready with help or suggestions. You do not hear more than a few sentences before you begin searching for a solution.

Judging

You prejudge someone as being stupid or neurotic or unqualified, so you do not pay much attention to what they are saying. You have already written them off. Judgements should be made only after you have heard and evaluated the content of the speaker's remarks.

Mind-reading

You may not pay much attention to what people say and, in fact, you often mistrust it. You spend more time trying to work out what the other person is 'really' thinking or feeling.

Filtering

You listen to some things and not to others. You pay enough attention only to hear what you want to hear.

Rehearsing

You are rehearsing what *you* will say next, so you do not have time to listen. Your attention is on the preparation and crafting of *your* next comment. You continue to look interested, but your mind is at work ... elsewhere.

Dreaming

You are half-listening and something the speaker says triggers a chain of private thoughts. Effort is needed to stay tuned in to conversations. Listening means concentrating and showing commitment to the speaker.

Sparring

You argue and debate with the other person. He or she never feels heard because you are so quick to disagree. You take a strong stand and are very clear about your beliefs and preferences.

Being right

You will go to any lengths to avoid being wrong. You cannot listen to criticism, you cannot stand being corrected and you cannot take suggestions to change. Since you cannot acknowledge that your mistakes are mistakes, you just keep making them.

Derailing

You suddenly change the subject. You get bored with the conversation or you feel uncomfortable with the topic, so you derail it.

There are many opinions and points of view in this chapter. If you have really listened to all that we have indicated, then you probably didn't need the advice in the first place!

Reading

7

LEAG	MEG	SEG	NEAB	WJEC	NICCEA	Topic	Date attempted	Date completed	Self Assessment
✓	✓	✓	✓	✓	✓	**Examinations and changes**			
✓	✓	✓	✓	✓	✓	**Coursework**			
✓	✓	✓	✓	✓	✓	**'Differentiation'**			
✓	✓	✓	✓	✓	✓	**An approach to the subject**			
✓	✓	✓	✓	✓	✓	**Speaking and listening**			
✓	✓	✓	✓	✓	✓	**Reading**			
✓	✓	✓	✓	✓	✓	**Ways and means**			
✓	✓	✓	✓	✓	✓	**Writing**			
✓	✓	✓	✓	✓	✓	**Practical writing**			

7.1 Social pressures

There are several human activities that have to be learnt to enable us to lead civilised lives. The extent to which we attain these skills depends upon our own natural or innate abilities, the amount of self-interest that we possess, the pressures and expectations of those around us, and the quality of the instructions that we receive.

Think for a moment of the features of speaking and listening outlined in the previous section. They are part of one of those basic, vital skills that people should and do strive to perfect. There are the enormous benefits to be derived from being able to communicate effectively. Then think of the other forces that motivate people. Consider the need to be able to move easily. Much effort is spent, and pleasure gained, from helping children to walk and run. A large service industry depends solely upon the demand from adults that they pass the driving test. Everyone needs to be able to count money and to know its value. Information and skills concerning the supply, preparation and consumption of food should be common knowledge. These are among the basic requirements that are needed for life to be stimulating – for where would we be without contact with others, mobility, financial security or a healthy diet?

The ability to read well is vital. The problem that occurs in this area is that it demands much application of time and effort in the early stages, when its benefits are not immediately recognisable to those who are learning. For a number of years one can 'get by' without literacy skills. Information can be conveyed by alternative means – talk, pictures, general awareness. It is possible to survive, but not to thrive, without being able to read and write well. Then suddenly the demand for qualifications and the need for examination techniques loom. By then it can be too late.

The ways in which individuals approach reading differ considerably. If you can read this, then you can probably think back to your own patterns of behaviour connected with dealing with words. The grasping of the shape of letters that led to the 'trial and error' concept of words and their patterns. Then came the sense of 'pleasure in accomplishment' that came with the repeated reading of certain passages or books. Gradually from the perfecting of parts came the sense of 'overview' in which complete sections could be comprehended. Finally came the moment of realisation that a relatively effortless skill was operating successfully.

7.2 The 'ABC' of reading

There are three important aspects about reading that need stating:

A *Awareness* of the powers conferred upon those who can read well and the various expectations of the examining boards.

B *Breaking down* the barriers to understanding by showing how simple analysis can lead to literary appreciation.

C *Constructing* ideas to show the concepts that authors use in order to write effectively.

This chapter will first consider the potential for individual development that is promoted by reading, and suggest ways and means of fulfilling the examination requirements. Then it will look at a simple method of beginning analysis before an assessment is made of how authors construct the various frameworks to convey their ideas. It's all a question of mind over matter – or, to put these words in a slightly different form with a somewhat different meaning, you mind because you matter!

7.3 Awareness of …

Awareness of … the consequences of reading

Everyone agrees that reading is a good thing. Some people need convincing that this skill is worth working at in order to perfect it. There are certain features that need stressing:

- it can be a pleasure in itself;
- the precision of carefully chosen words sharpens our insights into life;
- the inquisitive powers of the mind are harnessed;
- imagination is stirred;
- the mental training leads to skills much in demand by society.

In the countries with advanced economic systems there is a decreasing demand for strenuous human physical labour. Machines supply the effort. What is needed is a strong workforce of technically efficient, well-trained, thoughtful people who can respond to information and ideas. Consider some of the groups of people who earn their living by using words:

- advertisers;
- analysts;
- broadcasters;
- consultants;
- designers;
- graphic artists;
- journalists;
- lawyers;
- representatives;
- secretaries;
- teachers;
- writers.

Some of these groups are having to apply systems directly to their work and have little scope for innovation. Others are expected to think for themselves and to use words in inventive ways that arrest attention. They are well paid and in demand. The basis for their success is a lively mind fostered by literary skills.

Livelihoods will continue to be made for as long as humans continue to evolve. 'Word-trading' and 'idea-creating' will be at the heart of the thousands of new jobs that have to be produced in order to maintain relatively high employment. The neglect of reading skills can limit prospects.

Awareness of ... the different ways of reading

It is easy to think of reading as being solely whatever reading activity applies to our own life or interest – studying a text, looking at a newspaper, lying curled up in bed with a book. As it happens the art of reading involves so many aspects of day-to-day living that we must be aware of the ways in which we direct our minds.

At one end of the scale is **skimming** – the glance at the advertisement, the quick look over the notice, the flick through the newspaper or magazine, the thumb-through of a book to see whether it contains relevant material or interest, the dipping into reference material.

At the other end is **studying**, in which time and energy are spent consciously weighing precise meanings, noting the main and detailed points, and committing certain aspects to memory.

In between is what we could term **surveying**, in which the intention is serious, but what matters is being able to see the essentials, the outline and the potential of a passage. It may not involve exploring something in depth; neither the occasion nor the subject may demand it.

There are two broad factors that matter in determining our approach to reading: **pace** and **depth**. Some reading material should be dealt with quickly, some has to be pondered over. It is necessary to make a decision about this in order to 'gear' one's mind to the task. Then the brain will take in information in an effective way – in a sense, it is programmed. Too many people see reading as an activity that is conducted at a single, and monotonous, speed. One of the features of so-called **speed-reading** is to practise regulating the flow of words absorbed according to the significance of the task.

So remember the three 'S' words – *skim, survey, study* – and regulate or manage your reading speed accordingly.

Awareness of ... habits

When people are at school or college, full- or part-time, they have both an incentive to read and plenty of stimulus material around them. However, in some places of work and in some homes there are distinct limitations. Books are not readily at hand and instead television may provide the sole medium of entertainment. It can monopolise the living room and, consequently, dominate life. It is then not so easy to acquire the reading habit, which is one of the most effective ways of self-improvement.

There are several ways of cultivating the reading habit. The first thing is to establish that you are in charge of what you want. If you want to read effectively, then the solution is in your mind, your will power and your actions. It becomes a matter of resolution. Secondly, there are some observations and suggestions that could help:

Portability

Books, magazines and newspapers are easily carried around. They are not electrical, they do not need power or fuel, they have no maintenance costs and they are found in every town – to be bought from shops and to be borrowed by arrangement from libraries. They are relatively inexpensive, when new; they may be very cheap or free when secondhand. Things to read have a tendency to be at hand when required, especially if we wish them to be.

Opportune moments

Business leads to busyness. Yet, busy as we may be, there are always moments to be found or created when one can read – at the beginning or end of the day ... on buses or trains ... sandwiched between meals and restarting work ... while waiting for someone to get ready ... while ovens warm up, cakes cool down or washing-up dries ... in half-an-hour between programmes. The week may be full of hours, but has plenty of spare minutes.

Fixed points

The patterns of individual lives vary as much as people themselves. Yet we can all see that there is a basic structure or rhythm about the times when we work, sleep, eat, go out, and feel at our best, and those times when we would rather not be seen, let alone have to *do* things. Within this cycle of everyday actions there could well be fixed points when the reading habit can be indulged. Perhaps it could be with the Sunday papers in bed; late on a Friday evening after a favourite magazine has been delivered; before going out on a Thursday evening; on the journeys to and from home at the weekends; while waiting for the lift after work. It doesn't matter 'when', just that it *happens*.

Exploration

There is an ever-expanding market. New technology has meant the appearance of new magazines and papers. Over 65 000 new titles a year are published by the book trade in the UK alone. Booksellers are opening new branches throughout the country. There is a growth of interest and as people become better educated the range of written material becomes more extensive. Look around: join those who browse and buy or borrow; search in the local secondhand bookshop for something of interest; read the book reviews that appear every week in the papers; have an occasional change of daily paper; buy a different magazine every now and then; take note of the fact that Britain has the largest sale of newspapers per head of population in the world ... and then join the queue!

Collecting

If a subject appeals, you might like to collect books on it. The same applies to the work of authors and to regular writers in the press. The more interests you have, the more you will read about them and increase the reading habit.

Taking note

Reading should be a pleasure. A preoccupation with taking notes on what has been read soon converts an interest into a chore. However, just *take note* of what you read, make jottings or keep in mind occasional ideas and references. These will soon build into a network of responses and help create a rich mental stock of material.

Mould tendencies into habits and, once established, they will create a state of mind that, all being well, will help you work out whatever you want. In your case it is, perhaps, the effective management of language and the ideas that it promotes.

Awareness of ... what is required

Let us just remind ourselves of some of the reading attainments that the National Curriculum wishes candidates to achieve by the time of Key Stage 4, when the GCSE is taken:

Response to literature

Candidates should read a range of fiction, poetry, literary non-fiction and drama, including pre-20th century literature, explaining their preferences. They should show insights, personal responses and an understanding of the author's approach. At the higher levels they should be able to make comparisons within texts and between different texts.

Response to non-literary and media texts

Candidates should show whether subject matter is presented as fact or opinion; indicate recognition of features of presentation; and, at the higher levels, be able to judge and evaluate the techniques used.

Research and information retrieval

Candidates should use appropriate methods to select, retrieve and combine information from a wide range of reference materials; and, at the higher levels, they should show discrimination and the ability to evaluate material as well as to make effective and sustained use of the information.

Knowledge about language

Candidates should show an awareness of an author's choice of particular words, and how, in time, words can change in use and meaning; they should indicate an awareness of writers' use of sound patterns and literary devices; and, at the higher levels, they should reveal some knowledge of the changes in English grammar and of the attitudes in society towards appropriateness and correctness in language use.

7.4 Barriers to understanding

There are three basic barriers to effective understanding: ignorance, laziness and fear.

Ignorance

Ignorance usually involves a poor vocabulary. There is normally a gulf between writers and readers which exposes differences in their actual knowledge about words. A writer obviously uses words as the primary force of expression. He or she gets to know them well. Readers do not necessarily have the same incentive. Hence there is a difference, which can grow into a problem.

Vocabularies can be classified, as *basic, extended, technical,* and *obsolete*. Most people have mastered the first, the **basic** vocabulary, for it consists of only about a thousand words and enables fairly straightforward business to be undertaken. The **extended vocabulary** relies upon an education, some reading and listening, as well as a desire to further knowledge of words and their meanings. Writers need to have this type of vocabulary, but it is unlikely to total more than 20 000 words. Many of the 500 000 words that make up the English language are to be found in **technical vocabularies**, for a great number of words originate from crafts and trades, many long since defunct. Of course, a vast number of words are now **obsolete** and their inclusion in a piece of writing sounds archaic or results simply from the writer being pedantic, displaying obscure knowledge for the sake of effect.

If you feel uncomfortable about the words that you find in an ordinary passage or writing in a newspaper or magazine, then you must strive to increase your vocabulary. It's relatively simple to have a dictionary at hand and to make use of it. If ten words are looked up in the dictionary each day and then brought into the individual's extended vocabulary, within six months a fine, 'professional' working vocabulary will have been developed.

Laziness

Laziness is a common barrier to mental development. Never underestimate the power of inertia. Thousands of novels have been written; millions started. Millions of books have been read; billions of first chapters commenced. The mind is very powerful in finding reasons why it is not practical to continue with the task that needs attention. We all develop systems of thought that lead us surely and gently to relax and to put off the difficult parts of life. It's little wonder that we supposedly use only 10 per cent of the capacity of our brains. The figure, already quoted, of 98 per cent of our thoughts being the same today as they were yesterday, is not surprising.

The key to success is to work out strategies of making what appears to be demanding into something that is pleasurable. There are people who claim that they have 'never done a day's work in their lives'. Some are among the workshy; others are expressing gratitude that the tasks they have undertaken have always given them pleasure or stimulation. If you can convert reading from a chore to a treat, then any sense of 'work' is well and truly out!

Fear

Fear makes fools of us all. This saying is particularly true when it comes to reading. Even though we do not have to read aloud and can gloss over our mistakes within the privacy of our minds, there is a strong sense of being put off, even repelled, by what appears to be beyond us. The only guidance that we can give is to suggest that you 're-frame the picture' and try to transform the feeling of fear of the unknown into one of being intrigued by the mysterious. Reading will open new worlds to you, and teach you much about other people and places as well as about your own potential; it will not expose your own limitations to public awareness. Shortcomings are a matter between yourself and the book – or, in the case, of public examinations, between yourself and the anonymous, distant, never-to-be-met-in-person examiner. Let go of your fears.

Breaking down the barriers

In the passages for reading practice we suggest that you follow certain procedures and begin to adopt a systematic approach. Remember that you are being prepared as part of an examination technique – for this is 'studying', rather than 'surveying' or 'skimming'.

First reading

Go through the passage thoroughly. At the end, try to develop in your mind a simple, overall view of the subject – a sort of mental snapshot. Some people find it helpful to devise a title that attempts to sum up the content of the material read.

Second reading

Recall the advice given at American level crossings where railways meet roads: 'Stop, look and listen'. Put it into practice in the following way. Pause for a moment and try to clear your mind ('Stop'). Then, as you begin reading, visualise what is happening and develop a series of mental pictures ('Look'). At the same time imagine that you can hear any sounds referred to in the passage ('Listen'). In short, attempt to bring the words alive.

Analysis Now that the second reading has been completed, the analysis begins. It is important to do this *before* you attempt to answer any questions. In fact you may be given plenty of time to examine and assess the passage before you see the questions themselves. The approach is simple. Take the following five words, which begin with the same letter, and list them:

When? Where? Who? What? Why?

Then jot down these notes on a single sheet of paper, with equal spacing between the five sections:

- *When?* Time: which year or century? which season? what time of day?
- *Where?* Place: where in the world?
- *Who?* People: how many and what are their names, if mentioned?
- *What?* Happenings: what happens?
- *Why?* Purpose: why has the author written this passage or article?

Now that the framework of the analysis has been outlined, it is necessary to break down the passage more finely. So prepare yourself for the next stage ....

Third reading

Use the sheet of paper divided into the five sections: let it act as a marker as your eyes follow the words of the passage. Think of it as a net that is trawling through the sentences, ready to 'catch' relevant ideas that are to be noted in the appropriate sections. By the end of this exercise you should have gathered information that already appears in the passage to be studied, but which understandably you did not take in during the first two readings. Remember that you are looking for details connected with the following five major aspects:

When? The element of time that gives the setting of the passage historically, that indicates the season of the year, that refers to the morning, afternoon, evening or night. Not all of these features are likely to appear, but some probably will and your notes should record them.

Where? The features of place will possibly be mentioned: look for references and note specifically, if it's appropriate, the continent, country, town or village. It may be that the author has used only general references to land or sea, to rural, urban or suburban areas. If the passage yields any clues, jot them down on the sheet.

Who? People matter: conduct your own census. How many appear? Indicate their names, how they are related to one another, their jobs, their distinctive clothing, their manner of speaking.

What? Happenings occur. Work out the major movements that take place. Who does what to whom? What is the outline of conversations between people? What preferences do the individuals reveal? Remember the advice to 'stop, look and listen'. Add directives to *taste* and *smell*. Note any references to the senses of seeing, hearing, touching, tasting, smelling.

Why? The author's purpose may not be clear, and from one short passage it may be impossible to detect anything about this element. However, try to work out whether his or her intention is to provide one or more of the following: pleasure, insight, analysis, explanation, guidance, persuasion.

You will by now have broken the passage into certain definite parts. You will probably have seen certain features for yourself. The important aspect of exploring something below the surface should have occurred.

Now comes the moment to *practise* these skills. Remember the stages:

- first reading: 'overview';
- second reading: 'insights';
- third reading: the five 'W' words.

A sample passage

I Spy

Graham Greene

CHARLIE STOWE waited until he heard his mother snore before he got out of bed. Even then he moved with caution and tiptoed to the window. The front of the house was irregular, so that it was possible to see a light burning in his mother's room. But now all the windows were dark. A searchlight passed across the sky, lighting the banks of cloud and probing the dark deep spaces between, seeking enemy airships. The wind blew from the sea, and Charlie Stowe could hear behind his mother's snores the beating of the waves. A draught through the cracks in the window-frame stirred his nightshirt. Charlie Stowe was frightened.

But the thought of the tobacconist's shop which his father kept down a dozen wooden stairs drew him on. He was twelve years old, and already boys at the County School mocked him because he had never smoked a cigarette. The packets were piled twelve deep below, Gold Flake and Players, De Reszke, Abdulla, Woodbines, and the little shop lay under a thin haze of stale smoke which would completely disguise his crime. That it was a crime to steal some of his father's stock Charlie Stowe had no doubt, but he did not love his father; his father was unreal to him, a wraith, pale, thin, indefinite, who noticed him only spasmodically and left even punishment to his mother. For his mother he felt a passionate demonstrative love; her large boisterous presence and her noisy charity filled the world for him; from her speech he judged her the friend of everyone, from the rector's wife to the "dear Queen", except the "Huns", the monsters who lurked in Zeppelins in the clouds. But his father's affection and dislike were as indefinite as his movements. Tonight he had said he would be in Norwich, and yet you never knew. Charlie Stowe had no sense of safety as he crept down the wooden stairs. When they creaked he clenched his fingers on the collar of his nightshirt.

At the bottom of the stairs he came out quite suddenly into the little shop. It was too dark to see his way, and he did not dare touch the switch. For half a minute he sat in despair on the bottom step with his chin cupped in his hands. Then the regular movement of the searchlight was reflected through an upper window and the boy had time to fix in memory the pile of cigarettes, the counter, and the small hole under it. The footsteps of a policeman on the pavement made him grab the first packet to his hand and dive for the hole. A light shone along the floor and a hand tried the door, then the footsteps passed on, and Charlie cowered in the darkness.

At last he got his courage back by telling himself in his curiously adult way that if he were caught now there was nothing to be done about it, and he might as well have his smoke. He put a cigarette in his mouth and then remembered that he had no matches. For a while he dared not move. Three times the searchlight lit the shop, while he muttered taunts and encouragements. "May as well be hung for a sheep," "Cowardy, cowardy custard," grown-up and childish exhortations oddly mixed.

But as he moved he heard footfalls in the street, the sound of several men walking rapidly. Charlie Stowe was old enough to feel surprise that anybody was about. The footsteps came nearer, stopped; a key was turned in the shop door, a voice said: "Let him in," and then he heard his father, "If you wouldn't mind being quiet, gentlemen. I don't want to wake up the family." There was a note unfamiliar to Charlie in the undecided voice. A torch flashed and the electric globe burst into blue light. The boy held his breath; he wondered whether his father would hear his heart beating, and he clutched his nightshirt tightly and prayed, "O God, don't let me be caught." Through a crack in the counter he could see his father where he stood, one hand held to his high stiff collar, between two men in bowler hats and belted mackintoshes. They were strangers.

"Have a cigarette," his father said in a voice dry as a biscuit. One of the men shook his head. "It wouldn't do, not when we are on duty. Thank you all the same." He spoke gently, but without kindness: Charlie Stowe thought his father must be ill.

"Mind if I put a few in my pocket?" Mr Stowe asked, and when the man nodded he lifted a pile of Gold Flake and Players from a shelf and caressed the packets with the tips of his fingers.

"Well," he said, "there's nothing to be done about it, and I may as well have my smokes." For a moment Charlie Stowe feared discovery, his father stared round the shop so thoroughly; he might have been seeing it for the first time. "It's a good little business," he said, "for those that like it. The wife will sell out, I suppose. Else the neighbours'll be wrecking it. Well, you want to be off. A stitch in time. I'll get my coat."

"One of us'll come with you, if you don't mind," said the stranger gently.
"You needn't trouble. It's on the peg here. There, I'm all ready."

The other man said in an embarrassed way, "Don't you want to speak to your wife?" The thin voice was decided, "Not me. Never do today what you can put off till tomorrow. She'll have her chance later, won't she?"

"Yes, yes," one of the strangers said and he became very cheerful and encouraging. "Don't you worry too much. While there's life ..." and suddenly his father tried to laugh.

When the door had closed Charlie Stowe tiptoed upstairs and got into bed. He wondered why his father had left the house again so late at night and who the strangers were. Surprise and awe kept him for a little while awake. It was as if a familiar photograph had stepped from the frame to reproach him with neglect. He remembered how his father had held tight to his collar and fortified himself with proverbs, and he thought for the first time that, while his mother was boisterous and kindly, his father was very like himself, doing things in the dark which frightened him. It would have pleased him to go down to his father and tell him that he loved him, but he could hear through the window the quick steps going away. He was alone in the house with his mother, and he fell asleep.

First reading: overview

While a 12-year-old boy is attempting to steal cigarettes from his father's shop he is disturbed, hides and witnesses his father being taken away by two strangers.

Second reading: insights

1 It is obvious that both father and son are doing something wrong under cover of darkness.
2 They have certain other similarities.
3 A searchlight probes the night sky and a policeman's torch shines around the darkened shop.
4 The boy does not have a full view of what is happening and his partial understanding is evident.
5 He experiences a significant change – from 'he did not love his father' (line 17) to the remark in the final paragraph, 'It would have pleased him to ... tell him that he loved him' (84–5).
6 The limitations of sight are compensated for by the multiple sounds of the sea, footsteps, voices, movements.

Third reading: the five 'W' words

When?
World War 1 – late at night.

Where?
On the coast, fairly close to Norwich.

Who?
1 Charlie Stowe: son – fearful – furtive – clenches his collar when under pressure – fortifies himself with adult sayings and proverbs – realises that something significant is happening.
2 Mother: fast asleep and inactive – when awake is said to be boisterous and noisy and is considered by her son to be well liked by everyone.
3 Father: furtive – tendency to go out at night (line 78) – holds his collar while under pressure – encourages himself with

sayings and proverbs – realises that what is happening will be significant and have future implications (line 73).
4 Policeman: shines torch through door.
5 & 6 Two strangers: men with bowler hats and belted raincoats – they are official but quite gentle – one of them adopts the way of speaking using sayings ('While there's life …').

What?
- A father and son are stopped while undertaking apparently criminal activities – the former by the authorities, the latter by the circumstances in which he finds himself.
- The boy is spying out the stocks of cigarettes in his father's shop and takes some. The father has been out in the dark again and has been arrested, probably on suspicion of spying.
- The son knows more about the father's activities than vice versa.
- The boy senses the highly-charged atmosphere, especially the sounds, smells, touch and tastes.
- Proverbs, sayings and well-used expressions are frequently used.

Why?
The author wants to *reveal* the connections between a son and his father; to *explore* how under these strange circumstances the boy realises his feelings of love; and to *demonstrate* how language can contain many suggestions. 'May as well be hung for a sheep' (line 42) makes reference to the one-time practice of executing sheep-stealers, although by this time hanging was reserved for murderers and traitors. 'I Spy' are the first two words of the game – 'I Spy With My Little Eye' – usually played between adults and children.

The next chapter of the book will consist of passages that will provide opportunities for you to practise this approach. It is necessary first to consider one further aspect – the framework of literary appreciation.

7.5 Constructing ideas

At the beginning of section 7.2 the so-called 'ABC' of reading was mentioned. Attention was drawn to 'awareness of powers', 'breaking down barriers' and 'constructing ideas', and these phrases were intended to focus on basic elements of communication.

One of the skills that you may be required to show is the ability to write about what you have read. This may take the form of a narrative in which you recast the original ideas of the author in words of your own. It may be that you are asked to give your opinion or state your preferences about the subject matter. Possibly you will be requested to let the passage before you act as a 'springboard' for your own thoughts or for the recounting of similar experiences.

On the other hand you may be required to write an **appreciation** of the passage, and this demands a special approach. In this case you should display through your own words that you are able:

1 to understand the content of the passage, short story or book;
2 to realise something of the aim or intention of the author;

3 to recognise some of the methods used;
4 to perceive features of the tone, ironies and images used;
5 to identify some of the devices employed by the writer.

In short, you are not primarily asked to repeat, reply to or react to the passage, but to *analyse* it. Obviously this is a sophisticated process and can become technical and complicated. The purpose here is not to baffle, but to direct you towards a simple framework on which ideas can be constructed.

Memorise the sequence of letters *C-A-M-T-I-D* and then list the following:

Contents   Aims   Methods   Tones   Ironies   Devices

When planning your 'appreciation', bear each of the above in mind and make a series of notes that will explore them. Here are some explanations and extensions of the topics.

Contents

Use the type of material that you created while breaking down the passage in section 7.4. Show the examiner or reader that you have understood the substance of the passage and that you can highlight its essential meaning.

Aims

All authors want to hold their readers' attention. Some are particularly keen to *persuade*, especially if they are teaching, preaching or advocating. The motive of the documentary or textbook writer is to *educate*; while the driving force behind manuals and practical guides is the giving of *advice*. The purpose of many authors is to *stimulate* ideas and attitudes in others, to *analyse* human motives, and to *entertain* an audience. Calculate which applies in the case of the passage that you are investigating.

Methods

Consider four aspects:

1 *First or third person?* Is the 'I' form used, to denote a more personal involvement of the author or the character through whom he is speaking?

2 *Subjective or objective?* Does the author *directly* participate in the matters of the text or does he or she try to be *detached*?

3 *Narration, description, analysis or comment?* Is the author attempting to tell a story, set a scene, expose underlying reasons or make direct personal observations?

4 *Brief or long-winded?* Where possible the style should be concise (short), precise (accurate) and incisive (with a sharp cutting edge).

Tones

The ways in which authors approach their subject matter vary considerably. At one extreme there are feelings of intensity and feverish commitment; at the other, tones of indifference and casual detachment. In between there is a complete range of emotions and mental states involving such feelings as: optimism, pessimism, depression, cheerfulness, detachment, bitterness, encouragement, restraint, effusiveness, carefulness, abandon, humour, austerity, frivolity, seriousness, reverence, respect, provocativeness, calmness, coolness, awe.

Ironies

These may be defined as:

- a situation or utterance that has an unforeseen significance;
- a condition in which one seems to be mocked by fate or by the facts;
- a figure of speech in which the intended meaning is the opposite of that expressed by the words used, often taking the form of sarcasm of ridicule;
- a contradictory outcome.

For the purposes of this exercise, ask yourself whether the author is being straightforward or whether she or he is being offhand, creating emphasis by stating the opposite to what is really intended, or showing signs of sarcasm or ridicule. Perhaps future references or occurrences are anticipated by apparently innocent remarks.

Devices

This demands almost a section of itself! Authors will use techniques in order to emphasise, catch attention, vary their style or explain with greater clarity. For the purpose of this exercise bear in mind the following twenty features and see whether any examples appear in the passages that you are studying:

- *Alliteration* A sequence of words beginning with the same letter or sound. (Example: 'Now nobody knows'.)

- *Analogy* A detailed similarity between things otherwise different. (Example: the activities of a person's life compared with a journey by sea.)

- *Anti-climax* Something that descends from the sublime to the ridiculous. (Example: 'After a final, monumental effort he reached the summit and then peeled a banana.')

- *Archaisms* Expressions that are out of date. (Examples: 'The man on the Clapham omnibus'; 'Are you courting?')

- *Clichés* Expressions that have lost force through over-use. (Examples: 'like a red rag to a bull'; 'mad as a March-hare'.)

- *Colloquialisms* Remarks used in everyday conversations. (Examples: 'It's nice to see you'; 'You don't say!'; 'Have a great time.')

- *Euphemism* The use of a name to mellow a supposedly impolite term. (Examples: 'toilet', 'lavatory', or 'convenience' for 'urinal'; 'passing on' for 'death'; 'the worse for wear' for 'drunk'.)

- *Hyperbole* Exaggeration. (Example: 'He put on weight until he was the size of a house.')

- *Idioms* Distinctive phrases, expressions and meanings of a language. (Example: 'It's raining cats and dogs' to describe heavy rain.)

- *Innuendo* A suggestion that is hinted at, but not directly expressed.

(Examples: 'He enjoys the company of women'; 'She is fond of her drink'.)

- *Jargon* Words used by a group of specialists, sometimes to impress. (Examples: 'frequency modulation'; 'induction manifold'; 'rhetorical devices'.)
- *Metaphors* Attempts to describe one thing in terms of another. (Examples: 'That man is a beast'; 'A maze of streets'.)
- *Onomatopoeia* Words that imitate the sounds that they are describing. (Examples: 'crash'; 'murmur'; 'whistle'; 'shriek'.)
- *Paradox* A statement that apparently contradicts itself. (Example: 'The more you know about people, the less you understand them!')
- *Repetition* The reiteration of a word or phrase for emphasis. (Example: 'Pick up your books, and pick them up now!')
- *Similes* Metaphors that are introduced by *like*, *as*, or *as if*. (Examples: 'Some men are like beasts'; 'The streets are as if a maze.')
- *Symbols* Words used as an emblem to stand for a fuller meaning. (Examples: 'heart' or 'rose' for love; 'crown' for ultimate achievement; 'pits' for worst moments or occasions.)
- *Understatement* An expression that uses modesty or limitation for effect. (Examples: 'we were not displeased' for 'we were delighted'; 'a little misunderstanding' for 'a complete disagreement'; 'a little local difficulty' for 'a civil war in a distant country'.)
- *Verbiage* The use of too many words. (Example: 'The excessive expenditure of verbal resources can have a limiting, tiring and trying effect upon both listeners and readers.')
- *Vogue words* Words that are in fashion and which often disappear from common usage after a short while. (Examples: 'ambience'; 'politically correct'; 'awareness'; 'accessible'; 'disadvantaged'.)

7.6 Putting these ideas into practice

You may care to apply this approach to analysing the short story 'I Spy', for it will help you start in a methodical way. The ideas presented here are not meant to be complete or comprehensive in themselves, but they are systematic. In any series of examinations, systems will be devised to enable the markers and assessors to do their work effectively and fairly. You are strongly advised to have a system of your own to ensure that you consider the vital aspects of every question that you are asked and that, in the heat of the moment, you have a checklist which will serve you well.

7.7 Future strategy

This concludes the 'reading' section. It is desirable for you to continue to practise the skills that you have developed over the years. A three-pronged strategy is proposed.

First, consider how so much stimulating reading material is to be found in newspapers and magazines. Every day, highly competent writers produce countless words to promote endless ideas. These are to be found on the shelves of newsagents and libraries, and, what's more, they change daily. Beg, borrow or buy *The Times, The Guardian, Daily Telegraph, The Independent* or *The Financial Times* (and, if you live in Scotland, the *The Herald* or *The Scotsman*). At the weekend try to secure *The Sunday Times, The Observer, Sunday Telegraph* or *The Independent on Sunday* (with *Scotland on Sunday* being available for some). When you are next in the library get into the habit of reading an article or two in *The Spectator, The Economist, The New Statesman* or *The Literary Review*. Your mental horizons will expand, your grasp of ideas and constructions will strengthen and your ability to generate material for your own written work will increase.

Secondly, always have a book 'on the go'. Keep it in a handy place – your briefcase or bag or by your bedside – and keep a bookmark in its place so that access can be immediate. Using the spare moments of the day, much can be achieved.

Thirdly, you will have to undertake some 'formal' exercises in order to gain experience for the examinations. Your tutors and teachers will direct you accordingly and show you the type of question that your examination board is likely to set. In order to 'train' for these occasions you may care to apply the approaches suggested in sections 7.4 and 7.5 by looking at material that has been included in the next chapter, entitled 'Ways and means'.

Ways and means

8

LEAG	MEG	SEG	NEAB	WJEC	NICCEA	Topic	Date attempted	Date completed	Self Assessment
✓	✓	✓	✓	✓	✓	Examinations and changes			
✓	✓	✓	✓	✓	✓	Coursework			
✓	✓	✓	✓	✓	✓	'Differentiation'			
✓	✓	✓	✓	✓	✓	An approach to the subject			
✓	✓	✓	✓	✓	✓	Speaking and listening			
✓	✓	✓	✓	✓	✓	Reading			
✓	✓	✓	✓	✓	✓	Ways and means			
✓	✓	✓	✓	✓	✓	Writing			
✓	✓	✓	✓	✓	✓	Practical writing			

'Ways and means' is an old expression that refers to the method of achieving something. In Parliamentary terms it applies to the providing of money. In this chapter we provide samples of the sort of reading material that is a requirement for the English Language examination; examples of how they can be approached; opportunities to achieve what is required; and ways and means of working things out. Money may not be the direct product of success in this area, but skills and qualifications are usually rewarded.

Refresh your memory by reconsidering the three stages of 'breaking down' a passage in order to see some of its parts:

1 *Overview:* The essential features.
2 *Insights:* 'Stop, look and listen'.
3 *The five 'W' words:* When? Where? Who? What? Why?

The selection of material here is meant to reflect the range of the National Curriculum requirements in which examples of different types of reading matter are given. Your examination board may not expect you to master the complete range, but the skills of interpretation expected by them are standard. Bear in mind that the Graham Greene short story in Chapter 7 is representative of 20th century prose in the 'response to literature' area.

We suggest that you attempt to read and work out (or 'break down') the following passages *before* you look at the notes beneath them. Writing assignments are provided in order that you can practise responding to the passages. At some stage of being examined you have to be able to demonstrate that you have understood what you have read.

8.1 Twelve passages to work out

1 Response to literature: poetry

My Wicked Uncle

His was the first corpse I had ever seen,
Untypically silent in the front room.
Death had deprived him of his moustache,
His thick horn-rimmed spectacles,
The easy corners of his salesman dash –
Those things by which I had remembered him –
And sundered him behind a sort of gauze.

His hair was badly parted on the right
As if for Sunday School. That night
I saw my uncle as he really was.

The stories he retailed were mostly
Wicked-avuncular fantasy;
He went in for waistcoats and Brylcreem.
But something about him
Demanded that you picture the surprise
Of the chairman of the board, when to
'What will you have with your whisky?' my uncle replies,
'Another whisky please'.

He claimed to have been arrested in New York
Twice on the same day –
The crookedest chief steward in the Head Line.
And once, so he would say,
Sailing from San Francisco to Shanghai,
He brought a crew of lascars out on strike
In protest at the loss of a day's pay
Crossing the International date line.

He was buried on a blustery day above the sea,
The young Presbyterian minister
Tangled and wind-swept in the sea air.
I saw sheep huddled in the long wet grass
Of the golf course, and in the empty freighters
Sailing for ever down Belfast Lough
In a fine rain, their sirens going,
And as the gradual graph of my uncle's life
And times dipped precipitately
Into the black earth of Carnmoney Cemetery.

His teenage kids are growing horns and claws –
More wicked already than ever my uncle was.

Derek Mahon

Overview

On the occasion of his uncle's death, the poet considers the true nature of the man. He sees him in a new light, as a man who liked to create appearances and whose reputation was, perhaps, deliberately cultivated to be 'larger than life'.

Insights

Stop
This poem refers to a unique moment in family life.

Look
The undertaker has changed aspects of the uncle's appearance and taken away some of the visual features for which he was well-remembered – the moustache, hairstyle and glasses.

Listen
The silence of the front room contrasts with the noisiness associated with the uncle. His burial is on an appropriately 'blustery' day that, in some ways, reflects his temperament; but mourners are not mentioned, only sheep and empty ships.

The five 'W' words

When?
Probably the latter part of the 20th century, referring to the uncle's earlier life.

Where?
There is a Northern Ireland setting for the funeral, but reference is made to the uncle's exploits in different parts of the world.

Who?
The poet; his uncle; the chairman of the company for which he worked; the lascar crew with whom he worked; the young minister who buried him; his teenage children.

What?
The poet sees matters in a new light. The uncle's reputation was based upon self-narrated stories mainly inspired by fantasy. He wanted to appear 'wicked' in the sense of being roguish or playfully mischievous. He had what he considered to be a 'salesman dash', the exaggerated features of a person who feels that he must be noticed by others.

Why?
One of the purposes of the poem is to show how changes take place. The poet has a different perception of his uncle. It contrasts with what he previously thought and with what the uncle wished to project. There are constant changes in society and the 'life and times' of his uncle altered considerably. Not only did he make the ultimate change from life to death, but he showed how certain ways of behaviour, of dress and manner become outdated and disregarded. Whether his children are more 'wicked' in the genial sense or are actually malicious is not explained. What is certain is that they differ from their father and see life in a different way.

Writing

- Imagine that you are a local newspaper reporter and that you have to write a straightforward account of the life of the deceased. You will have to be inventive, but try to remain authentic.
- Pretend that you are the author of this poem. Write a letter to relatives in Australia informing them of your uncle's death and indicate what you felt about him as a person.
- Consider the word 'wicked'. Devise one paragraph that explores its meanings in the sense of 'evil and malicious' and another that brings out its meanings with the 'mischievous and roguish' implications.

2 Response to literature: poetry

Chaucer's description of The Miller from The Prologue to *The Canterbury Tales*

> The Miller was a stout carl, for the nones,
> Ful big he was of braun, and eek of bones;
> That proved wel, for over-al ther he cam,
> At wrastling he wolde, have alwey the ram.
> He was short-sholdred, brood, thikke knarre,   5
> Ther was no dore that he nolde heve of harre,
> Or breke it, at a renning with his heed.

His berd as any sowe or fox was reed,
And ther-to brood, as though it were a spade.
Up-on the cop right of his nose he hade   10
A werte, and ther-on stood a tuft of heres,
Reed as the bristles of a sowes eres;
His nose-thirles blake were and wyde.
A swerd and bokeler bar he by his syde;
His mouth as greet was as a greet forneys.   15
He was a jangler and a goliardeys,
And that was most of sinne and harlotryes.
Wel coude he stelen corn, and tollen thryes;
And yet he hadde a thombe of gold, pardee.
A whyt cote and a blew hood wered he.   20
A baggepype wel coude he blowe and sowne,
And ther-with-al he broghte us out of towne.

This was written in the late 14th century and language has obviously changed since then. Some of the words have remained unaltered and some have just had a letter or two amended. If you enjoy working things out, then here's an opportunity.
  Line references:

1 *carl*: fellow;   *for the nones*: for the occasion
2 *eek*: moreover
4 *the ram*: the prize he won for overcoming all opponents at wrestling
5 *a thikke knarre*: a muscular fellow
6 *harre*: hinges
8 *reed*: red
10 *cop*: tip
11 *werte*: wart;   *heres*: hairs
12 *eres*: ears
13 *nose-thirles*: nostrils
14 *bokeler*: shield;   *bar*: carried
15 *forneys*: furnace
16 *jangler*: loud talker;   *goliardeys*: coarse buffoon
17 *harlotryes*: obscene subjects
18 *tollen thryes*: take three times the permitted toll or charge
19 *thombe of gold*: discoloured by handling corn samples as well as a sign of the way he acquired his wealth
20 *whyt*: white;   *blew*: blue

Our reading of this passage could be along the following lines.

Overview

Here is a portrait of an assertive, aggressive figure who likes to be seen, for he is leading the group of people out of the town; and to be heard, either by playing bagpipes or talking loudly. He is a big man, with a certain presence!

Insights

Stop
This type of man would arrest your attention anywhere.

Look
He seems to be as thick as he is tall, with a broad head, mouth, beard and shoulders. His nose, tipped with a wart which, in turn, is tipped with bristly red hairs, is certainly distinctive.

Listen
To the noises that he makes.

The five 'W' words

When?
Chaucerian times in the late 14th century, but there is a timelessness about attention-seeking wrestlers who don't mind what people think of them or their activities.

Where?
On the pilgrimage to Canterbury.

Who?
A portrait centred very much on the man himself – his looks, interests and forceful ways. Here's an individual who appears to indulge in a hobby of heaving doors off their hinges or battering them with his head.

What?
This is a description, but you can imagine that things will happen wherever this man goes.

Why?
Chaucer tries to bring alive the vital, outrageous features of this man so that we do not forget him easily. He may have been based upon a real person or represent a certain type of brute.

Writing:

- Write an account of The Miller in modern English.
- How would he be likely to earn his living in the 20th century?

3 Response to literature: non-fiction

from *Political Register* (16 March, 1811)

The words were: "that in proposing this amendment, he by no means intended to defeat the ends of punishment. It would only give to the Courts Martial *an alternative*, where they should think it necessary, to imprison, instead of resorting to any *corporal punishment*."—That is to say, *to flogging*. Why do you mince the matter? Why not name the thing? *Flog* is *flog*, and *flogging* is the active participle of the verb to *flog*. *Flog, flogging, flogged*. That is the word; and, it means, in this sense of it, to whip the naked back (and, sometimes, *other parts*) of a soldier, with a thing called a *cat*; that is to say, with nine strong whipcords, about a foot and a half long, with nine knots in each, and which cords are fastened, like the thong of a whip, to the end of a stick about two feet long. With this cat-o'-nine-tails the soldier, being tied up to a thing for the purpose, by his hands and thighs, is flogged, out in the open field, or parade, while the regiment are drawn up round him.—This is the plain, unadorned, unexaggerated thing; and its name is *flogging*. Why, then, call it by any other name? Why call it "*corporal infliction?*" These words may mean anything touching the body. The word *flogging* we all understand; and, as to *delicacy* of expression, if the word *be* indelicate, what must the *thing* be?

WILLIAM COBBETT

Overview

The author is responding strongly to an amendment that has been proposed, probably in Parliament. He wants to make clear his point and, metaphorically, lay bare the language.

Insights

These are words that are intended to be heard – either because they have been spoken or because they lend themselves to the orator's art. The audience is virtually asked to *stop* and consider the matter. Then they are to *listen* to the key word repeatedly and then they are to *look* at the way in which the activity takes place. The implication is that this activity should be stopped!

The five 'W' words

When?
Date supplied.

Where?
The act of flogging takes place in the army, in front of regiments on the parade grounds or in the camps.

Who?
The author is responding to another speaker who has used the words 'corporal punishment'. He refers to a soldier being 'punished'.

What?
Most of the passage is about the detailed examination of language and what the words 'flogging' and 'cat' actually mean in the context of an army punishment.

Why?
It is meant to expose a barbarous form of punishment, to show exactly what happens and to ridicule the ways in which carefully chosen words (euphemisms) can be used to cover the real, and in this case savage, nature of things.

Writing

- Imagine that you are an army officer of the time. Counter Cobbett's arguments by maintaining a case for strong military discipline.
- 'Pollution of the environment' is a polite way of referring to the destruction of natural things. Write on the subject of 'Pollution' with the same fervour as Cobbett.

4 Response to literature: drama

from *Death of a Salesman*

BIFF: What are you talking about? You're not even sixty, Mom.
LINDA: But what about your father?
BIFF (*lamely*): Well, I meant him too.
HAPPY: He admires Pop.
LINDA: Biff, dear, if you don't have any feeling for him, then you can't have any feeling for me.
BIFF: Sure I can, Mom.

LINDA: No. You can't just come to see me, because I love him. (*With a threat, but only a threat, of tears.*) He's the dearest man in the world to me, and I won't have anyone making him feel unwanted and low and blue. You've got to make up your mind now, darling, there's no leeway any more. Either he's your father and you pay him that respect, or else you're not to come here. I know he's not easy to get along with – nobody knows that better than me – but ...

WILLY (*from the left, with a laugh*): Hey, hey, Biffo!

BIFF (*starting to go out after Willy*): What the hell is the matter with him? (HAPPY *stops him.*)

LINDA: Don't – don't go near him!

BIFF: Stop making excuses for him! He always, always wiped the floor with you. Never had an ounce of respect for you.

HAPPY: He's always had respect for –

BIFF: What the hell do you know about it?

HAPPY (*surlily*): Just don't call him crazy!

BIFF: He's got no character – Charley wouldn't do this. Not in his own house – spewing out that vomit from his mind.

HAPPY: Charley never had to cope with what he's got to.

BIFF: People are worse off than Willy Loman. Believe me, I've seen them.

LINDA: Then make Charley your father, Biff. You can't do that, can you? I don't say he's a great man. Willy Loman never made a lot of money. His name was never in the paper. He's not the finest character that ever lived. But he's a human being, and a terrible thing is happening to him. So attention must be paid. He's not to be allowed to fall into his grave like an old dog. Attention, attention must be finally paid to such a person. You called him crazy –

BIFF: I didn't mean –

LINDA: No, a lot of people think he's lost his – balance. But you don't have to be very smart to know what his trouble is. The man is exhausted.

HAPPY: Sure!

LINDA: A small man can be just as exhausted as a great man. He works for a company thirty-six years this March, opens up unheard-of territories to their trademark, and now in his old age they take his salary away.

HAPPY (*indignantly*): I didn't know that, Mom.

LINDA: You never asked, my dear! Now that you get your spending money someplace else you don't trouble your mind with him.

HAPPY: But I gave you money last –

LINDA: Christmas-time, fifty dollars! To fix the hot water it cost ninety-seven fifty! For five weeks he's been on straight commission, like a beginner, an unknown!

BIFF: Those ungrateful bastards!

LINDA: Are they any worse than his sons? When he brought them business, when he was young, they were glad to see him. But now his old friends, the old buyers that loved him so and always found some order to hand him in a pinch – they're all dead, retired. He used to be able to make six, seven calls a day in Boston. Now he takes his valises out of the car and puts them back and takes them out again and he's exhausted. Instead of walking he talks now. He drives seven hundred miles, and when he gets there no one knows him any more, no one welcomes him. And what goes through a man's mind, driving seven hundred miles home without having earned a cent? Why shouldn't he talk to himself? Why? When he has to go to Charley and borrow fifty dollars a week and pretend to me that it's his pay? How long can that go on? How long? You see what I'm sitting here and waiting for? And you tell me he has no character? The man who never worked a day but for your benefit? When does he get the medal for that? Is this his reward – to turn around at the age of sixty-three and find his sons, who he loved better than his life, one a philandering bum –

HAPPY: Mom!

LINDA: That's all you are, my baby! (*To Biff.*) And you! What happened to the love you had for him? You were such pals! How you used to talk to him on the phone every night! How lonely he was till he could come home to you!

BIFF: All right, Mom. I'll live here in my room, and I'll get a job. I'll keep away from him, that's all.

LINDA: No, Biff. You can't stay here and fight all the time.

BIFF: He threw me out of this house, remember that.

LINDA: Why did he do that? I never knew why.

BIFF: Because I know he's a fake and he doesn't like anybody around who knows!

LINDA: Why a fake! In what way? What do you mean?

BIFF: Just don't lay it all at my feet. It's between me and him – that's all I have to say. I'll chip in from now on. He'll settle for half my pay cheque. He'll be all right. I'm going to bed.

He starts for the stairs.

LINDA: He won't be all right.

BIFF (*turning on the stairs, furiously*): I hate this city and I'll stay here. Now what do you want?

LINDA: He's dying, Biff.

ARTHUR MILLER

Overview

The key to the passage is the opening question – 'But what about your father?' What follows concerns what is wrong with him: his state of mind, character, feelings, relationships and work; and how his wife feels that 'attention must be paid'.

Insights

Stop
Very strong feelings are being expressed about all-important issues of life ... and death.

Look
Every topic involves the father (Willy Loman) but he is almost off-stage, away from the intense conversation conducted between Linda, his wife, and their sons, Biff and Happy.

Listen
To the changes of the pitch of the voices as emotions vary, to the only time that the 'central' character speaks and to the only laugh referred to in the extract.

The five 'W' words

When?
The working conditions and monetary values suggests the mid-20th century.

Where?
In the Loman family home in the United States of America. There are a few American words and expressions as well as the direct references to Boston and dollars.

Who?
Willy Loman – father; Linda – wife; Biff and Happy – sons; Charley – family friend; 'His old friends, the old buyers that loved him so ...
they're all dead, retired' – people who once featured in Willy Loman's work as a salesman.

What?
The mother issues an ultimatum – 'Either he's your father and you pay him that respect, or else you're not to come here.' This leads to a fervent discussion that involves:

1. Willy's mental health – 'spewing out that vomit from his mind'.
2. The 'terrible thing [that] is happening to him' – exhaustion.
3. His loss of earning power, inability to make ends meet, and need to borrow money pretending that it's his pay.
4. The apparent loss of love between father and son, culminating in the boy having been thrown out of the house.

Linda is assertive throughout the passage until she is obviously perplexed by the accusation of Biff who says, 'Because I know he's a fake and he doesn't like anybody around who knows!' Finally she makes a dramatic revelation of her own – 'He's dying, Biff.'

Why?
The author is revealing various aspects of the salesman's life and the ways in which his mind, body, effectiveness, work and relationships are deteriorating. At this point of the play he is being seen through the eyes of others.

Writing

- Imagine that you are Charley, the friend, and that you have overheard these remarks through the walls of the house. Sum up what has been said in order to tell your wife of the Lomans' troubles.
- Work out from this exercise why Willy Loman has become 'exhausted'.

5 Response to literature: Shakespeare

from *Measure for Measure* (Act I: scene 4)

Enter LUCIO.

Lucio. Hail, virgin, if you be, as those cheek-roses
Proclaim you are no less! Can you so stead me
As bring me to the sight of Isabella,
A novice of this place, and the fair sister
To her unhappy brother Claudio?   5
Isabella. Why 'her unhappy brother'? let me ask,
The rather for I now must make you know
I am that Isabella and his sister.
Lucio. Gentle and fair, your brother kindly greets you.
Not to be weary with you, he's in prison.   10
Isabella. Woe me! for what?
Lucio. For that which, if myself might be his judge,
He should receive his punishment in thanks:
He hath got his friend with child.
Isabella. Sir, make me not your story.
Lucio.   It is true.   15
I would not, though 'tis my familiar sin
With maids to seem the lapwing and to jest,
Tongue far from heart, play with all virgins so:
I hold you as a thing ensky'd and sainted;
By your renouncement an immortal spirit,   20

    And to be talk'd with in sincerity,
    As with a saint.
Isabella. You do blaspheme the good in mocking me.
Lucio. Do not believe it. Fewness and truth, 'tis thus:
    Your brother and his lover have embrac'd: 25
    As those that feed grow full, as blossoming time
    That from the seedness the bare fallow brings
    To teeming foison, even so her plenteous womb
    Expresseth his full tilth and husbandry.
Isabella. Some one with child by him? My cousin Juliet? 30
Lucio. Is she your cousin?
Isabella. Adoptedly; as school-maids change their names
    By vain though apt affection.
Lucio.   She it is.
Isabella. O! Let him marry her.
Lucio.   This is the point.
    The duke is very strangely gone from hence;   35
    Bore many gentlemen, myself being one,
    In hand and hope of action; but we do learn
    By those that know the very nerves of state,
    His givings out were of an infinite distance
    From his true-meant design. Upon his place,   40
    And with full line of his authority,
    Governs Lord Angelo; a man whose blood
    Is very snow-broth; one who never feels
    The wanton stings and motions of the sense,
    But doth rebate and blunt his natural edge   45
    With profits of the mind, study and fast.
    He, to give fear to use and liberty,
    Which have for long run by the hideous law,
    As mice by lions, hath pick'd out an act,
    Under whose heavy sense your brother's life   50
    Falls into forfeit: he arrests him on it,
    And follows close the rigour of the statute,
    To make him an example. All hope is gone,
    Unless you have the grace by your fair prayer
    To soften Angelo; and that's my pith of business 55
    'Twixt you and your poor brother.
Isabella. Doth he so seek his life?
Lucio.   Has censur'd him
    Already; and, as I hear, the provost hath
    A warrant for his execution.
Isabella. Alas! what poor ability's in me   60
    To do him good?
Lucio.   Assay the power you have.
Isabella. My power? alas! I doubt, –
Lucio.   Our doubts are traitors,
    And make us lose the good we oft might win,
    By fearing to attempt. Go to Lord Angelo,
    And let him learn to know, when maidens sue,   65
    Men give like gods; but when they weep and kneel,
    All their petitions are as freely theirs
    As they themselves would owe them.
Isabella. I'll see what I can do.
Lucio.   But speedily.
Isabella. I will about it straight;   70
    No longer staying but to give the Mother

Notice of my affair. I humbly thank you:
Commend me to my brother; soon at night
I'll send him certain word of my success.
Lucio.   I take my leave of you.
Isabella.   Good sir, adieu. [*Exeunt.*   75

WILLIAM SHAKESPEARE

Line references:

2   *stead*: help
4   *novice*: a nun who has not yet taken her final vows
10 *weary*: wearisome, tedious
14 *friend*: lover
15 *story*: object of ridicule
18 *seem the lapwing*: be deceptive
19 *Tongue ... heart*: not expressing my real feelings
20 *ensky'd*: heavenly
21 *renouncement*: renunciation of the pleasures of this world
25 *Fewness and truth*: to speak truly and briefly
28 *seedness*: seed-time, time of sowing
29 *teeming foison*: abundant crop
30 *tilth and husbandry*: cultivation
34 *Adoptedly*: by adoption
35 *vain*: informal, joking
43 *givings out ... design*: his utterances were very different from his real intentions
47 *snow-broth*: a mixture of snow and water
48 *wanton stings and motions*: lustful and sensual desires
49 *rebate*: tone down; *edge*: appetite
52 *run by*: ignored; *hideous*: savage
54 *heavy sense*: severe terms
58 *grace*: attractive power
59 *pith of business*: essential business
62 *censur'd*: sentenced
79 *Mother*: Mother Superior of the Convent
82 *my success*: how I have got on

This passage obviously comes into a different category. It needs more preparation time and has to be worked on before its meaning can be worked out. Use the notes and carefully try to translate the lines into modern English before attempting to apply the suggested strategy of 'breaking down' the passage.

Overview

Lucio has arrived at Isabella's convent to bring news of her brother's imprisonment and sentence of execution for having made her friend, Juliet, pregnant. Her help is needed.

Insights

Stop
This is about a serious and delicate matter, literally involving life (in particular, its creation), death (in particular, the threat of execution), and the need for urgent action to be taken.

Look
Lucio is not directly involved in the business, but is the conveyor of

bad news. He plays a decisive role in getting Isabella to respond to his requests.

Listen
He explains fully, talks a lot and almost seems to enjoy his role as both messenger and persuader.

The five 'W' words

When?
Shakespearian times.

Where?
In the entrance to a convent that is situated in a country or state governed by a duke who has departed and left Lord Angelo in charge. The names of the characters suggest Italy.

Who?
Lucio – acting as a messenger; Isabella – a nun in training; Claudio – her brother; Juliet – Isabella's friend who has been made pregnant by Claudio; Angelo – the acting governor of the state.

What?
Lucio arrives at the convent, does not know the person he is addressing, but is very familiar – 'Hail, virgin, if you be … !' When he establishes that it is Isabella he continues in much the same direct tone, informs her immediately of Claudio's imprisonment and even makes his own observation about the matter of pregnancy:

> For that which, if myself might be his judge,
> He should receive his punishment in thanks

There are more diplomatic ways of approaching serious and delicate matters!

Lucio acknowledges his way of joking with all young women and goes on to explain in a full and elaborate way the relationship of her brother and lover. Isabella interrupts him and comes quickly to the point:

> Some one with child by him? My cousin Juliet?

Her advice is straightforward:

> O! Let him marry her.

This introduces the second part of the passage, the reason why the usually neglected law concerning conception out of wedlock has suddenly been imposed. The new, temporary governor, Angelo, has, according to Lucio, a cold-blooded attitude, repressed sexual desires, and a wish to impose his authority by making an example of someone who has broken the law. Having informed Isabella in considerable detail, Lucio makes a fairly sweeping comment:

> All hope is gone

This leads to his request for her prayers … soon to become an appeal to go to see Angelo … followed by the advice that she should 'weep and kneel'… and then the instruction that it should be done promptly. She appears to be humble and obedient in her responses to this fairly direct, assertive series of requests.

Why?
Shakespeare is drawing our attention to a critical piece of news that

begins an important action, the departure of a novice from a convent to appeal to the governor of the country. Certain personal features are stressed. Lucio appears to be an impulsive man in the way in which he conducts himself in a situation that would normally encourage formal manners. Claudio and Juliet have been unrestrained in some of their earlier behaviour. Isabella obviously decided, earlier in her life, to devote herself to a disciplined way of life, while Angelo would appear to have a naturally cold, rigorous attitude that makes him a harsh, decisive authoritarian figure. Towards the end of the scene the audience is left wondering whether Lucio's earnest appeal to Isabella – 'soften Angelo' – will be successful.

Writing

- Give a personal sketch of Lucio based upon the information given in this extract.
- Imagine that you are Isabella. Trace the patterns of thought that run through your mind as your meeting with Lucio proceeds.

6 Response to literature: Charles Dickens

from *Our Mutual Friend*

In these times of ours, though concerning the exact year there is no need to be precise, a boat of dirty and disreputable appearance, with two figures in it, floated on the Thames, between Southwark Bridge which is of iron, and London Bridge which is of stone, as an autumn evening was closing in.

The figures in this boat were those of a strong man with ragged grizzled hair and a sun-browned face, and a dark girl of nineteen or twenty, sufficiently like him to be recognisable as his daughter. The girl rowed, pulling a pair of sculls very easily; the man, with the rudder-lines slack in his hands, and his hands loose in his waistband, kept an eager look-out. He had no net, hook, or line, and he could not be a fisherman; his boat had no cushion for a sitter, no paint, no inscription, no appliance beyond a rusty boat-hook and a coil of rope, and he could not be a waterman; his boat was too crazy and too small to take in a cargo for delivery, and he could not be a lighterman or river-carrier; there was no clue to what he looked for, but he looked for something, with a most intent and searching gaze. The tide, which had turned an hour before, was running down, and his eyes watched every little race and eddy in its broad sweep, as the boat made slight headway against it, or drove stern foremost before it, according as he directed his daughter by a movement of his head. She watched his face as earnestly as he watched the river. But, in the intensity of her look there was a touch of dread or horror.

Allied to the bottom of the river rather than the surface, by reason of the slime and ooze with which it was covered, and its sodden state, this boat and the two figures in it obviously were doing something that they often did, and were seeking what they often sought. Half-savage as the man showed, with no covering on his matted head, with his brown arms bare to the elbow and the shoulder, with the loose knot of a looser kerchief lying low on his bare breast in a wilderness of beard and whisker, with such dress as he wore seeming to be made out of the mud that begrimed his boat, still there was business-like usage in his steady gaze. So with every lithe action of the girl, with every turn of her wrist, perhaps most of all with her look of dread or horror; they were things of usage.

"Keep her out, Lizzie. Tide runs strong here. Keep her well afore the sweep of it."

Trusting to the girl's skill and making no use of the rudder, he eyed the coming tide with an absorbed attention. So the girl eyed him. But, it happened now, that a slant of light from the setting sun glanced into the bottom of the boat, and, touching a rotten stain there which bore some resemblance to the outline of a muffled human form, coloured it as though with diluted blood. This caught the girl's eye, and she shivered.

"What ails you?" said the man, immediately aware of it, though so intent on the advancing waters; "I see nothing afloat."

The red light was gone, the shudder was gone, and his gaze, which had come back to the boat for a moment, travelled away again. Wheresoever the strong tide met with an impediment, his gaze paused for an instant. At every mooring chain and rope, at every stationary boat or barge that split the current into a broad-arrow-head, at the offsets from the piers of Southwark Bridge, at the paddles of the river steamboats as they beat the filthy water, at the floating logs of timber lashed together lying off certain wharves, his shining eyes darted a hungry look. After a darkening hour or so, suddenly the rudder-lines tightened in his hold, and he steered hard towards the Surrey shore.

CHARLES DICKENS

Overview

On a dark evening two dark figures in a small boat are closely examining the dirty waters of the River Thames in their search for something.

Insights

Stop
The people seem absorbed by their task and it's the girl who is skilfully handling the boat.

Look
This is certainly what the couple, a father and daughter, are doing! Consider the number of words in the second paragraph connected with the act of looking.

Listen
They appear to work, for the most part, in silence. 'He directed his daughter by a movement of his head.' The father speaks twice, obviously at significant moments. The daughter says nothing, she just 'shivered'.

The five 'W' words

When?
Dickensian times – autumn – evening.

Where?
On a stretch of the River Thames between Southwark Bridge and London Bridge.

Who?
Father – a strong, quiet, hairy man wearing clothes begrimed with mud. There is a 'business-like' air about this person referred to as 'half-savage'. For most of the passage he makes no use of the rudder, but allows his daughter to determine the movements of the boat.
Daughter – a silent young woman who can handle a rowing boat with considerable ease and who has the confidence of her father. They watch one another closely as well as the surface of the river. Her one movement, perhaps out of character, is to give a shudder.

What?

During their investigations of the surface and currents of the river in order to find something floating, the father keeps his eye on his daughter's facial expressions. She, too, watches his movements and signs. At the critical moment when she shivers, he notices it immediately. The cause of her response is a slant of light that has revealed a stain on the bottom of the boat. For a moment it appeared to be the 'outline of a muffled human form'.

Why?

The author creates a feeling of heightened atmosphere in which two characters are doing something that they frequently undertake, in a place and way that they know well. We, as readers, are the ones 'left in the dark' for we can only guess that they are doing something stealthily, under cover of darkness. The stain that looked as though it is of 'diluted blood' suggests something sinister. This 'crisis' passes, but at the end of the extract, an hour or so later, 'the rudder-lines tightened'. The father suddenly responds and takes charge. A sense of mystery prevails.

Writing

- Imagine that you are on the bank of the river witnessing the scene involving the absorbed searchers. Carefully tell what you have seen.
- Describe this situation through the eyes of the girl.

7 Response to non-literary and media texts: profile

Back to the lonely sea and the sky

At 71, Michael Richey survived the sinking of his yacht *Jester* in a storm. Now, at 75, he's fighting the elements in the Single-handed Transatlantic Race. *Frank Page* reports

When Michael Richey's tiny yacht *Jester* was being battered almost to destruction by a force ten storm some 300 miles west of Land's End in 1986, he was able to maintain a remarkably philosophical attitude. "The violence had reached alarming proportions," he wrote later, "and I wondered how much more the boat would stand. I viewed the prospect with some equanimity, although without enthusiasm, wondering how the last moments might pass. It had, I reflected playfully, at least a certain style."

Such British sang-froid is typical of Michael Richey. He and his boat made ten single-handed transatlantic passages and five voyages to the Azores and back together over the 24 years that he owned her. During that time they survived violent storms, an attack by killer whales off the Grand Banks, several knockdowns and at least one 360-degree roll-over. Sometimes Michael was injured; often he suffered from exposure. Yet you will never hear him put any blame for anything that happened on *Jester*, or on anyone else. And you will never hear him complain about bad luck. When, eventually, *Jester* was lost during the 1988 Single-handed Transatlantic Race, the skipper would blame only himself.

Jester had been knocked down and badly damaged in a severe gale some 470 miles southwest of Halifax, Nova Scotia. Not only was she half-full of water, but one of her side-hatches had been stove in, leaving her open to the sea and in peril of being completely swamped. Michael activated his emergency radio beacon and was pinpointed by a US Coast Guard airplane and then rescued by a 60,000-ton bulk carrier.

But there is a happy ending to the sad story, for there is now a new *Jester*, built almost exactly like the old. As you read this,

Michael Richey should be well on his way from Plymouth to Newport, Rhode Island in the 1992 *Observer* Single-handed Transatlantic, which started from Plymouth on 7 June. *Jester*'s is the only name to have appeared in the entry list of every race in the four-yearly series since it began in 1960. I went to see Michael and the new boat in Brighton Marina, and quickly sensed his enormous affection for this *Jester* which looks and feels so much like the old.

The original *Jester* was designed by Colonel Blondie Hasler, a former Royal Marines officer, who wanted to create a yacht which could be cruised single-handedly in far more comfort than a conventional craft. Built in 1953, she had a Folkboat hull with fully-enclosed superstructure. A fully-battened Chinese lugsail on an unstayed hollow wooden mast had all its lines – halyard, hauling parrel, downhauls and sheet – within reach of the crew standing in the central hatch.

Blondie Hasler sailed *Jester* across the Atlantic in the first two *Observer* races, finishing second to Sir Francis Chichester in 1960 and fifth behind Eric Tabarly in 1964. Then Michael Richey, prompted by Sir Francis, bought *Jester* and sailed her in the next six races. Though the yacht would never be likely to take a high place in the finishing list, she did provide Michael with plentiful material for his learned articles on navigation.

For navigation is his passion. He served as a navigating officer in the Navy during the war. After demobilisation in 1946 he became one of the top navigators in ocean racing, and in 1947 joined the newly-formed Royal Institute of Navigation as executive secretary. He directed the affairs of the Institute through to 1982 and continued to edit its Journal for another four years after that. Now aged 75, he is semi-retired, though he still writes a regular column on navigation for *Yachting Monthly* and has several book projects on the boil.

On the new *Jester* there are several differences from the original. The hull is cold-moulded rather than carvel-built and a sophisticated modern hatch on the foredeck replaces the more vulnerable fitting which was simply sucked out of the yacht in that almost-calamitous 1986 storm. But the Hasler-designed whaleback coachroof is exactly like the old one.

Michael Richey will not use an electronic GPS (global positioning system) which takes signals from geo-stationary satellites to provide an instant fix on his position.

"I don't really understand GPS," he says. "But I do think yachtsmen are quite right to use it. And I think Captain Cook would have used GPS if it existed in his day. Really its development is no more revolutionary than the chronometer." But supposing the electronics fail? "Then buy two – you can get a couple for less than the price of a good sextant." He does use a small pocket computer, rather than printed tables, to work out his positions from sun or star sights. "That's really still the traditional method, because tables are only what some other computer has already worked out."

Bearing in mind that the fastest boats now do the Single-handed Transatlantic in little over a fortnight, I asked him if he had a target time for himself and *Jester*.

"About 50 days," he replied, with a slightly rueful smile.

Overview

This article considers the enthusiams, disposition and attitudes of a man, Michael Richey; the technical features of his yachts, the old and new *Jesters*; the details and dangers of transatlantic voyages.

Insights

Stop
This is about a man in his mid-70s who continues to undertake adventures that would frighten most people.

Look
At the power and ferocity of the sea and the elements, and then picture the dimensions of the yacht.

Listen
For the tones of affection about the craft of sailing and the technical terms which you have probably never heard before.

The five 'W' words

When?
The dates mentioned are from 1946 until almost 50 years later.

Where?
The interview was conducted at Brighton Marina and the references are mainly about the single-handed yacht races and journeys across the north Atlantic.

Who?
Michael Richey; Blondie Hasler; other lone voyagers.

What?
The interview focuses on Michael Richey's survival in 1986, his determination to continue, the designs of his yachts and his methods of navigation.

Why?
To illustrate how certain individuals love to undertake particular activities regardless of effort, age or danger.

Writing

- What motivates Michael Richey?
- Single-handed transatlantic sailing is just one activity of many difficult tasks that people set for themselves. Consider a challenge that *you* would like to undertake.

8 Response to non-literary and media texts: instruction

How to face a live audience
Fighting her nerves, **Margaret Coles** plunges into public speaking – and lives to tell the tale

SPEAKING in public is a prospect that terrifies most of us. A polished performer can make it look the easiest thing in the world, but we know that if we had to do it we would shake, sweat, drop our notes, forget our jokes and make complete idiots of ourselves.

"It is perfectly natural to be nervous," says Cristina Stuart, managing director of Speakeasy Training and author of *Effective Speaking*. "The secret is not to let it show – and that's a skill that can be acquired."

To find out how, I joined six managers from a cross-section of industry on a two-day Speakeasy training session that embraced every aspect of presentation on a public platform: preparing the speech, using the voice effectively, breathing and relaxation, using visual aids, handling the audience.

The first thing to do, Cristina Stuart tells us, is to get the body language right. "People read body language, it's stronger than words. However you look or move, you will be signalling your feelings. If your inner panic shows itself in fidgety feet and fiddling fingers, your audience will feel uncomfortable, because they want and expect you to be in control. They won't have confidence in you, your ideas or your product. They won't listen well and will quickly forget what you said."

The key to good body language is eye contact. "If you want your audience to have confidence in you, you have to look them in the eye," says Cristina. "When you don't, they feel, probably unconsciously, that you don't care whether they listen or not and because they don't feel involved by you their concentration lags."

Participants had been asked to bring a prepared speech, which they gave before a video camera. They were helped to analyse their performance and identify things they needed to work on. Later they were asked to step in front of the camera again, this time to talk without any preparation.

"John, I'd like you to simply describe the inside of your home. I want you to use bigger gestures, be overdramatic, over the top, have fun. Use your height." Cristina smiles encouragingly as John tries to make bigger gestures while describing his lounge. Cristina: "Put your hands by your sides for a moment. Look at the audience. Bring your feet round. Bring your hands down. OK – marble fireplace... . " John starts again.

When Cristina plays back the video, she turns the sound down. "Can you see why I asked you to overdo it? Was any of that over-done?" "No, not at all!" "You see, you can afford to do that."

Charles is next. He is allowed to sit, because he is going to be working on his voice. "You can say anything else, but not 'er'." Charles begins, describing the hallway, the carpets, curtains, furniture... . "Oh, you've conquered that one, that's marvellous, no 'ers' at all – but it's going very fast and it is a bit of a monotone. Try to see if you can get some colour into your voice."

Charles describes the fireplace, the wallpaper. "Slow down," Cristina interjects. "Try to get colour into your voice. Very slow. Slow." Charles's pace begins to slow and he manages to use a variety of pitch and tone. "Good. How did it feel?" "It felt slow." The group, however, found it much better to listen to: they said they felt much more involved in what he was saying.

For the next turn before the camera, the participants were asked to prepare the sort of speech they might have to give in the course of their work. They were offered a formula – identifying their objective, in order to select the right material; thinking about the audience – how much they knew about the subject, how much they needed to know, if any decision-maker would be present; creating a structure by jotting down ideas and thoughts and then choosing material in order of importance.

This time they performed far better and looked much more confident. David Froude, a director of a group of estate agents, said: "I had a feeling that I didn't present myself very well in speeches but I didn't know why. Halfway through the course I began to realise why I wasn't doing well, and by the end of the course I started doing it right.

"For me, eye contact was the main thing that was wrong. I didn't look at individuals, but rather, through them or over them. And I needed to work on my tone of voice and emphasis – my voice was too low, and not varied and expressive enough.

"When you are in the audience you can tell if the speaker is looking at you and if he is interested or just looking blankly. Towards the end of the course I was noticing if people were paying attention, and if someone wasn't looking at me I looked at him until he did, so I was able to command their attention better. On the voice, I learned how to vary the tone and pitch and how to project, to make it more interesting.

"It was nice to be part of a small group; I found the group comment very useful, because they were managers at the same sort of level, but we did not know each other, so nobody had an axe to grind."

John Dunlop, general manager of the Post Office's consultancy services group, was on the course because "there is now much less reliance on the written word. My job involves communicating with a team, drawing them in, putting across ideas which they then develop, and I want to improve my skills in that direction."

A month after the course he said: "It was good for me because we had plenty of individual tuition and useful comments and lots of practice. The notes for planning a presentation gave a good, sensible step-by-step approach. I've been going through them again and find them very practical and helpful. I've been doing much more research and preparation, and thinking more about my audiences, and I've been more relaxed. I've made a couple of presentations since the course, and they have gone very well."

Cristina Stuart says: "Many people think speakers are born, that speaking can't be taught, but it can. Everyone is nervous, but when you see yourself on video you realise that nerves don't show up to the same extent that you feel them. The feeling of nervousness comes from the thought, 'I'm going to fail'. The thought comes from an attitude that says, 'Everyone is better than I am' or 'I have to be perfect'. If you can say, 'I don't have to be perfect to be successful', you take the pressure off yourself. The secret of controlling nerves is to have a more positive image of how things are going to go. You have to prepare and practise, but it will always look artificial until you can say, 'I may not be a great orator, but I can do a good job'."

The importance of being able to communicate effectively to an audience is now recognised by public and private organisations. The Civil Service puts it high on its training agenda "because the days when

Civil Servants were nameless and faceless gurus have gone," says Jonathan Lawson, head of information at the Cabinet Office. "Nowadays there is so much public exposure, through contact with the media and lobby groups and parliamentary committees, that lucid presentation is essential." The Civil Service runs its own courses, which are so highly regarded that top industrialists attend.

Overview

This article leads us from references to being terrified about public speaking to feeling reassured that there are ways and means of being successful.

Insights

Stop
Don't panic!

Look
Individual, specific pieces of advice are given.

Listen
To the people interviewed who now feel in greater control.

The five 'W' words

When?
Now.

Where?
Anywhere in the UK.

Who?
Cristina Stuart, the managing director of Speakeasy; some of the participants on one of her courses.

What?
Methods stressed; the importance of body language – eye contact – pitch and tone of voice – speed of delivery – material – needs of audience – attitudes of mind.

Why?
To emphasise that the application of certain methods can improve confidence in an area of human activity where fears are evident.

Writing

- Prepare a speech for a class or group in which you are advising them on how to speak in public. Incorporate your own views with some of those from the passage.
- Describe the content, delivery and effect of the worst speech or lesson that you have ever heard.

9 Response to non-literary and media texts: appeal

Why can't we sit still any more?

by Mary Killen

As the spectating season comes upon us – Wimbledon, Glyndebourne, Lord's, a new white-collar crime is set to wreck the harmless enjoyment of enthusiasts. Fidgeting. Cricket fan and Battersea Conservative MP John Bowis is among those who wrote to The Times this week to draw attention to the now quite prevalent, but previously unthinkable, practice of spectators actually moving about during overs at Lord's.

All Londoners who attend performances of sport or stage will be familiar with the rapidly-reducing attention spans of audiences. What has caused it?

Not so long ago audiences *did* sit to attention. "Silence in class!" and "Sit up Straight!" were almost like mantras in the consciousnesses of anyone whose school had managed to exert the slightest degree of discipline over its pupils.

It sank in at an early age that the correct response when being addressed, lectured to or performed to, was polite attention and concentration and this naturally applied outside the schoolroom too.

Now, all over London's theatre and cinemaland and soon, no doubt, at Wimbledon, we will see the increasingly-pernicious effects of the three-minute culture as audiences find it more and more difficult to prevent their minds from restlessly wandering and to sit through a performance in peace. Chewing, rustling, talking and – when they don't dare do any of those – coughing and throat clearing, the weed's way of attempting disruption.

It is partly the fault of television which is always adapting itself to our lazy and saturated brains. More programmes are being divided into "bites" or segments – Noel Edmonds' Telly Addicts, Masterchef, Antiques Roadshow. Children's television on Saturday mornings is the most insidious – a weekly three-hour training course in butterfly-braining young minds.

Leading the field in mental corruption are the Americans, whose television news programmes have to restrict coverage of each item to under 25 seconds. The audience loses interest after that and becomes impatient for the next item.

But the brain is like a muscle and we must use it or lose it, as the Oldie magazine warns its readers this week. You can test the accuracy of the muscle theory by trying to read Proust when out of practice. It takes a good few days to get that brain power up again to concentrating for 120 seconds at once – the length of time it takes to read an average Proustian paragraph with multiple tangents all threading back to a central idea.

How long will it be before hardly anyone can read Proust because the muscles have simply atrophied in just the same way as most women of my generation have lost the muscles for hand-washing jumpers and have to take them to be dry-cleaned or get their mothers, whose arms were trained in the days before washing machines, to do it?

We lament the lack of ability to concentrate, not so much as an authoritarian requisite, as because absorption can lead to great mental ecstasy through relief from oneself. As Proustian John Gross says: "Proust gives you another life."

We were not always expected to pay attention: Gross, who is also a theatre critic, reminds me that in the early 19th century people went to the theatre for openly social reasons, and screens were provided in boxes so that they could even shut off the irritating spectacle on the stage.

The performance was very much by the way, which is why the second acts of operas like La Traviata had "sex scenes" written in: pretty ladies dancing and kicking their legs in the air as a way of getting men in from the bar. It was not until the late 19th century that audiences were expected to concentrate.

Which brings us to a marvellous irony. In the 20th century the venue where art and society converge is the Royal Opera House. It is *the* place to be seen and yet talk is *verboten* and even leg-crossing is frowned on. Those who attend Covent Garden for openly social reasons don't usually do it more than once.

The seats at the Royal Opera House, which is in line for closure for refurbishment, have not been changed for more than 100 years when they were designed to accommodate pelvises of much smaller girth than today's. As one opera goer remarked: "It seems odd to see these plutocrats and businessmen sitting through five hours of intense discomfort. I feel that when they refurbish they should introduce a business class of seat with reclining facilities for those who are going to be spending five hours on Wagner. It's bloody uncomfortable at the moment."

I believe that Glyndebourne's recent popularity is because audiences know they can always escape into the wonderful grounds. It is always interesting to note the number of empty seats after the first interval.

Talking of escaping into the open air reminds me of the high point of the fidgeting season: Wimbledon. As the sun beats down on spectators at the end of next month we can only wonder how many times an hour the umpire will find it necessary to shout "Quiet please!"

As I watched the Wimbledon semi-finals on TV last year with some teenagers, the umpire kept appealing for the audience to stop making 'line calls" as this was very confusing for the players. "I'd be calling out Game, Seat and Match! if I were there" chortled one of the Etonian yobs in the room. And then he loped off in search of divertissement.

As John Bowis wrote in his letter to the Times: "One yearns for the days of those ripe and gnarled tyrants who struck terror into the schoolboy heart". But authority figures have been so demystified and debunked of late that it is hard to imagine anyone being genuinely frightened of such a figure.

from the *London Evening Standard*

Overview

Behavioural patterns change and by the late 20th century many people have, perhaps, lost the knack of being able to concentrate for longer than three minutes ... or less.

Insights

Stop
Leisure time, in general, and spectating, in particular, have increased. Television has enabled us to view public events while remaining in private places.

Look
At our own behaviour as well as of those around us.

Listen
Does this article ring true?

The five 'W' words

When?
Early 1990s.

Where?
Public gathering places.

Who?
Audiences, especially at national or prestigious events.

What?
The decreasing demand for long periods of concentration has led to parts of some people's brains being ineffective through lack of use. Changes in expectations, teaching methods, timing of stimulus material, authority and individual preferences have been matched by changes of behaviour.

Why?
Questions are posed about these changes and whether humankind has actually benefited when, apparently, there has been a general loss of certain mental attributes and skills of effective concentration.

Writing

- 'Why should we keep still? ... Ways of behaviour change ... We deserve to be entertained!' Continue this reply to Mary Killen, giving an alternative opinion.
- What makes you inattentive? Outline the types of events that would make you feel tired, bored and keen to escape from feeling trapped.

10 Response to non-literary and media texts: argument

The following extract is taken from an article that appeared at the time of a national scandal involving the alleged adultery of a politician.

from *Wedded bliss-ters*

Why do romantic novels always end with marriage? Because the people who write them know that that's the end of the really good stuff – all the juice has been squeezed. And it's high time that the rest of us admitted that marriage is the boring and unworkable institution that it is. Let's stop pretending that marriages are made in heaven, that they signify perfect love and that they last forever.

Enough of this falsehood that a marriage is a success if it lasts – however ghastly – and a failure if it ends – however nice it was while it lasted. This is not, after all, a standard that we apply to anything else.

Everybody who is married or has ever been married knows that marriage breeds contempt, children and divorce. But if you say so out loud it seems to upset people terribly. The messenger is blamed. The messenger is accused of spreading some terrible disease, like moral typhus, that Little Britishers won't catch, if they only shut their ears and eyes.

Men get particularly hot and bothered on the subject of divorce figures, because they have been deceived into thinking that they are some desirable prize, capable of conferring a great honour on women in the form of the marriage contract. After all, we are supposed to be luring them into the M-word with all our feminine wiles, not questioning the institution with our feminist logic.

Let's face it, married people are unutterably dull. Their souls denuded of hope, their sex lives of denuded interest and, worst of all, their fridges are stuffed with food not champagne. The light has gone out of their eyes because they always know who they'll be sleeping with that night.

Marriage is for people who've given up the struggle. You can spot them in restaurants a mile off: they're the silent ones. I don't know why the waiter asks, "Smoking or non-smoking?" when, "Talking or not talking?" would seem a more relevant question.

The only thing that they seem to enjoy wholeheartedly is bickering. They are rude to each other, preferably in front of an audience, and they expect you to put up with it. They arrive at dinner parties arguing about who is drinking and who is driving, and proceed from there. They make little digs at each other and you are supposed either to take sides, affect not to notice, or to find it amusing in some way. Actually single people are so unaccustomed to rows that it quite traumatises them.

There are three stages in the life of a couple who have contracted marriage, and none of them is pretty. Firstly there is the initial incubation period, when people do a lot of hand-holding and name cooing, and take up too much room on the pavement. Then they actually wed and behave relatively normally apart from an alarming level of smugness that seems designed to make the unmarried feel as though they have failed in some way. But don't worry, this doesn't last because they soon move into the full-blown marriage stage, clinically known as MH (mutual hatred).

Marriage is not a word, it is a sentence and there's only one section of society that benefits from it – the law. If there were no marriage there would be no D-I-V-O-R-C-E and that means many lawyers would be out of a job – what better way to chart society's progress towards civilisation? Also, there would be no need for all those guilt-pedlars, otherwise known as counsellors.

The only excuse for getting married is to have children. Then you enter another level of boredom, *competitive* boredom. You tend to meet other similarly circumstanced people with whom you can chat freely about school runs, the relative merits of nannies, the social implications of giving small boys guns and other equally fascinating subjects.

The marriage contract should expire automatically after five years because five years is the maximum length of time two people are any good to each other. At the end of *Sleeper*, Woody Allen's film set 200 years in the future, Diane Keaton explains that scientists have discovered that there is a chemical in our bodies that makes us get on each other's nerves after a while. Do we really need scientists to explain this to us?

SALLY ANN LASSON

Overview

This is strong stuff! The writer is attacking a universally-acknowledged institution and making it seem repellent. The pun in the title contrasts wedded 'bliss' with the word 'blisters' (a swelling caused by friction), which also has the meaning of 'to attack sharply'. Her well-ordered, vigorous and vehement article contains the essential ingredients of argument. Is it true?

Insights

Stop
The passage is contentious and needs thinking about, not immediate acceptance.

Look
The views expressed here are that relationships begin with one emotion, mutual attraction, invariably to end with another, resentment.

Listen
This is a piece of writing you can undoubtedly hear being spoken in words loud and clear, together with many of the background noises that the writer mentions or implies – cooing, bickering, boring, screaming and, then, silence.

The five 'W' words

When?
The 1990s, during the earlier years of some people's married lives.

Where?
Anywhere, although the conversational topics cited suggest an affluent area of England.

Who?
Partners in marriage.

What?
The writer suggests that there are inevitable stages in marriage in

which the 'chemistry' follows a certain course that leads to failure. These are, in her view, predictable, and are outlined.

Why?

A case is argued that is based upon opinion, experience and observation. We have to decide its merits, relevance and truth.

Writing

- Take the role of someone who upholds the need for traditional marriage – you might choose to write as a clergyman or as a marriage guidance counsellor – and make your reply.
- What do *you* expect from marriage?

11 Research and information retrieval: comparisons

These skills are based upon using the facilities of a library and on being able to know where to find the reference books that matter. Chapter 21 considers these activities in detail, but one of the requirements is the ability to see connections between facts, ideas and viewpoints. The following exercise may illustrate and help.

MR GERALD BRENAN

Mr Gerald Brenan, CBE, MC, who died on January 19, at the age of 92, was a gifted writer whose best books arose from his lifelong concern with Spain and his understanding of its ways.

The Spanish Labyrinth (1943) is acknowledged, even by the most exacting Spanish historians, as being unrivalled for its analysis of the social and political background to the civil war.

Edward FitzGerald Brenan was born on April 7, 1894, in Malta, the son of an officer in an Irish regiment, who tyrannised over him and his mother. His childhood was nomadic, and by the time he was six he had also lived in Africa, Ceylon, India and Ireland.

He was sent to prep school, and then to Radley, both of which he hated for their rigid code, unthinking glorification of games, the hypocrisy of school religion, and their deplorable attitude to the mass of the people.

At the end of his last term, in 1912, he slipped away to France, and from there he begged and pilfered his way, with a friend and a donkey cart, down to the Balkans. This progress made him familiar with low taverns, dosshouses and prisons.

Coming hard on his school experience, it confirmed him in that lifelong compassion for the poor which made him such an acute observer of the Spanish condition.

Lack of funds forced him back home in 1914, and he was sent to a crammer's with a view to his entering the Indian Police. He took the entrance exam, but before he knew the result war broke out.

Joining the 5th Gloucesters he fought from 1915 to 1918 at Armentières, the Somme, Ypres, Passchendaele and the Marne. He was wounded at Ypres. But he returned to his battalion to take part in the final Allied offensive. Besides his MC he was awarded the Croix de Guerre. This period is described in a first volume of autobiography, *A Life of One's Own*.

After the Armistice, with the thought of returning to his father's stifling ménage at Cheltenham intolerable, he went to live in Andalusia, to prepare himself for his vocation as a writer. He thought his war gratuity would last longest there. As preliminary training he settled himself for a comfortable course of reading the world's great literature.

He lived alone in Yegen in the Alpujarras, where he punctuated his reading with long walks in those untenanted uplands. He also visited London where, through his old friends Ralph Partridge and Hope Johnstone, he became part of the Bloomsbury Circle.

A dominating feature of this phase of his life was a consuming love affair with the painter, Dora Carrington, later Lytton Strachey's companion. This is described with naked candour in his second volume of memoirs, *Personal Record*.

Brenan's creativity took a long time to flower. Throughout the 1930s he lived on a modest income from investments.

In 1931 he married an American poetess, Gamel Woolsey, and settled in a beautiful house at Churriana, outside Málaga. There he experienced the early stages of the civil war.

He and his wife returned to England, and during the Second World War he wrote *The Spanish Labyrinth*. It was immediately recognized as the most perceptive study of modern Spain to be published by a British writer, and its reputation has increased over the years.

After 1945 the Brenans went back to Spain, where they lived permanently after 1953.

Brenan produced many more books, including *South from Granada*, about his days in Yegen; *The Face of Spain*, a travel book with a difference; and his authoritative history, *The Literature of the Spanish People*, based on a vast amount of reading. His study *St John of the Cross* sheds fresh light on the life and works of the holy man and poet.

In his later life he was the centre of a lively group of visitors. In summertime his home was often full of inquiring people of all ages, and Brenan, a man of great generosity of spirit, always made his time available to those wanting to consult him on the subjects he knew well.

When his wife died in 1968 he sold his house and went to live nearby at Alhaurin el Grande, with another poet, Lynda Nicholson Price and, subsequently with her husband.

There he remained until 1984, when, in confused circumstances, he returned briefly to an old people's home at Pinner. From there he was persuaded to return by the generosity of Spaniards who admired him. Last year a group of Spanish and foreign historians in Málaga set up a Gerald Brenan Foundation to perpetuate the study of his works.

Brenan did, meanwhile, complete one work of imagination, *The Lighthouse Always Says Yes*, a novel about his life in Andalusia. But he will be remembered principally as a brilliant interpreter of Spain to the rest of the world.

By a Spanish woman, he had a daughter, whom he adopted.

MR LIONEL LESLIE

Mr Lionel Leslie, sculptor, soldier and author, big game hunter and explorer, died on January 17. He was 86.

Throughout his life he displayed an admirable indifference to conventional constraints. Even when he was advanced in years, an aura of Bohemian eccentricity surrounded him, which he himself encouraged.

Lionel Alistair David Leslie was born in London on June 27, 1900. His boyhood was spent at Castle Leslie, in county Monaghan, in whose woods was nurtured his sense of adventure and where the gamekeepers taught him to ride and shoot.

He was educated at Eton, which was not a happy time for him. His parents removed him and sent him to a grammar school near Kendal where one of his more friendly antics was to pelt charabancs, filled with happy trippers returning from a day on Lake Windermere, with clods of earth.

He became a recruit in the Inniskilling Fusiliers – in the reserve battalion commanded by his father – at the age of sixteen. From there he went to Sandhurst (where he was a boxing champion) and was commissioned into the Cameron Highlanders in 1922.

He was sent, first, to India and then to Burma from where, in 1925, he set off on the most adventurous of his expeditions. Taking with him two servants who spoke only Chinese, he crossed the frontier in the neighbourhood of Bhamo and made his way to the old walled city of Tengyueh, about a hundred miles within Yunnan.

He left the Army in 1926, and went to Africa where he made an effort to walk across the continent on foot, accompanied by a Masai warrior. He then joined an expedition to Labrador led by Gino Watkins. Leslie remained behind for a while to work on a "jackboat" engaged in rum smuggling from the island of St Pierre, off Newfoundland.

These adventures are described in his first book, *Wilderness Trails in Three Continents* (1931), with a foreword by Winston Churchill who was his cousin and godfather.

It was not until 1930, when he was in Morocco, that Leslie decided to fulfil his old wish to become a sculptor. He departed for Paris, where he spent the next four years as a pupil of the eminent French sculptor, Charles Despiau.

By 1933 he had two heads in the Paris Salon: one a portrait of the daughter of Lord Tyrell, the retiring British ambassador; the other of a Senegalese.

The following year he returned to London and shared for a time a Chelsea studio with the Russian sculptor, Dimitri Tsapline. A marble head of "Clara" was accepted by the Royal Academy in 1935. He also showed at the Royal Hibernian Academy and with the London Group.

Many of his sculptures were of animals, usually reduced to a compact shape that combined simplicity of form with an impression of strength. His human sculptures, among them Eskimo and Red Indian heads, were of similar style.

In 1939 he was recalled to the colours, and served in France and Egypt as well as in this country. He also spent some time in Italy, receiving escaped British PoWs back into the allied lines. For this work he was mentioned in despatches.

After the war he worked for a short time in Kensington as a road navvy, and he was able to give Churchill an account of the mind of the working man of the day. He and his wife, Barbara Enever – whom he had married in 1942 – then retired to the Isle of Mull where they set about the restoration of a derelict inn at Grasspoint. In the summer months they entertained the tourists with tea and tales; in the peace of winter, Leslie occupied himself with his sculpture, poetry and writing. He also made plaques to sell to the following season's sightseers.

He published, in 1961, the autobiographical *One Man's World*. It is an uninspiring book, partly redeemed by the author's recollections of life in Bohemian taverns in the 1930s, before it became fashionable to frequent such establishments.

He was particularly interested in the Loch Ness monster. Convinced that it was a creature of the night, he devoted much of one summer systematically scouring the entire loch under cover of darkness. He also went to Lough Fadda in Connemara, again in search of creatures of the deep. It was, alas, all to no avail. Looking nearer home, however, he did find the corpse of a killer whale washed ashore on Mull, whose skull he proudly mounted.

Leslie was a man of extreme modesty. He had written a first draft of his memoirs, but his publishers suggested that he was too kind in his recollections, and advised him to make it "spicier". Towards the end of his life, his eyesight began to fail. But he never lost his hardiness, tolerance or sharpness of mind.

He is survived by his wife, Barbara, and their daughter.

These two obituaries, or brief biographies of the deceased, were placed next to each other in an edition of *The Times* in January 1986. They are about fairly old men from similar backgrounds and with similar enthusiasms.

Writing

- There are about 20 similarities between these two men – from their ages to the lengths of their names, their upbringings, their travels, their interests and their families. List them.
- Imagine that you have witnessed a meeting between Messrs Brenan and Leslie. Relate what they talk about, bearing in mind the range and similarities of their experience and age.

12 Knowledge about language

One of the requirements of the National Curriculum is to have some knowledge of the ways in which the English language originated and developed. There are useful accounts in encyclopaedias as well as straightforward books on the subject. None is more amusing than Bill Bryson's *Mother Tongue,* published by Penguin. The quality newspapers often have articles about aspects of language. Here is one that appeared in *The Times.*

...and moreover
PHILIP HOWARD

English has far the largest vocabulary of any language. You have only to compare the OED with other national dictionaries to see that. This has come about because English is so widely spoken around the world that it takes in the local dialects of other languages and because it is universally used as the language of science and technology. So, the new vocabulary is coined in English. Nobody can hope to use more than a fraction of English. We try to get as much as we can manage of the central core, and then top it up with the particular words of our trades and idiolects.

Not even a polyglot polymath such as Thomas Macaulay deployed more than a small fraction of the English vocabulary, and he alarmed people even as a small boy by shooting off "quite printed words" as a linguistic missile firing multiple warheads. I wish I had a memory half as capacious as his. He said that if by some miracle of vandalism all copies of *Paradise Lost* and *Pilgrim's Progress* were destroyed, he would undertake to produce them both from recollection whenever a revival of learning and printing came. He was a dictionary in trousers. But even Tom only skimmed the shallows of the language.

Our memories and vocabularies are card indexes, consulted and then put back in disorder by authorities which we do not control. In the jungle of language there are no exact synonyms. Chubby is not precisely the same as buxom, fat, plump, and all other near-synonyms. One man's turnip is another man's swede. A rare undergrowth in the linguistic jungle consists of solitary words without antonyms. Why have we invented words for being feckless and reckless, but not feckful and reckful? Why are we disgruntled, but not its positive? Wodehouse actually created the back-formation in the *The Code of the Woosters*: "He spoke with a certain what-is-it in his voice, and I could see that, if not actually disgruntled, he was far from being gruntled." The word comes from the frequentative of grunt. It means to make little grunting noises as of a happy pig. It is pure accident that we have only just invented gruntled, as a joke.

The same with disgust and dishevelled. The dis- in the latter means not or un-. The shevelled comes from the French *cheveux* or hair. In English the word originally meant wearing nothing on the head, as in a history of King Arthur of 1450: "She was dishevelled and had the fairest head that any woman might have." Then it came to mean uncombed and with hair flowing free. Then it forgot about the hair, and took on its modern meaning. The language would be richer if we could say, admiringly, of a tidy person: "She's *so* shevelled." Why can we dismantle, but not mantle? "Wieldy" exists, as opposite of unwieldy, but we don't use it.

The same carelessness made us flabbergasted in the 18th century, without giving us a word for having our flabber ungasted. The experts suggest it is an invention made by coupling flabby or flap with aghast. If we need a word meaning having our flabbers ungasted, we shall make one.

The same uneven growth of lingo has made it possible for us to be undone, but not "done" in the opposite sense, and demoralised but never exactly moralised. The sick man is distempered and distraught, but not tempered and traught when he gets better. We can be nonplussed, but not plussed, and nondescript, but not descript. There is an opposite to inept, which is apt, but it does not mean the opposite of inept. Why no common corrigible? Ruthless, but no ruth. Actually, we used to have ruth: "Look homeward, Angel, now and melt with ruth." Even with its huge vocabulary, English has a class of words for which we have not yet felt the need of antonyms.

Beside these solitary single words with no opposites, there are double words that say the same idea twice. We could call them autotautologous words, which repeat themselves for emphasis. A skirt already means an edge, border, or extreme part. Yet since Spenser, we have felt the need for belt and braces by having outskirts. To bode already means to portend, or have an uneasy presentiment. To forebode repeats the idea internally. There is no rhyme or reason in the luxuriance of English.

It is appropriate to end this chapter by slightly amending the strategy employed to promote effective reading and understanding. Consider the suggested techniques applied to the passage above.

Overview

The *Oxford English Dictionary (OED)* shows how the language is teeming with words which are interesting both in their application and in themselves. There are many odd corners and some parts which have remained unexplored for generations.

Insights

Stop
Think of how these linguistic riches are for us to use and enjoy.

Look
At the ways in which writing skills can be improved by our thinking about words and their meanings.

Listen
Words speak for themselves and because the English language is both flexible and universal it has developed a centuries-old past, has a present usage that is lively and worldwide, and is assured of a most promising future. In fact, its future is, literally, in our hands, whether they are holding pens or fingering typewriters and word-processors.

The five 'W' words

When?
Now.

Where?
Here.

Who?

What?
Effective writing.

Why?
To enable our use of language and our future success to 'work out'.

Writing

- Use your dictionary to find twenty words that give you pleasure for their sound, meaning or shape. Find out something about their origins and indicate what appeals to you about them.

Writing 9

LEAG	MEG	SEG	NEAB	WJEC	NICCEA	Topic	Date attempted	Date completed	Self Assessment
✓	✓	✓	✓	✓	✓	Examinations and changes			
✓	✓	✓	✓	✓	✓	Coursework			
✓	✓	✓	✓	✓	✓	'Differentiation'			
✓	✓	✓	✓	✓	✓	An approach to the subject			
✓	✓	✓	✓	✓	✓	Speaking and listening			
✓	✓	✓	✓	✓	✓	Reading			
✓	✓	✓	✓	✓	✓	Ways and means			
✓	✓	✓	✓	✓	✓	Writing			
✓	✓	✓	✓	✓	✓	Practical writing			

9.1 General outline

Writing involves constructing sequences of words in various patterns to create effective communication between people. The needs and requirements of both writers and readers differ considerably according to time, place and relationship. The writing that we undertake usually falls into certain categories, which could be classified as:

1. *Practical*
    - a letter;
    - a report;
    - a short article;
    - a set of instructions;
    - an ordered explanation;
    - an outline of a point of view;
    - an outline of advice on some problem.

2. *Summarising*   Selecting relevant information and restating it accurately.

3. *Directed writing*   Structuring a composition, having been provided with 'source material' and detailed instructions.

4. *Expression*
    - narrative skills;
    - descriptive techniques;
    - argumentative methods;
    - dramatic ways;
    - impressionistic writing.

5. *Personal*   Conveying experiences through personal letter-writing.

The next five chapters of the book will consider these topics in this order. In fact, emphasis will be placed on the orderly way in which writing should be approached. However, we are well aware that effective writing involves more than the application of rules, the systematic layout of ideas and the involvement of 'tricks of the trade'. It's about such dynamic matters as the state of mind, mood and emotions, as well as the ability to generate ideas under pressure of time, regardless of place, and with regard to people and purpose. The process involves mystery as well as method!

9.2 Getting started

Problems arise because a number of conditions have to be fulfilled. Things have to be worked at or worked out. Little happens by chance. On one hand there are the physical requirements – the writing implements and paper, the table or desk and chair, the light and noise level, the availability of attractions and the lack of distractions. On the other there are the mental demands – being in the right frame of mind, with hope of success and fear of failure; having an inventive attitude; being stimulated, with enough energy to complete the task or a significant part of it.

Words have to be regimented. Where are they to be found? The answer lies within the vocabulary of the writer as well as in the columns of dictionaries. Vocabularies are extended by the use of brainpower and experience as we encounter the few thousand different words that are normally exchanged orally (by word of mouth) and the tens of thousands of different words that are given and received on paper. Then there are the 'dying' words that are occasionally revived by popular or fashionable use, and there are the many 'dead' ones that make some columns of the larger dictionaries look like 'verbal mortuaries'. Some words appear only on ceremonial occasions, some are reserved for legal matters and others make special appearances when technical information needs conveying.

There's a vast stock of words (about half a million in the English language) and some of them have to be selected to enable us to write. Perhaps the best analogy is to see our own store of words in terms of a wardrobe of clothes. 'What shall I put on?' is the equivalent to 'What shall I write?' Some people rarely change their clothes and others do so constantly. Some people use the same words in different combinations; others have the knack of being able to choose without difficulty and develop interesting word patterns. It's all a matter of balance in trying to develop a style that is sound, accurate, distinctive as well as individual, and experimenting with new approaches that will change our ways of expression.

Artists often feel daunted when confronted with a fresh piece of canvas. A clean sheet of paper or a blank word-processor screen has the same effect on many people. How should we get started and overcome these mental hindrances, 'word blocks' and 'idea shortages'? Here are seven thoughts on the topics, devised in an alphabetical sequence:

Awareness of the problems is vital, for it makes us realise that these are mental conditions shared by nearly everybody. Humankind may talk incessantly, but reading and writing are not generally engaged in impulsively. They are worked at.

Beautiful equipment helps. Bearing in mind that 'beauty is in the eye of the beholder', and according to what you can afford, you may like to choose pens, paper, and printing devices that give you pleasure. Look after them and try always to keep them at hand in appropriate places. This may seem to be a statement of the obvious, but it's strange how some people take years to learn a skill and then, within the space of a few moments, can mislay vital recording equipment and lose an opportunity.

Calmness matters, for we tend to perform any task more efficiently when we are relaxed (though not casual) in our approach. If you can convince yourself that writing is a form of therapy, then that's a good start. Remember also that there are certain times of the day when you are in a better state of mind. Work out when these are and use these 'personal prime times' to your advantage.

Delight in words, and remind yourself that out of the large stock available you will have a collection of your own that will be extended day by day. A person is partly judged by the company she or he keeps and this applies to the 'company' of words that each of us has built up. We all have our favourite words and it's important not to indulge ourselves with them too often: repetition certainly tires others.

Effectiveness depends upon the generating of ideas. We have to be inventive and to harness the mental powers that enable us to think. The human brain has its left and right parts. One side specialises in order; the other in forms of chaos. The orderly side helps us to structure our thoughts, to lay down rules and follow them, to give a clear presentation of what we mean and generally to encourage constructive patterns. The other side controls our imagination, our fantasies, our destructive urges and impulses. Effective writing means that we have to use the mechanisms of the former to give shape to the dynamisms of the latter. One is of little use without the other. In order 'to build castles', or anything structured, we have first to be able 'to build castles in the air', or dream in memorable ways. So never refrain from turning things over in your mind, attempting to break down ideas, exploring unexpected connections or just letting your thoughts wander off the beaten track ... if you have the powers to create meaningful forms of expression when relevant ideas need recording.

Focus on creating ideas. Try the device of 'tree growing' explained below in order to assist in this process. Although we recommend your using scrap paper for this activity, do remember that it helps to overcome the inhibition of making the first marks on the clean sheet in front of you.

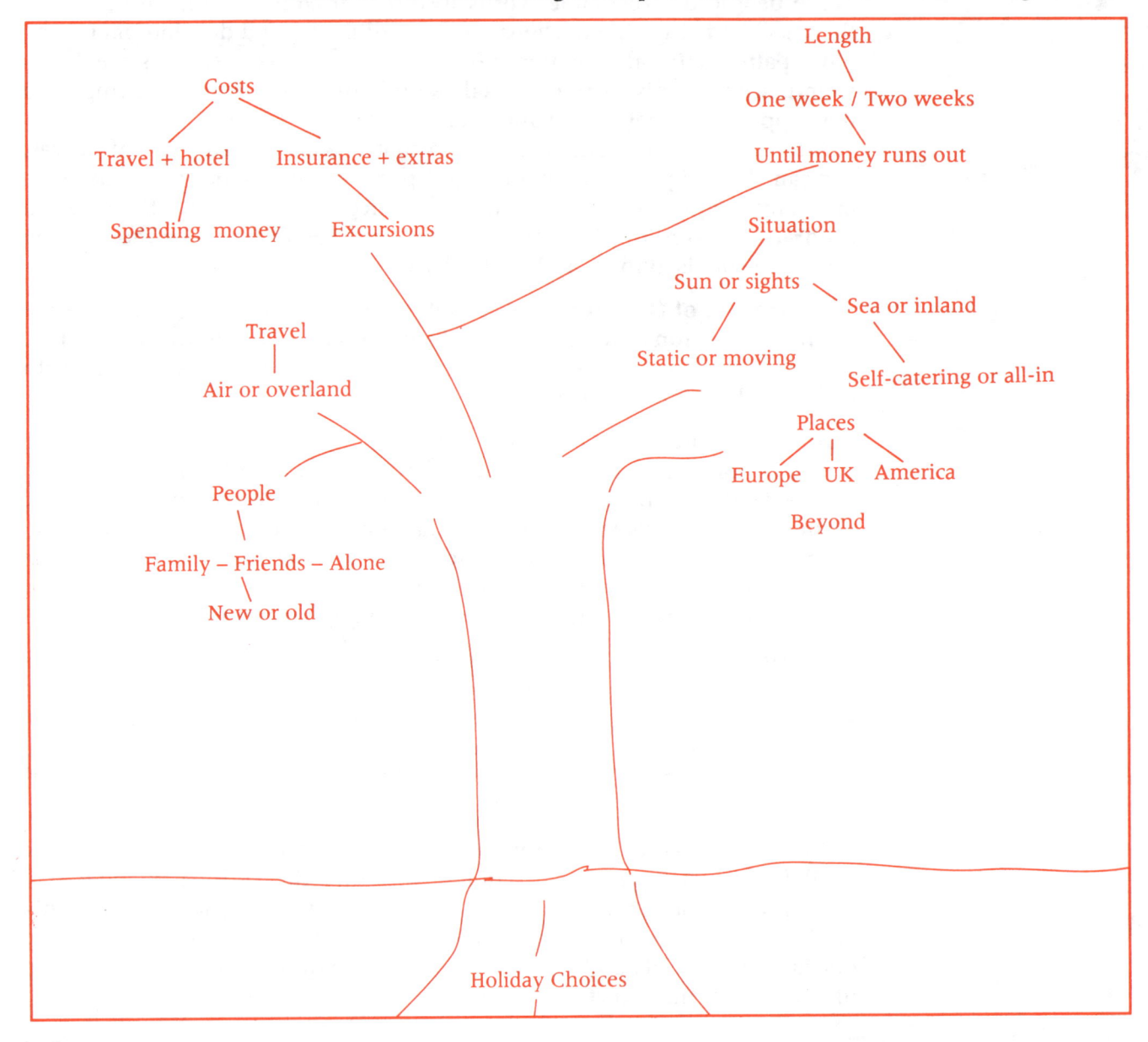

At the foot of your sheet, write down the topic on which you have to compose a letter, a report, an article, a composition or a story. Draw the trunk of a tree stemming from your word. Then at random throughout the top half of the sheet jot down ideas that may have application to the topic in question. Consider them to be the branches of the tree; where you think of closely related ideas in the same area, make them like the minor branches and twigs.

Train your mind to see:

- comparisons and opposites;
- similarities and differences of time and place;
- associations with people and animals;
- specific experiences that you have encountered;
- the most unlikely outcomes possible;
- impulsive as well as considered judgements.

In short, connect ... and disconnect.

Regard the groups of ideas that have evolved in the branch network of your tree as being clusters of fruit. Imagine that you are harvesting the crop and wish to pick the best first. Encircle the most important cluster first, number it with a '1' and then continue through the tree, ignoring the irrelevant or unfruitful parts, until you have a series of numbered circles that indicate an order of preference.

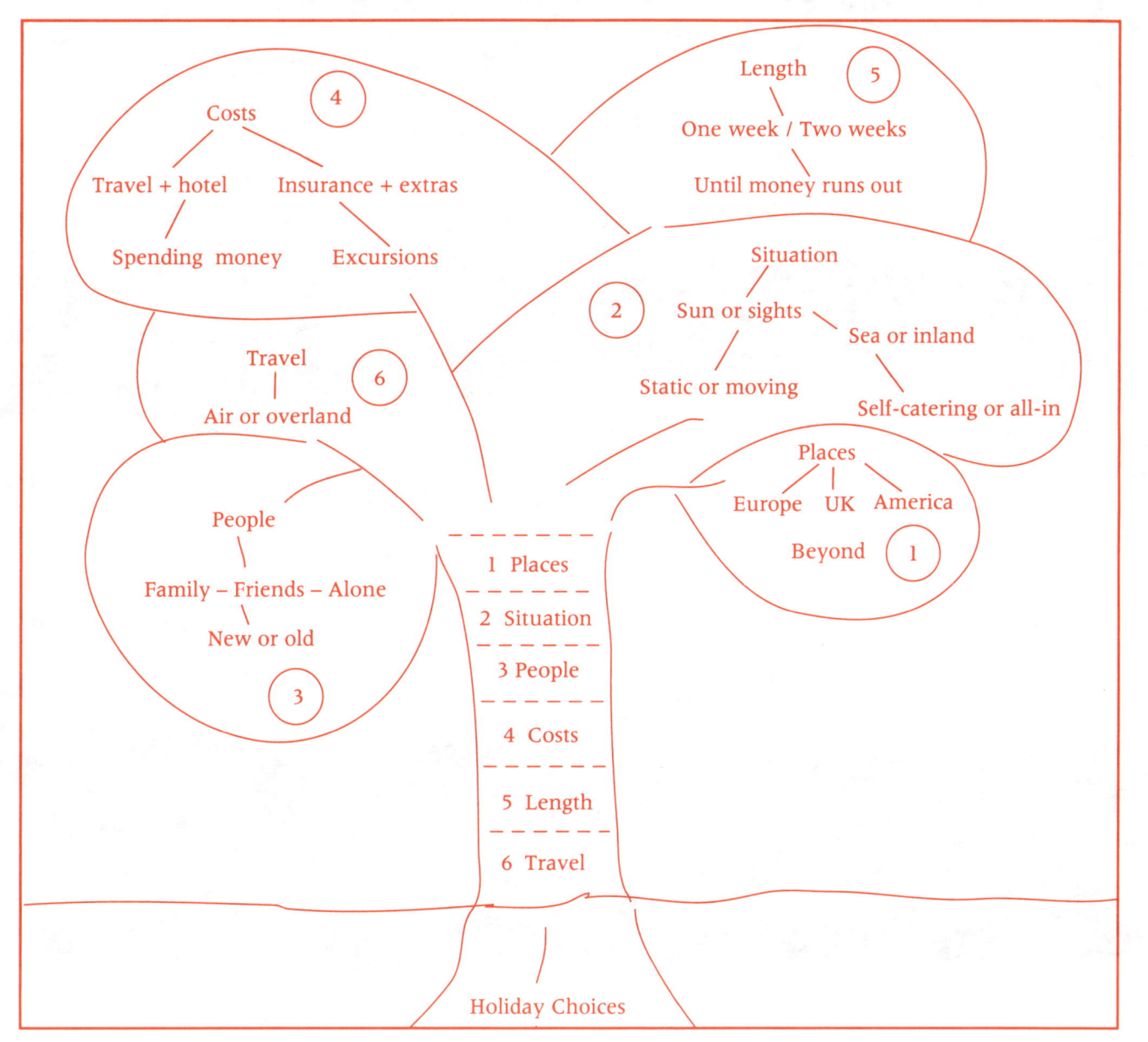

Finally, see yourself as a forester who has come to assess the value of the tree for its wood. Divide the trunk of your tree into the same number of parts as circles you have created. Give each part of the trunk a relevant nametag. So now there is a series of major points inscribed above the original topic that first appeared on the sheet. The detailed features of these main points appear in the system of branches depicted above.

This is a form of 'brainstorming', a way of trying to liberate thoughts, generate ideas and apply a simple system in order to harness the workings of a complicated process.

Grasp of the essentials is all-important. The so-called 'brainstorming' techniques mentioned above are particularly useful when imaginative work is required. Much of the 'ordinary' writing that we have to complete involves the systematic, well-ordered presentation of ideas where the *inclusion* of all relevant material matters more than inventiveness.

The steady application of our mental powers to the creation of carefully-crafted, detailed pieces of work will be appreciated by readers, examiners and employers. It should be a rewarding occupation – for these skills are special, constantly in demand and becoming increasingly more rare. Regard yourself as a 'specialist' and work at them!

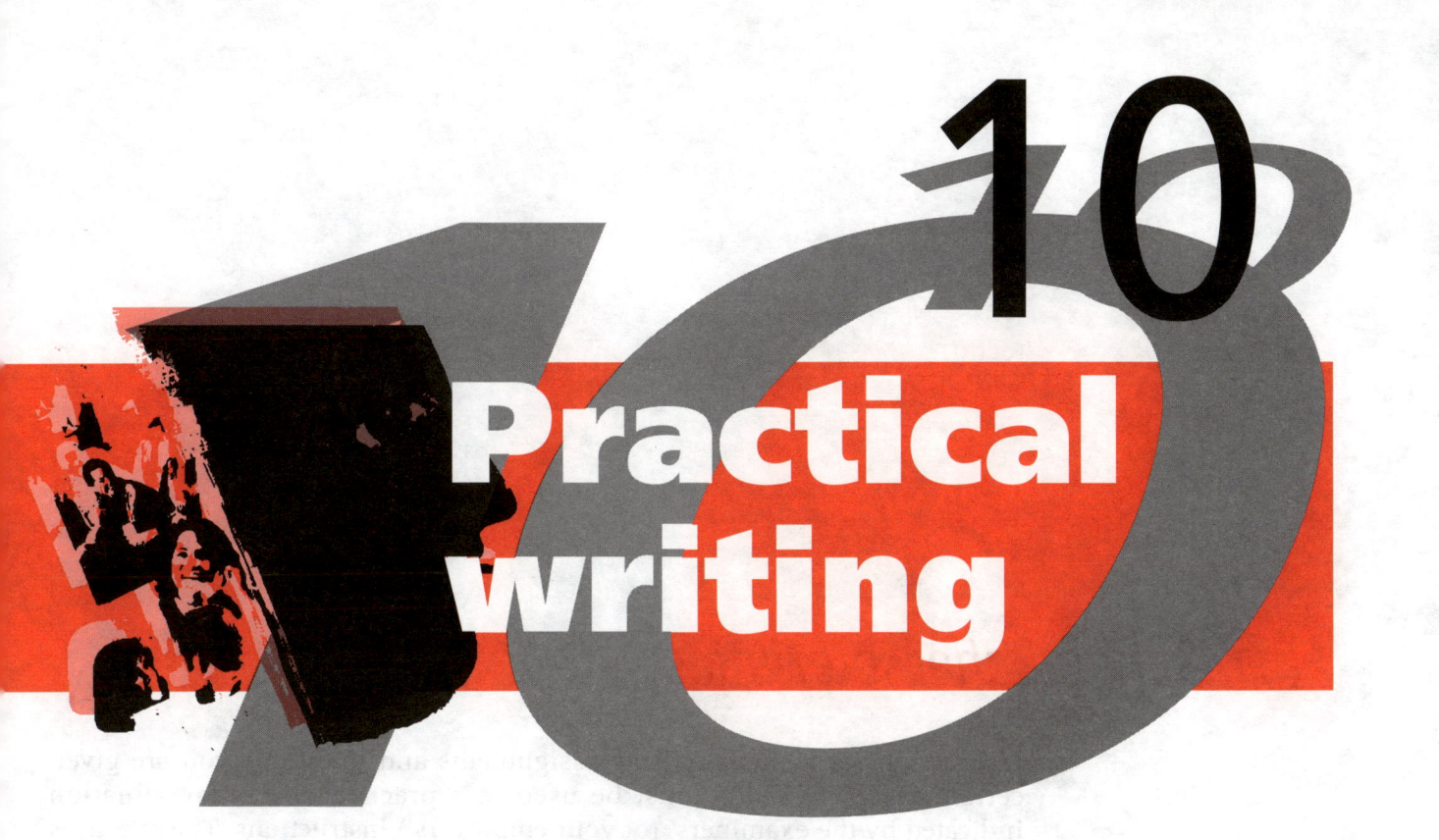

10 Practical writing

LEAG	MEG	SEG	NEAB	WJEC	NICCEA	Topic	Date attempted	Date completed	Self Assessment
✓	✓	✓	✓	✓	✓	Examinations and changes			
✓	✓	✓	✓	✓	✓	Coursework			
✓	✓	✓	✓	✓	✓	'Differentiation'			
✓	✓	✓	✓	✓	✓	An approach to the subject			
✓	✓	✓	✓	✓	✓	Speaking and listening			
✓	✓	✓	✓	✓	✓	Reading			
✓	✓	✓	✓	✓	✓	Ways and means			
✓	✓	✓	✓	✓	✓	Writing			
✓	✓	✓	✓	✓	✓	Practical writing			

10.1 General characteristics

In practical (or factual) writing assignments and questions you are given certain material which must be used in a practical, everyday situation indicated by the examiners' (or your employers') instructions. The exercises test your ability to write briefly, clearly and accurately. Because the instructions strictly control both the content and the purpose of your writing, practical writing is sometimes called 'directed writing'.

In this chapter we are looking at the specific forms or ways of approach – the letter, the report, the article, the advisory instructions, etc. – while in Chapter 12, entitled 'Directed writing', we shall consider some more complicated tasks that you might be set.

Purpose and form

Practical writing tests your ability:

- to write correct English
- to make accurate use of given information;
- to carry out instructions.

Style

A plain, 'no frills' style is appropriate to the practical purpose and factual content of practical writing. The letters, reports, instructions and the like that are called for are best expressed in simple terms, with no wasted words or elaborate descriptions. 'Transactional' writing (writing that gets things done) is successful when it is crisp, clear and very much to the point, so your use of language must be objective, unemotional and controlled.

10.2 Work out letters

If instructions are given for you to lay out your letter observing the conventions of letter-writing, do so. If no instructions are given, do so just the same!

Failure to comply with the conventions will lead to loss of marks in the examination. In matters relating to employment and applications for jobs, the failure to write correctly and in the accepted manner leads to far greater losses.

Work out 1

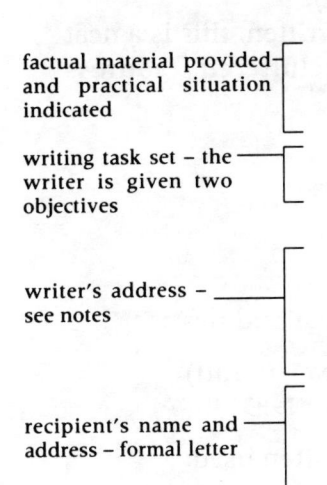

factual material provided and practical situation indicated

writing task set – the writer is given two objectives

There is a proposal to resite the market in your town by moving it from its present open-air site in the town centre to a covered hall being built by property developers. This proposal has caused bad feeling between its supporters and its opponents. Write a letter to the editor of your local newspaper, stating your own views and attempting to reconcile the two sides.

---

writer's address – see notes

                          12, Grove Road,
                          St Mary's Way,
                          Boroughtown.
                          BT7 12GR
                          31 March 1993

recipient's name and address – formal letter

The Editor,
  Boroughtown News,
    6, West Walk,
      Boroughtown.
      BT4 6WW

correct salutation for the editor

Sir,
    It is not surprising that the proposal to resite our market has caused so much bad feeling. Its supporters see only the advantages offered by a modern, spacious, weatherproof market. Its opponents regret the ending of a long tradition. Our market has been held in the Square for over three hundred years. Its stallholders give us excellent service throughout the year. The objectors also argue that the move will cause market prices to rise to pay for increased rents in the new hall.
    My own view is that the advantages of the move outweigh the disadvantages, but I sympathise with the objectors and I believe that their case merits a reasoned answer. If the market committee of the borough council would publish details of the new stall rents, the objectors would know whether their fears are justified. They also deserve an assurance that the layout of the new hall will be as convenient and efficient as the arrangements that we are used to.
    I believe that the present bad feeling would be greatly reduced if those two suggestions were followed up.

                            Yours faithfully,

                            Brian Jones

formal close Yours faithfully matches salutation Sir – no full stop after signature

---

The layout of addresses

Choose either of the following styles. Whichever you choose, be consistent. Do not start with one style and change to the other.

Style 1 12, Grove Road, St Mary's Way, Boroughtown. BT7 12GR	*Style 2* 12 Grove Road St Mary's Way Boroughtown BT7 12GR
• Closed punctuation. • Indented lines (except postcode). • The comma after the house number is optional. • No full stop after St – it is a contraction (= *Saint*), not an abbreviation.	• Open punctuation. • Blocked lines (i.e. not indented). • If well-written, this is a neat and uncluttered address layout.

The date

All letters must be dated. The date form shown is clear and neat:

    day (numerical)   month (in full)   year (in full)
    31   March   1993

There are many other date forms. The following are often used:

    31st March 1993   March 31st, 1993   31.iii.93

Economy and clarity argue for the form used in the work out.

The recipient's name and address

This must be included in formal letters; it is out of place in informal letters. It may be written above the body of letter, as in the work out, or below.

Salutation

The recipient of the letter must be 'greeted'. This greeting is called the **salutation**: *Dear So-and-so*. Formal ('business') letters require formal salutations. These are: *Dear Sir/Dear Madam*; *Dear Sirs* (to a company); *Sir* (to the editor of a newspaper). The correct salutations for 'non-business' letters are: *Dear Mr Jones*; *Dear Mrs Jones*; *Dear Miss Jones*; *Dear Ms Jones*; *Dear Tom*; *Dear Jane*; *Dear Uncle Fred*; etc.

Punctuation of salutation

When indented paragraphs are used in the letter, it is customary to end the salutation with a comma.

    Dear Mr Jones,
            Thank you for your letter ...

Note the capital initial for the first word of the letter. When the paragraphs are not indented, omit the comma at the end of the salutation.

    Dear Mr Jones
    Thank you for your letter ...

Formal close

Before 'signing off', the letter writer uses a **formal close**. The formal close must 'match' the salutation. Like this:

Dear Sir ⎫	Dear Mr Jones ⎫
Dear Madam ⎬ Yours faithfully	Dear Mrs Jones ⎬ Yours sincerely
Sir ⎭	Dear Sally ⎭

If the salutation does not name the recipient, the formal close is *Yours faithfully*. If the salutation does name the recipient, the formal close is *Yours sincerely*. Note that *Yours* begins with a capital Y, but *faithfully* and *sincerely* begin with small letters. There is no punctuation after the signature.

Work out 2

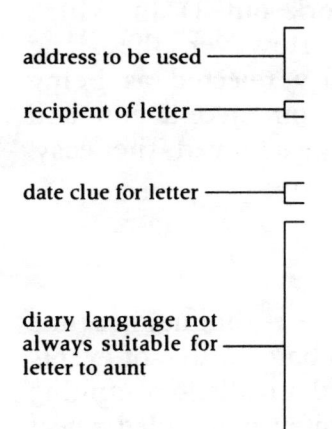

address to be used
recipient of letter

You are on holiday with some family friends, the Robinsons, at 6 Quayside Cottages, Hartsea, Devon. On a morning walk along the cliffs, you witness the rescue of a person cut off by the tide. Write a letter to your Aunt Amy, describing the adventure. Make use of these notes from your diary:

date clue for letter

diary language not always suitable for letter to aunt

Friday 13 August. Early walk along cliffs. Robinsons' dog Toby wittering away on cliff top. Barking like fury. Looked down. Figure on beach waving frantically. Faint calls. What to do? Return for help? Sound of helicopter. Hovered overhead. Then down cliff face. Winchman brought stranded walker up. Elderly woman. Bit shaken; not hurt. Took her to Robinsons. Surprise, surprise! Miss Agnes Smith – old family friend of theirs. Mrs R and Miss S quite overcome – shock/relief. Mr R's joke. Plans for party at Miss S's hotel tomorrow.

---

6 Quayside Cottages
Hartsea
Devon
14 August 1993

Dear Aunt Amy,

    I promised you a letter, but I didn't think I'd have quite such exciting news to send.

    Yesterday, I took the Robinsons' dog, Toby, for an early morning walk along the cliffs. Suddenly, he got very excited and started barking furiously. I looked over the cliff and saw a figure on the beach below, waving frantically at me. I could hear faint calls for help and I decided I must return to the cottage. I couldn't do anything on my own.

    Then I heard a helicopter in the distance. Quite soon, it was hovering overhead and then it descended the cliff face very slowly and carefully. The winchman was lowered and he lifted the stranded walker off the beach.

    When they got her to the cliff top, I saw that she was an elderly woman. She was a bit shaken, but she assured them that she was not hurt, so they asked me to guide her back to the village.

    Mrs Robinson came out to greet us and you can imagine how surprised she was to recognise the rescued woman as Miss Agnes Smith, an old family friend of theirs. It was quite a shock for them both and they were rather upset by it all, until Mr Robinson made them laugh by saying that this was an unusual way of paying calls!

    We're having a celebration party at Miss Smith's hotel tonight and I must start getting ready now.

With lots of love,
Your affectionate niece,
Jane

Layout and conventions

The information required for the address was included in the instructions. (Style 2 was chosen for the layout, but style 1 would have been equally correct.) The date clue was also important. Notice the use made of it by Jane. The salutation *Dear Aunt Amy* was matched by the signing off, which accurately reflected the kinship and good feeling between writer and recipient.

Style

This is an informal letter (contrast it with Work out 1) in which colloquialisms (*didn't, I'd,* etc) are appropriate. However, the slang expressions used in the diary notes were rightly rejected as being unsuitable in tone. Though not formal, this letter is from niece to aunt and slang would be ill-mannered. Jane very nicely achieved the easy, conversational style that the occasion required.

Contents

The letter-writer was instructed to describe the adventure, but neither time nor length allowed space for descriptive detail, so a bare outline of events was required. A brief introductory sentence supplied a realistic beginning for the letter. Similarly, the last clause of the final sentence provided a neat and convincing ending.

Work out 3

You notice this advertisement in your local paper:

> Junior assistant required to work initially in Accounts Department of small but growing local firm, specialising in the preparation of research reports for electronics industry. Must be mathematically competent and willing to undertake part-time study for further qualifications in areas to be agreed. Apply in writing to Box 27, Bramshall Clarion, Mill Lane, Bramshall, BM1 6ML, giving details of qualifications and experience. Two referees required.

You left school two years ago with eight GCSE subjects and since then have had work experience relevant to the post advertised. You have applied for admission to an electronics course at your local FE college and are waiting for the result of your application. Write a letter to the address given, applying for the advertised job.

16 Smith Street
Bramshall
BM2 6ST
30 June 1993

formal letter: recipient's name and address required

Box 27
The Bramshall Clarion
Mill Lane
Bramshall
BM1 6ML

formal salutation

Dear Sirs

letter 'headline' provided: reader can 'tune in' to contents at once

<u>Junior Assistant in Accounts Department</u>

I believe that my qualifications and experience make me a suitable candidate for the above post.

start with personal details: list all qualifications and other achievements in non-academic fields

highlight aspects of experience that suit you for job

I am 18 years old and left Bramshall Central Comprehensive School in July 1991 having taken eight GCSE subjects: English Language (B); English Literature (C); Mathematics (B); French (D); Geography (B); History (C); Science (C); Food & Nutrition (B). I was a member of the committee of the school's charity fund-raising group and also gained a life-saving award from the local swimming club.

I then worked with Comma Electric for a year, gaining varied experience in components assembly and in the Customer Relations department.

In the past year, I have had experience of part-time voluntary work in the Bramshall Youth Centre. I have now applied for admission to the first-year electronics course at Bramshall FE college and, if you appoint me to the vacancy in your firm, I shall ask to be transferred to the evening course in order to pursue the further qualifications to which your advertisement refers.

formal close: Yours faithfully

Yours faithfully,

Mary Young

clear and convenient way of listing referees

Reference may be made to the following:
1 Mr J. K. Tompkins, M.A., Headmaster, Bramshall Central Comprehensive School, BM4 5CC.
2 Miss A. C. Bednall, Personnel Officer, Comma Electric, BM6 1TE.

10.3 Work out reports

What the examiners are looking for

When a practical writing assignment takes the form of a report, the examiners expect you to be:

- accurate in carrying out the instructions;
- logical in the arrangement of the contents;
- clear and brief in expression.

A **report** must be written in continuous prose (not in note form), but headings and/or numbered sections may be used as an aid to clear presentation. The test of a well-written report is the ease and clarity with which it can be read and understood.

Assignments of this type are often set:

> Your student council committee has asked you to report on the cafeteria service provided in your school or college. Write your report, suggesting practical ways in which the service could be improved.

Layout: headings

By its very nature, a report is an essentially practical piece of writing, intended to be *used*. It has been asked for by some person or some organisation. It is on a precise subject. It is needed for a particular purpose at a particular time. Therefore, it must be accurately and clearly identified.

Always supply **headings** that provide the necessary details. The report called for in the question just quoted requires these headings:

To: Student Council Committee, Fairplace FE College
From: X. Y. Bloggs
Subject: College cafeteria service
Date: 15/9/93

Note that all-numeral date forms are acceptable on reports, memoranda and brief notes. On letters, the date form recommended in section 10.2 should be used.

Layout: internal

Headings and/or **numbered sections** are usually required in the body of a report. They are *essential* when it contains numerous and varied items, and even the comparatively straightforward reports asked for in your examination are made much clearer by such divisions. Internal headings and/or numbered sections act as 'signposts' to the logical order in which a report is set out: they assist the reader to comprehend the contents quickly and clearly.

Logical order: findings and recommendations

When you have assembled the material for your report, sort it into a logical order of presentation. In the question quoted above, you are instructed to do two things: (1) investigate the cafeteria service; (2) make practical suggestions for improvements. Logically, then, your report should consist of two main sections: (1) Findings; (2) Recommendations.

Since you will probably need to include more than one item under each of those internal headings, some such plan as this will be suitable:

1 *Findings*
　(i) or (a)
　(ii) or (b)
　etc. ⎫ arranged in a logical order when the material for the report has been assembled – see below

2 *Recommendations*
　(i) or (a)
　(ii) or (b)
　etc. ⎫ arranged in a logical order after the findings have been sorted out – see below

The precise nature and number of the subdivisions under each main heading cannot be decided in advance. After you have jotted down the material for your report, you can then work out the classifications into which it can sensibly be divided. For example: favourable items; unfavourable items. Then you can decide upon the *order* of presentation: favourable items before unfavourable items – or vice versa? Proceed from the most important item to the least important item (*descending* order)? Proceed from the least important item to the most important item (*ascending* order)?

Provided that you are aware of the necessity of establishing a logical order, a scheme to suit the nature of the report will emerge as you sort out your material.

Work out

practical situation indicated: instructions given

Your student council committee has asked you to report on the cafeteria service provided in your school or college. Write your report, suggesting practical ways in which the service could be improved.

Stage 1 of work out

Jot down the material as it occurs to you. In an everyday situation you would gather this material by observing, asking questions and making notes. In examination conditions you must draw on your experience of the system to provide the material for the report.

> poor quality of snacks, sandwiches especially – lack of variety and imagination – hot and cold drinks expensive and not good – food, except for standard hot meal at lunch, poor value for money – hot lunch very good, varied, plenty of it, but too expensive for most students to eat every day – long queues – takes far too long to get to food bar – seats uncomfortable, and not enough – too much noise – lack of social atmosphere – cafeteria closes at five, no chance of hot drink or snack after lectures, evening students not catered for at all.

Stage 2 of work out

Suggestions for improvements have been asked for, so the logical order of presentation seems to be: (1) favourable items; (2) unfavourable items. Recommendations will then follow logically from the latter. Again, looking for ways of sorting the material into sensible groups, you can see that the unfavourable items fall into three classes: (1) food; (2) surroundings and conditions; (3) opening hours. Of these, food is undoubtedly the most important, so take that first:

plan for report is emerging from close, analytical study of findings

1 *Findings*
   (a) Favourable items
   (b) Unfavourable items
      (i) food
      (ii) surroundings and conditions
      (iii) opening hours

The details of this 'display code' – '(a), (b), (b)(i)', etc. – will not necessarily be followed in the report itself. Here they are useful in setting out the emerging plan for the report.

Stage 3 of work out

The instructions asked for practical suggestions about ways of improving the cafeteria service. Now that the findings have been assembled and arranged in a logical order of presentation, the recommendations follow on logically. It is important to distinguish between what can and should be done immediately and what might be done in time and with extra funds. Those considerations suggest the logical order in which to present the recommendations.

recommendations follow logically from ordered presentation of findings and are themselves presented in a logical order

2 *Recommendations*
   (a) *Food* Detailed recommendations for immediate action can be made.
   (b) *Surroundings and conditions* Detailed recommendations for immediate and medium-term action can be made.
   (c) *Opening hours* Long-term problem because of serious financial implications. General recommendations can be made.

Stage 4 of work out: writing the report

REPORT

To: Student Council Committee, Fairplace FE College
From: X. Y. Bloggs
Subject: College cafeteria service
Date: 15/9/93

1 *Findings*

(a) Students consider that the hot lunch is a good meal, providing a variety of well-cooked dishes.
(b) Most students, however, rely on the snacks because they cannot afford the hot lunch. The snacks – especially the sandwiches – are of poor quality. They lack variety and they are over-priced. The same criticisms apply to the hot and cold drinks.
(c) Lunchtime queues are long and tiresome. The seating is uncomfortable and inadequate. There is too much noise in the cafeteria and a lack of social atmosphere.
(d) Cafeteria service closes at 5.00 p.m. Consequently, students cannot obtain refreshments after lectures, and evening students are not catered for at all.

2 *Recommendations*

(a) *Food* Immediate action can and should be taken to improve the quality and variety of the snacks and drinks. No additional funds are required to effect this improvement, just more care and imagination. A student/cafeteria staff liaison committee should be set up at once.
(b) *Surroundings and conditions* As a first step, more chairs should be provided. Then queues, overcrowding and noise could all be reduced by more thoughtful timetabling. If half the morning lectures ended at 12 noon and the other half at 1.00 p.m. (with a consequent adjustment to afternoon lectures), the pressure on the cafeteria would he halved. Lunch service would have to be extended to 2 hours, but this should not cost more than present resources would allow.
(c) *Opening hours* I recognise that an extension beyond 5.00 p.m. would be costly, but I recommend that this problem be taken to the college authorities for urgent action as soon as financial conditions permit.

10.4 Work out articles and newspaper reports

Qualities to be aimed at

Note, first, that the examiners' instructions often refer to a piece of writing intended for a newspaper or magazine as 'a report'. Such a report is very different from the kind of report worked out in section 10.3. Its heading (or **headline**) is brief and eye-catching. It is not divided into sections and subsections (though it is clearly paragraphed and may have **subheadings**). It does not make recommendations.

An **article** is less concerned with events than is a newspaper or magazine report. For example, you would probably be asked to write a *report* of a village meeting called to discuss a local issue and to write an *article* about one of the speakers at that meeting. A report is more 'newsy' than an article. However, the distinction is not always sharply drawn. Instructions phrased like this are common:

> Write an article, suitable for your school or college magazine, reporting the major events (sporting *or* academic *or* artistic) of one term in the past year.

An *article* and a newspaper or magazine *report* are very similar. The theoretical distinction between them does not affect the qualities looked for in your answer.

An article or report written for a newspaper or magazine must be accurate, lively and readable.

Two kinds of assignments

In one kind of assignment you are supplied with the information that you must use in the article. In such cases pay very careful attention to the instructions. Careless reading costs marks, a point illustrated by the following instructions:

1 Write an article for your school or college magazine, selecting your information from the notes below.
2 Write a report for your local paper, using all the information given below.
3 Write a report for publication in your college magazine, based on the notes supplied and any other information that you may wish to add.

The other kind of assignment stipulates the subject on which your article must be written, but leaves you to provide all the information. For example:

> Write an article for your local paper, reporting a measure proposed by the council and the strong feelings (for and against) that this has provoked.

Note that you are *not* asked for *your* opinions. Objective reporting is required. (Compare that assignment closely with the one set in section 10.2, page 74.)

Work out

> Write an article for your local paper about Councillor Brown, your newly elected mayor, selecting your information from the facts supplied below:
>
> Brown, Arthur Henry. b. Fairplace, 30 November 1950. Third son of William Henry Brown, foreman fitter Fairplace Engineering and a member of Fairplace Borough Council until his death in 1965. Educated at Fairplace Central School. Left at 16. Apprenticed to Fairplace Engineering. Later joined export sales division. Widely travelled. Numerous international conferences. Eventually managing director, his present post at Fairplace Engineering. Keen sportsman: Fairplace R.U.F.C. 1st XV; F. cricket club, captain 1st XI. Also F. dramatic soc. and civic soc. Member of Borough Council for past 10 years, Independent (Castle Ward), chairman library committee, member watch committee. In acceptance speech stressed desire to attract more industry to F. Hoped his year in office would be remembered for industrial expansion: 'more jobs and better jobs'. Married Mary Jones (Fairplace-born) in 1974. Three children (two daughters, one son) now attending F. Sixth Form college.

Stage 1

The problem of *order* must be solved first. Think about the nature and purpose of the set task. You have to present facts about the new mayor in a way that will interest readers of your paper. A straightforward chronological arrangement of facts – (1) birth; (2) education; (3) early career; and so on – would work, but it might be rather dull reading. Can you think of a more interesting order? Here is one possibility:

NEW MAYOR'S AMBITIONS FOR FAIRPLACE

Paragraph 1: A local family man

Paragraph 2: Successful career – wide experience of industry and foreign travel led to top job

Paragraph 3: Yet, a Fairplace-centred life – local activities and local politics

Paragraph 4: His ambitions for his term of office

Paragraph 5: Conclusion: Councillor Brown, a mayor for our town and our times

The paragraph headings used in that outline will not appear in the article. They are useful signposts at this stage, when the objective is to group together and then to set out in a logical and interesting order the items of information supplied. You can probably improve on the suggested outline, but it does point out the possibilities for a livelier article than strict chronological order seemed to offer.

Stage 2

The reader's attention must be gripped by the beginning of the article and, an outline plan having been settled on, it is a good idea to try out one or two opening sentences. You do not have to distort the facts or to copy the broken English of the tabloids to be interesting. 'Fairplace's new mayor is a Fairplace man.'/'A truly local man is now Fairplace's first citizen.'/'Rooted in local life, our new mayor brings wide experience to his high office.' You may not use any of the trial openings exactly as worded (none of those seems very satisfactory), but jotting them down tunes you in to the spirit of the article and helps you to get off on the right foot.

Stage 3

Think hard about your ending. Have it clearly in mind before you begin to write. Aim for a pithy and memorable summing up of the body of the article. No repetition, of course; but something that will stay in the reader's mind as epitomising the content and tone of the article. Look back at the outline: paragraph 5 may suggest a good way of ending.

Stage 4: write the article

NEW MAYOR'S AMBITIONS FOR FAIRPLACE

Arthur Henry Brown was born on 30 November 1950 in the heart of the community whose first citizen he now is. The third son of William Henry Brown, foreman fitter at Fairplace Engineering and borough councillor until his death in 1965, he was educated at the Central

School, leaving at the age of 16 for an apprenticeship with his father's employers. His marriage in 1974 to a Fairplace girl, Mary Jones, strengthened these local ties, and their three children (two daughters and a son), students at Fairplace Sixth Form College, now follow in the family's footsteps.

Councillor Brown's apprenticeship was succeeded by an outstanding career in the export sales division, involving worldwide travel and attendance at many international conferences, before he was appointed to his present post of managing director of Fairplace Engineering, the firm that he joined as a school-leaver.

Despite his many business commitments, he has always been involved in Fairplace activities. He played for the rugby club's 1st XV and was captain of the cricket club's 1st XI. His membership of the dramatic and civic societies was a reflection of his interest in the arts and in local history. Ten years ago, his election as a councillor (Independent, Castle Ward) led to service on the watch and library committees and the chairmanship of the latter.

His much-applauded acceptance speech, as mayor, epitomised his long and many-sided involvement with the life of our town. Above all, he said, he wanted his term of office to be remembered for the prosperity that would follow industrial expansion. 'More jobs and better jobs for Fairplace', in his own words.

Regardless of party ties, the people of Fairplace have welcomed their new mayor. An energetic and forward-looking man, deeply rooted in the community and devoted to its welfare, Councillor Brown is a mayor for our town and our time.

10.5 Work out instructions, descriptions, explanations, etc.

Typical assignments

1. Give instructions (not in note form) on how to do *one* of the following:
   (a) replace a faulty plug on an electrical appliance;   (b) prepare a simple meal;   (c) book a holiday;   (d) build a kite.

2. Describe the layout of and the services offered at *one* of the following:
   (a) a public library;   (b) a 24-hour petrol station and associated shop;   (c) a theme park;   (d) an out-of-town shopping centre.

3. What advice would you give to a first-year student at your school or college to help him or her to settle in as quickly and happily as possible?

4. Write a leaflet for distribution to your fellow-students, urging them to support a campaign for better library and leisure facilities.

5. You have been asked to speak briefly for or against *one* of the following:
   (a) that the voting age should be reduced to 16;   (b) that the compulsory registration of dogs should become law;   (c) that drug-taking in sport should be more closely monitored and penalised. Write your speech.

6. A visitor from overseas has asked you to suggest a place of interest in your locality suitable for an excursion. Write a brief description of an outstanding building or of an attractive place that would be worth a visit.

7   A relative or friend about to travel abroad for the first time has asked for your advice. Write helpfully on *one* of the following:
    (a) health and medical matters;   (b) language problems;   (c) travelling light.

8   You want to encourage a friend to take up your own favourite activity or pastime. Describe its attractions and rewards.

9   Advise a friend who is thinking of buying a piece of audio equipment on how to make a good choice.

What you must do

Although the instructions may be worded in very different ways, practical writing is always a test of your ability to organise your material and to write clearly and to the point.

You must work out your **plan** before your begin to write. To work out a satisfactory plan, you must:

- arrange the individual items into sensible groups;
- decide on a logical order of presentation.

Parts, stages, steps

When a straightforward subject has been set, thinking along these lines will help you to organise your material. Suppose you have chosen to describe the layout and equipment that you would expect to find in a well-planned kitchen. A number of unorganised items will spring to mind at once. They can be arranged into organised groups by thinking of the *parts* in relation to the whole. The essential parts of a kitchen are: cooker, sink(s), refrigerator, worktops, seating, lighting, utensils, storage-space, and so on. An organising idea has been found. If you are giving advice on how to perform some transaction, such as applying for a passport or a driving licence, divide the transaction into its *stages*. If you are giving instructions on how to build a kite or make a dress, divide the process into *steps*.

More complicated subjects

The parts/stages/steps approach will not always work. For example, numbers 3, 4, 5, 6 and 9 above are so worded as to require a different solution of the organisational problem. Giving instructions on how to build a kite (1d) is best done in a series of steps, whereas 'advice ... to help him or her to settle in as quickly and happily as possible' (3) must be organised differently. The plan has to take strict account of the task set, a point illustrated in the following work out.

Work out

9   Advise a friend who is thinking of buying a piece of audio equipment on how to make a good choice.

Stage 1

Jot down thoughts just as they come:

> double tape-deck – compact-disc (CD) provision – remote-control – graphic equaliser – audio-analyser – headphones – detachable speakers – size of equipment and portability – power of watts – loudness with extra base-speaker – radio – stacking systems – provision for old methods (records) – provision for new, advanced systems – price – reputation of manufacturer and supplier.

Stage 2

Look for a way of organising the items. The essential parts of a piece of audio equipment can be grouped by function: (1) sound quality; (2) systems that can be played (types of audio tapes, compact discs, records); (3) appearance; (4) price and models.

After a few moments, it is clear that the system of grouping tried out above is of limited help in organising the material for this particular question. Organisation into parts grouped by their function would be a sound enough base for a plan if the task were to describe an audio player, but that is not what the instructions require. We have to advise on a good *choice* of player. We must try to find another way of organising the material.

A good choice can't be made until you know:

- what you want to do with the player;
- what kind of recordings and sound qualities you want;
- where it is to be played;
- how many people will be listening;
- whether the features of the machine have to suit the room it's to be in;
- whether it has to incorporate provisions for old as well as new methods of reproducing sound;
- what can be afforded.

We think we have now found a way of organising material into a suitable answer.

Stage 3

Keeping in mind the task set, group the items accordingly and decide on the order of presentation.

1. Good choice depends on what kind of activity the player will be used for.
2. The importance of sound-reproduction quality has to be assessed.
3. Any limitations of space or demands of decor need to be considered.
4. The factors of price and brand have to be estimated.
5. Conclusion: decide on use, looks and cost, then you can decide what features are essential.

Stage 4

An outline plan has been worked out, grouping the items and getting them into a logical order of presentation. The writing can now be done.

Advice on choosing a piece of audio equipment

Your choice of audio equipment depends on what you want to use the machine for. If your priority is for personal listening, then a small, portable player equipped with headphones is what you want. However, if you wish to share the sounds with others, then you will have to consider having separate speakers and a larger piece of equipment. How important is the ability to record as well as to reproduce sound?

Before you select anything, decide about the quality of the sound that you want. You may be a purist who demands a very high standard or you may just want to hear the music loud and clear. It's a good idea to consider the space that you have available to accommodate both the machine, its accessories and potential volume. Does its capacity and appearance suit your room?

If the make and cost of the equipment strongly affect your choice, then certain decisions will be made easier. There are many systems and models to choose from, but the main determining factors will be your needs and the amount of money that you wish to spend.

11 Editing, summary and redrafting

LEAG	MEG	SEG	NEAB	WJEC	NICCEA	Topic	Date attempted	Date completed	Self Assessment
✓	✓	✓	✓	✓	✓	Examinations and changes			
✓	✓	✓	✓	✓	✓	Coursework			
✓	✓	✓	✓	✓	✓	'Differentiation'			
✓	✓	✓	✓	✓	✓	An approach to the subject			
✓	✓	✓	✓	✓	✓	Speaking and listening			
✓	✓	✓	✓	✓	✓	Reading			
✓	✓	✓	✓	✓	✓	Ways and means			
✓	✓	✓	✓	✓	✓	Writing			
✓	✓	✓	✓	✓	✓	Practical writing			

11.1 Essential skills

Good answers to any questions depend on your ability:

- to select and extract relevant information from a given source;
- to restate that information accurately and coherently.

In Chapter 12, on 'Directed writing', you are required to select relevant information from various sources and to make use of it for specified purposes. For example, you may be told to take what is needed for a given purpose from maps, or diagrams, or tables of figures, or articles, and then use it in, say, a report, or a letter, or a 'feature' suitable for a newspaper or a magazine. Successful performance of such tasks is based on your ability to edit. This may involve rewording, summarising and then shaping or redrafting the material in question.

Editing is the process of preparing a piece of work for publication. It often involves extracting the essential points from a given source and then rewording them *briefly* without falsifying them. They must be set out in a clear and logical sequence.

Because it is a process that we all have to use frequently in our working lives, the examiners rightly expect candidates to be competent 'editors'. Any examination question or coursework assignment based upon editing and summarising, for example, is a rehearsal for an activity on which efficient communication depends.

For example, you may need to make a summary of papers, correspondence, articles, books or parts of books in order to **abstract** information needed for working purposes. So there is nothing 'artificial' about an examination question that requires you to demonstrate your ability to do this. The examiners are simply asking you to show that you are capable of going to the heart of the given material and rewording its essential information for use in different circumstances.

This is one of those tasks that has been made easier by the introduction of the word-processor. The correcting of mistakes, the redrafting of sections and the counting of words makes the challenge of creating the deadly-accurate and finely-tuned alternative version something that can be undertaken on the screen, by your own hands, before your very eyes!

11.2 Simplifying and shortening

The National Curriculum demands that you display the abilities to edit and redraft written material. This would normally involve two processes:

- simplifying;
- shortening.

The former means that you should make the material easier to understand and the latter that you select and condense what you consider to be the main points. The skill of presenting ideas in an easy-to-follow, brief and accurate manner is of inestimable value.

The key to good editing is being able to **summarise** effectively. Fluency in language is a valuable asset, but brevity commands attention. In all that you write you should aim to make your words clear to others. It is a vital part of the writer's very purpose to be meaningful and readily understood by the audience that is being addressed. However, the art of summary – of being precise – needs the application of both mind and technique. You have to direct your own mind by willpower; we will show you how to master the techniques by some straightforward methods. They will need practice. Yet as the stages are mastered you will grow in confidence, handle editing with increasing pleasure, and spend a decreasing amount of time on redrafting.

11.3 Definition and description

A **summary** is a short, pithy restatement of the *chief points* made by a writer (or speaker); a *concise summing up* of the contents of a passage of writing, or of information derived from maps, diagrams or tables. It must be written in *continuous prose* (*not* in note form). As far as possible, it must be written in the summariser's *own words* (*not* in the words of the original passage).

A good summary is:

- *Accurate* It includes all the chief points of the original passage and, although they must be expressed in the summariser's own words, they must *not* be altered. However much the summariser may dislike or dispute the facts set out or disagree with the ideas or opinions expressed in the passage, they must not be tampered with. The 'slant' and the 'feel' of the original passage must not be changed.

- *Brief* The summariser must condense the original passage by selecting the essential points and expressing them in economical language. Minor points must be omitted. All decorative writing, figures of speech, verbal flourishes, illustrations and examples must be omitted. In a summary there is room only for the essential meaning – the bare bones – of the original passage.

- *Clear* It must be *clearly planned* so that its successive items follow each other in a logical sequence. It must also be *clearly expressed* in plain, easily understood English.

11.4 The skills required

Summarising employs all the skills required for general competence in the use of language, for it is a test of reading comprehension and writing aptitude. To make a good summary you must be able:

- to understand what you read;
- and then to express your understanding in words of your own.

The first step in summarising is to arrive at thorough comprehension of the passage. Then, and only then, you are ready to plan and write your summary. Those two operations demand:

- the **judgement** to distinguish between *essential points* (which must be included) and *minor points* (which must be omitted);
- the **organising ability** to work out a *coherent* and *logical* plan;
- the **writing skill** to frame *clear* sentences, *correct* in grammar, punctuation and spelling;
- the **word power** to *condense* the passage while restating its essential contents, and to select *appropriate* expressions to reflect the 'slant' and the 'feel' of the passage.

Each of those points is discussed and demonstrated in later sections of this chapter.

11.5 Different kinds of summary

Whole-passage summary ('précis')

Note: The word *précis* (French) is still in common use as a synonym for *summary*.

Typical instructions: whole-passage summary (précis)

Summarise (make a précis of) this passage in clear and correct English. Some words and phrases in the original writing cannot be accurately or economically replaced, but you must not copy out long expressions or whole sentences. Use *your own words* as far as possible. Your summary *must not exceed 150 words*. State at the end the exact number of words you have used.

The **word limit** may be expressed in other ways. For example, '… in about 150 words'. In that case, you should aim at being not more than 5 words above or below the stipulated number.

Whole-passage summary requires you to include in your summary all the chief points expressed in the passage set.

Selective summary

Often, the examiners' instructions direct attention to one particular subject dealt with in the set passage or passages. In that case your answer must be based exclusively on the information that is supplied about that specified subject. No other information in the passage is relevant.

For example, the set passage might recount the history of a legal reform (the abolition of child labour, say), proceeding from the early days of the struggle to enlist public support to its passage into law and its effects on society. A question set on that passage might ask you what you learn from it about either the early stages of the reforming process, or the parliamentary battle, or the subsequent developments. Your answer must be confined strictly to the specified subject.

Another kind of question demands the selection and rewording of material occurring in various places throughout a passage or passages. For example, in an account of the career of a famous person there might be details of how, at various stages of his or her life, particular qualities of character and personality led to success or failure. The instructions might tell you to say what part one quality (rashness, say) or another (ruthlessness, perhaps) played in his or her career.

Instructions of that kind demand close attention and an alert mind. The examiners are testing your ability to follow their precise wording by extracting and rephrasing only the particular information required. Much that is important in the passage as a whole must be disregarded in your answer, because it is irrelevant to the task you have been set. You will lose marks if you include any point that does not bear directly on the particular topic you have been told to write about.

If you have practised summarising in the ways suggested here, you will be unlikely to make that mistake when tackling tests of understanding and directed writing.

Typical instructions: questions based on selective summary

1 This passage gives an account of the various courses of action open to the leaders of the new party. Say, in your own words, what you learn about their reasons for rejecting the policies that were pressed upon them by an influential group of their supporters.

Use in your answer only that part of the passage that is concerned with the specified subject. Much that is important in the passage as a whole (for example: other courses of action open to the party leaders; the policies that they adopted) is irrelevant to the task you have been given.

2 Study these letters exchanged between Mr J. K. Smith and the Northtown planning authority. Bring out in your own words their points of disagreement about the roofing materials to be used on the house that Mr Smith seeks planning permission to build.

Other matters may be covered in the correspondence (design of roof and windows, colour of paintwork, access road to the house, and so on), but the subject matter of your answer must be restricted to the topic specified in the instructions.

11.6 Summarising method (step by step)

Practice in whole-passage summarising ('précis writing') is the best way of learning the art of summary. While you are learning how to make a good summary of a whole passage, you are at the same time mastering the kind of thinking and the language techniques needed for answers based on a selective summary.

- *Step 1* Get the **gist** of the passage. State it briefly and in your own words.
- *Step 2* Get to grips with the writer's **purpose** by 'tuning in' to the 'slant' and 'feel' of the passage.
- *Step 3* Make a **skeleton outline** of the writer's presentation of the **main theme** by noting each **key point** as it occurs in the passage.
- *Step 4* Use your list of key points as the framework of a **detailed plan** for your summary.
- *Step 5* Write a **draft** of your summary.
- *Step 6* **Prune** and **polish** the draft.
- *Step 7* Write the **final version** of your summary.

That list of the necessary steps may look daunting, but each step is explained and demonstrated later in this chapter.

Summary writing is an essential skill and you must take pains to learn it. Method is vital: nobody can make a good summary 'off the cuff'. With practice, you will speed up and become so versed in these well-tried procedures that you will find it second nature to apply them efficiently in your examination.

11.7 Applying the method

Step 1: Get the gist of the passage

Write (*in your own words*, as far as possible) a brief statement of the main theme(s) expressed in the passage. (The **theme** is the basic, bedrock subject.) Your statement should sum up in as few words as possible ('encapsulate') what the passage is essentially about: the very heart of the matter. You will find it helpful to begin your statement of the theme with some such formula as 'The writer argues that ... ' or 'This passage gives an account of ... '. Such an opening helps you to make an objective and accurate statement of the writer's main subject matter.

Step 2: Get to grips with the writer's purpose

The need to be objective and accurate was emphasised in section 11.3: 'However much the summariser may dislike or dispute the facts set out ... they must not be tampered with.' You may not like the factual contents of the passage. You may even know or think you know that they are wrong, but *it is not your job to alter or correct them in any way*. If the passage states that the moon is made of green cheese, you must not query it or comment on it in your summary. When you make a summary you must reproduce *faithfully* the gist of the original. Your concern is with what the writer says, *not* with what you think he or she ought to have said.

The subject matter is not always factual. It may be an expression of ideas, opinions, arguments for or against a point of view or a course of action. Again, you must reproduce the writer's 'slant' accurately, however much you may disagree with it. It may arouse strong feelings in you – either for or against – but *you must not allow those feelings to appear in your summary*.

Again, without actually stating a point of view, the writer may indicate his or her standpoint indirectly. The passage may be satirical (mildly or savagely, in whole or in part). It may be objective or subjective; part factual, part persuasive. It may be warmly enthusiastic or 'tongue in cheek' writing. There are many possibilities, but whatever the 'feel' of the passage, *you must reflect it accurately and without comment* in your summary.

So, keeping in mind your brief statement of its theme, read through the passage again, looking for the writer's point of view and purpose in writing. As you read, note key words, phrases, sentences that indicate the 'feel' of the piece. Ask yourself these questions: '*What* is the writer trying to do?'; '*Why* is the writer trying to do this?'; '*How* is the writer trying to do this?'

Step 3: Skeleton outline – key points of the main theme

Keep in mind your statement of the main theme as you look for the key points. Include every one that bears on that statement. If in doubt about a point, include it; you will prune later. You can list the key points either by underlining them in the passage or by jotting them down on rough paper.

Step 4: Make a detailed plan for your summary

Base the **plan** on your list of key points. When writing the plan:

- Use *your own words* as far as possible.
- Include sufficient *detail* to enable you to write your draft summary from your notes *without referring to the passage*.

There are two good reasons for that advice. First, if you use the writer's words in your notes, you will be in danger of incorporating them in your summary. Second, if you have to refer to the passage as you write your draft, you will be in danger of departing from the scheme of key points worked out in Step 3 and will probably mix minor points and other irrelevant matter in with the key points.

A good summary plan is:

- *coherent* – all the items that sensibly go together are grouped together (they stick together or 'cohere'): they are *not* 'dotted about' in various parts of the summary;
- *logical* – each part follows on sensibly from the preceding part: the summary is presented in an ordered sequence, *from* its beginning, *through* its middle, *to* its end.

Step 5: Write a draft of your summary

Stick to your plan. Do not be tempted to alter it as you go along. Revisions come later (Step 6). Choose your words carefully and think out well-framed sentences. The language of summary is:

- clear and easily understood;
- condensed – no wasted words of long-winded expressions;
- correct – in grammar, punctuation and spelling.

Step 6: Prune and polish the draft

1 Check the length of your answer. If you have included only the essential information and written clear, economical English, you

should have used about one-third of the number of words in the original. A 'long summary' is a contradiction in terms. A summary is always a *brief* account of the chief points made in the passage on which you are working.

2 Prune by removing unnecessary words. Look especially for overworked, verbose expressions and tautologies (see sections 16.2, 16.3, 16.4, 16.7 and 16.8).
- *check up on* = check
- *period of time* = period
- *in this day and age* = now *or* nowadays
- *advance forward* = advance
- *reverse backwards* = reverse

Apart from such misuse of language, some perfectly good expressions must be pruned because brevity is so important: figurative language, illustrative examples, rhetorical questions and repetitions, decorations – all of which have a part to play in writing *of a different kind*.

3 Condense wherever possible. Search your vocabulary for *compendious* words (see section 11.8). Make every word tell:

| Those who argued in favour of a nuclear generation plant raised powerful objections to their opponents' plan, which offered them some but not all of the resources for which they were contending. | The nuclear lobby objected strongly to their opponents' suggested compromise. |

4 Check for errors of grammar, punctuation and spelling.

5 Look out for and remove *all* colloquialisms, slang, quotations, direct speech.

6 Finally, ask yourself these questions:
- Would this summary be readily understood by *a reader who had not seen the original passage*?
- Would it convey to that reader *the essential meaning* of the passage?

If the answer to both questions is 'yes', you have written a good draft of which you can now make a fair copy and which you can confidently hand in.

Step 7: Write out the final version

1 Head your summary with a suitable title and underline it. Keep it *short*. Do not try to write a 'clever', 'punchy', newspaper-type headline. A plain, accurate, brief title is what is wanted. It does *not* count towards the number of words used.

2 Write the final version in your best and clearest handwriting. Be sure to incorporate all the corrections and improvements made as you pruned and polished the draft.

3 If you have been given a word limit, state at the end the *exact* number of words in your summary, *excluding the title*. Do *not* be tempted to falsify the number. If it looks wrong (and the examiners have a shrewd idea of how many words occupy how many lines of the answer sheet), it will be checked.

11.8 The language of summary

Plain, clear, brief

1. *Plain*, because a summary is a restatement of the bare bones – the *essential* meaning – of a given passage. So, no 'frills' of any kind: no figures of speech; no illustrative examples; no rhetorical questions or repetitions; no 'decorative' writing.

2. *Clear*, because *a reader who has not seen the original passage* must be able to grasp its essential meaning quickly, easily and accurately *from the summary alone*.

3. *Brief*, because the *word limit* imposes a strict discipline and not a word must be wasted. (If no word limit has been stated, keep within one-third of the original length.)

That description sums up points made in earlier sections, but certain other features of the language of summary must now be singled out for special attention.

Condensed

See section 11.7, step 6. The use of **condensed language** (language that boils down a lot of meaning into very few words) is necessary. You must take every opportunity of contracting clauses into phrases and phrases into single words. **Compendious words** (*compendious* = 'space-saving') are needed to encapsulate the essential meaning of longer expressions.

You must also *remove* all **redundant** (or **superfluous**) **words. Verbose language** (language that uses more words than are necessary) is always a fault: in summary, it is fatal:

1	The popular press is full of crime stories, violence in the streets, scandals, thefts and horrifying incidents of every kind.	The popular press is full of sensational items.
2	She made a list of things she needed, such as butter, cheese, raisins, salt, sugar, flour and frozen foods.	She made a list of groceries she needed.
3	The auctioneer moved on to the old barn where harrows, ploughs, seed-drills, rakes and mowers were stored.	The auctioneer moved on to the old barn where agricultural implements were stored.
4	The ship was crowded with people who were leaving their native land for a new home.	The ship was crowded with emigrants.
5	Jean decided to train as a teacher of spinning, weaving, basket-making, china-painting and similar skills.	Jean decided to train as a handicrafts teacher.
6	He was handicapped in examinations by his inability to recall accurately facts and theories that he had learnt.	He was handicapped in examinations by his bad memory.

7	The book tells how Ben Gunn was put ashore and abandoned on an uninhabited island as a punishment.	The book tells how Ben Gunn was marooned.
8	Her small, unexpected good fortune was quickly and wastefully spent on tastelessly showy ornaments.	Her windfall was soon squandered on garish ornaments.
9	Brown says his new job involves a great deal of very hard work.	Brown says his new job is laborious.
10	We tried in vain to persuade the conflicting parties to agree to submit their respective cases to the decision of an independent umpire.	We failed to persuade the adversaries to go to arbitration.
11	The treasurer reported that there were serious financial difficulties in respect of the prospect of completing the new housing estate by the target date that had been set.	The treasurer reported that lack of funds was endangering the completion of the new housing estate on time.
12	In the majority of instances, householders informed the council through the investigating officers enquiring on the council's behalf that they were satisfied and had no complaints in the matter of the scheme regulating the system of differential rating.	Most householders told the council that they were satisfied with the differential rating scheme.

Correct and appropriate

Errors in grammar, punctuation and spelling will cost you marks in questions based on summary (as in all the other questions), but correct language alone is not enough: it must also be *appropriate*. The language of summary is formal (without being stiff or pompous). Therefore, you must not use:

- **colloquialisms** – 'free and easy' expressions suited to conversation and informal writing;
- **contractions** – 'didn't' for 'did not'; and so on;
- **abbreviations**;
- **slang**.

Reported speech

The language of summary is **impersonal**. Therefore, you must *not* use **direct speech**. Any direct speech in the passage that contributes to the essential meaning must be turned into **reported** ('indirect') **speech** in the summary.

Direct speech is a direct representation in writing of the words *actually spoken*. Reported speech is a *report* in writing of what was said:

- *Direct speech* Jones said, 'I shall be forced to resign.' (*Quotation marks round the words actually spoken.*)
- *Reported (indirect) speech* Jones said that he would be forced to resign (*No quotation marks, because the words are not actually quoted here.*)

The rules

1. A 'saying' verb followed by 'that' introduces reported speech. The use of an *expressive* 'saying' verb helps to convey the tone and flavour of the speech being reported:
   - The customer *maintained* that the goods were faulty when delivered.

2. The **tense** of the 'saying' verb governs the tenses of the verbs that follow. When the 'saying' verb is in the past tense, the other verbs must also be in the past tense. When the 'saying' verb is in the present tense, the other verbs must be adjusted to fit the sense:
   - The witness *declared* that he *had* often heard the accused threaten to set fire to the factory and that he *had* not *been* in any doubt that the threats *were* serious.
   - Our agent in Brussels *reports* that the new regulations *will* favour our products and that he *foresees* a steadily growing market.

3. All pronouns and possessive adjectives must be in the **third person**: *I* becomes *he/she*; *we* becomes *they*; *my* becomes *his/her*; and so on.
   - *Direct speech* The retiring president said, 'I am grateful for the support that I have always received from you, the officers of the association. Your help and friendship will remain a precious memory.'
   - *Reported speech* The retiring president expressed *his* gratitude for the support that *he* had received from the officers of the association, adding that *their* help and friendship would remain a precious memory.

4. All expressions indicating nearness in place and time in direct speech are 'distanced' in reported speech: *here* becomes *there*; *this* becomes *that*; *today* becomes *that day*; and so on.
   - *Direct speech* Councillor Brown said, 'My supporters have not sent me here to prolong these conditions. They expect decisive action before this year is out.'
   - *Reported speech* Councillor Brown said that his supporters had not sent him *there* to prolong *those* conditions. They expected decisive action before *that* year *was* out.

5. Colloquialisms, contractions and slang expressions used in direct speech must be removed in reported speech. If they contribute to the essential meaning, a formal equivalent must be substituted.
   - *Direct speech* At this point, the sergeant blew his top. 'Don't dodge the question!' he yelled at the suspect.
   - *Reported speech* The sergeant now angrily accused the suspect of being evasive.

6. As the examples have made clear, quotation marks must never be used in reported speech.

The following demonstration gathers together all the rules. Note that a rearrangement of the order of the original passage helps to condense the material. Note, too, the use of compendious words and the way in which the 'flavour' of the direct speech is reflected in the shortened version.

- *Direct speech:*

'May all the plagues of Hades fall upon you!' the furious Hassan shouted at the trembling courier. 'You arrive with a message from my brother, asking for instant help, and I find that you have been over a week on the way. This letter should have been in my possession last Tuesday at the latest. I've half a mind to string you up with my own hands!'

'Pardon your wretched slave, pardon!' howled the distraught courier. 'The river at the frontier was in high flood and I could by no means cross until the waters subsided. You know how swift and faithful I have been in your service for many a long year.'

- *Shortened version in reported speech:*

Hassan cursed the terrified messenger and threatened him with execution, saying that his brother's request for immediate help, which should have arrived no later than the previous Tuesday, had taken over a week to deliver. Begging for mercy and reminding Hassan of his past services, the messenger protested that he had been delayed by a flooded river.

11.9 Work out 1 (step by step)

Write a summary of the following passage in good continuous prose, using not more that 120 words. State at the end of your summary the number of words you have used. The passage contains 348 words.

When social historians look back, they will be astonished at our almost obsessive concern with sufficient supplies of energy. Our planet is, after all, one vast system of energy. The sun's rays that fall on the roads of North America contain more energy than all the fossil fuel used each year in the whole world. The winds that rage and whisper round the planet are a vast energy reserve caused by unequal solar heating of blazing tropics and arctic poles.

Nor should we forget the energy locked up in plants. Indeed, in some developing lands, ninety per cent of the energy is derived from wood. Experimentally, a U.S. Naval Undersea Centre has an ocean-farm project cultivating seaweed. The hope is that the solar energy captured by the plant on an ocean-farm of, say, 470 square miles could theoretically be converted into as much natural gas as is consumed in America at present. All in all, the fear of running out of energy must be said to have a social, not a rational base. Modern citizens simply do not see that their whole life is surrounded by a variety of energy reserves which not only exceed present sources but have a further advantage that they are not exhausted by use. A ton of oil burnt is a ton lost. A ton of seaweed will be growing again next year. Even more reliably, the sun will rise and release an annual 1.5 quadrillion megawatt hours of energy. There can be no running out of such resources.

But can they be harnessed? A tornado is a fine exhibit of energy unleashed but it is hardly a useful one. The fundamental question with all renewable sources of energy is how to develop the technologies for using and storing them at reasonable cost. Perhaps the first need is for citizens to open the eyes of their imagination and conceive of energy in new shapes, forms and sizes. If they do, they will find that the technologies *are* available, *will* become cheaper, and *could* even lead to a more civilised mode of existence.

BARBARA WARD

Step 1

Discover the theme. Make a brief statement of the gist of the passage.

> Writer argues that our worries about supplies of energy are unnecessary, since nature provides abundant renewable supplies if we learn how to tap them.

Notes

1 This is an objective statement, beginning with a formula ('Writer argues that ...').
2 The summariser's own words are used.

Step 2

Read the passage again, slowly and carefully. Jot down (or underline in the passage) expressions that highlight the writer's ideas, views and aims. Get to the heart of the subject matter.

> they will be astonished/our almost obsessive concern/Our planet ... vast system of energy/fear of running out of energy ... social ... not rational/simply do not see ... whole life surrounded ... energy reserves/exceed present sources ... not exhausted by use/no running out of such resources/can they be harnessed?/fundamental question ... to develop the technologies/open the eyes of their imagination/conceive of energy in new shapes/technologies *are* available/*will* become cheaper/*could* even lead to a more civilised mode of existence.

Notes

1 The writer believes people misunderstand the true position.
2 She uses facts to back this up.
3 She wants to persuade people to look at the position differently.
4 All those points are made clear by scrupulous examination of *what* the writer says and *how* it is said.

Step 3

Keeping the statement of the theme in mind, make a skeleton outline of the key points.

> 1 ... social historians ... will be astonished at our almost obsessive concern with sufficient supplies of energy.
> 2 Our planet is ... one vast system of energy.
> 3 All in all, fear of running out of energy must be said to have a social, not a rational base.
> 4 Modern citizens simply do not see ... not exhausted by use.
> 5 There can be no running out of such resources.

6 But can they be harnessed?
7 The fundamental question ... reasonable cost.
8 Perhaps the first need is for citizens to open the eyes of their imagination ... energy in new shapes, forms and sizes.
9 If they do ... more civilised mode of existence.

Notes

1 *Only* key points are included. All supporting points and illustrative examples are omitted (e.g. 'The sun's rays ... the whole world'/'The winds ... arctic poles'/'A ton of seaweed ... next year').
2 This effects a considerable reduction of the original material; but there are nine major points, so condensed writing will be required.
3 Question: How vital is the 'social historians' point? Not sure, so include it *at this stage*.

Step 4

Make a plan for the summary. Base the plan on the list of key points. Use your own words in the plan as far as possible, and include sufficient detail to be able to write a draft of the summary without referring to the passage.

1 Future social historians will be very surprised by our constant worries about not having enough energy resources.
2 Since the planet is a huge reservoir of energy, it is not reasonable to be afraid of running out of energy. There must be a social reason for our fears.
3 People today do not see that there are many different sources of energy all around them. These sources are not only greater than those now used, but they cannot be used up because they constantly grow again or they are permanent forces.
4 There are technical problems of how to make use of these sources economically, but the chief problem is getting people to use their imagination and think about energy in new ways.
5 If they can manage to do that, they will see that we have the techniques to exploit the natural resources and that they will get cheaper and could make life more civilised.

Notes

1 The plan is based on the key points, but it 'telescopes' some of them: nine key points become a five-point plan.
2 There is a lot of repetition of words in the plan (e.g. 'energy'/'sources') and this must be removed in the draft. The detail of the plan is important; polishing comes later.
3 A good deal of rephrasing will be needed – compendious words must be found to boil down the meaning of some straggling expressions which waste words.
4 Connecting phrases and linking words will be needed to turn the separate points of the plan into a piece of good, continuous prose.

Step 5

Write a draft of the summary, working from the plan. Refer to the passage *only* if stuck; but it should not be necessary to do so.

Future social historians will be very surprised by our constant worries about not having enough energy resources. Since the planet is a huge reservoir of energy, it is not reasonable to be afraid of running out. There must be a social reason for our fears. People today do not see that there are many different sources of energy all around them and that not only are these greater than those now used, but they cannot be exhausted because they grow again or they are permanent forces. There are technical problems of how to use them economically, but the first necessity is for people to use their imagination and think about these new forms of energy. If they do that, they will realise that we have the essential technologies and that they will become cheaper and could make life more civilised.

Step 6

Prune and polish the draft.

1. *Word count* The word limit is 'not more than 120 words' and there are 139 word in the draft. Hard pruning is required.

2. *Look for unnecessary material* First, check the 'social historians' point listed as 'doubtful' at Step 3. Further thought shows that it ties in with 'a social reason', so it makes an important point and must stay. All the other material seems essential, so words cannot be saved by pruning the subject matter.

3. *Look for wasted words* The language of the draft needs to be much tighter in construction and more condensed in expression. For example: '... it is not reasonable to be afraid of running out'/'... because they grow again or they are permanent forces'. The first is loose; the second is both loose and ambiguous. Disciplined rewriting will save words and put the meaning across much more crisply.

4. *Look for badly chosen words* One leaps out at once: *reservoir*. There is nothing wrong with the word itself, of course, but *in this context* it seems to suggest that the natural energy sources are all to do with water-power; and that is *not* what the writer says. Again, is there confusion in the use of 'techniques'/'technologies'? Does 'very surprised' give the right 'feel'? Is it strong enough?

5. *Is the draft a connected and readable piece of prose?* The last two sentences are not linked firmly enough to bring out their logical connection. Apart from that, the 'flow' of the draft seems satisfactory. The ideas and the argument move steadily forwards.

6. *Check grammar, punctuation and spelling*

7. *Final tests to be applied* Would this summary be readily understood by a reader who had not seen the original passage? Yes. Would it convey to that reader the essential meaning of the passage? Yes.

Step 7

Write the final version.

1. *Head* the summary with a *suitable* (brief, plain, accurate) title.
2. *Write out* the final version in your best and *clearest* handwriting, remembering to incorporate all the improvements of Step 6.
3. *State* at the end the exact number of words used, *excluding the title*.

THE EARTH'S UNTAPPED AND RENEWABLE ENERGY RESOURCES

Our besetting anxiety about energy supplies will astonish future social historians. Since Earth is itself a huge energy system, our fear that our supplies may fail is not reasonable. Its cause is social. People today are blind to the fact that all around them are different kinds of energy, far greater than those now used. These natural sources of energy can never fail, for they are renewable and therefore inexhaustible. There is the problem of how to exploit them economically, but the first necessity is for people to think imaginatively about these new possibilities. Then they will realise that we have the essential technologies, which will get cheaper and which could make human life more civilised.

(116 words)

11.10 Work out 2 (with notes)

Summarise this passage in clear, concise English, *using your own words as far as possible*. You may retain words and brief expressions which cannot be accurately or economically replaced. Do *not* take whole sentences from the passage and simply replace key words. Write your summary in about 110 words and state at the end the exact number of words you have used. Spend about 45 minutes on this question.

A man can stand being told that he must submit to a severe surgical operation, or that he has some disease which will shortly kill him, or that he will be a cripple or blind for the rest of his life; dreadful as such tidings must be, we do not find that they unnerve the greater number of mankind; most men, indeed, go coolly enough even to be hanged, but the strongest quail before financial ruin, and the better men they are, the more complete, as a general rule, is their prostration. Suicide is a common consequence of money losses; it is rarely sought as a means of escape from bodily suffering. If we feel that we have a competence at our backs, so that we can die warm and quietly in our beds, with no need to worry about expenses, we live our lives out to the dregs, no matter how excruciating our torments. Job probably felt the loss of his flocks and herds more than that of his wife and family, for he could enjoy his flocks and herds without his family, but not his family – not for long – if he had lost all his money. Loss of money indeed is not only the worst pain in itself, but it is the parent of all the others. Let a man have been brought up to a moderate competence, and have no specialty; then let his money be suddenly taken from him, and how long is his health likely to survive the change in all his little ways which loss of money will entail? How long again is the esteem and sympathy of friends likely to survive ruin? People may be very sorry for us, but their attitude towards us hitherto has been based upon the supposition that we were situated thus and thus in money matters; when this breaks down there must be a restatement of the social problem so far as we are concerned; we have been obtaining esteem under false pretences. Granted, then, that the three most serious losses which a man can suffer are those affecting money, health and reputation. Loss of money is far the worst, then comes ill-health, and then loss of reputation; loss of reputation is a bad third, for, if a man keeps health and money unimpaired, it will generally be found that his loss of reputation is due to breaches of parvenu conventions only, and not to violations of those older, better established canons whose authority is unquestionable. In this case a man may grow a new reputation as easily as a lobster grows a new claw, or, if he have health and money, may thrive in great peace of mind without any reputation at all. The only chance for a man who has lost his money is that he shall still be young enough to stand uprooting and transplanting without more than temporary derangement.

Samuel Butler, *The Way of All Flesh*

LOSS OF MONEY IS THE WORST OF ALL MISFORTUNES

The prospect of a major operation, fatal illness or crippling disability is more courageously borne than financial disaster. Indeed, that worst of sufferings, loss of money, is followed by all other miseries. Health is lost because habitual comforts are removed. Friendships and social regard are destroyed because sympathy alone cannot sustain former relationships once they are seen to have been based on false financial assumptions. Loss of money is worse than loss of either health or social standing. With money, illness is endurable. Lost social standing is easily recovered or readily dispensed with if money and health are preserved, but financial ruin can be survived only by those young enough to start again elsewhere.

(113 words)

Notes

1. The opinions expressed in the passage are contentious, deliberately challenging the usual points of view on these matters. The summariser must not be jolted out of an objective approach to the task. The writer's opinions must be restated accurately, without alteration or comment.
2. Because the writing is itself condensed, the word limit is hard to observe. In fact, the summary is just below the upper limit ('about 110 words' allows a plus or minus of 5 words). The material omitted consisted mainly of supporting points and illustrative examples (e.g. 'Suicide is …'/'Job probably felt the loss …'/'as easily as a lobster …').
3. Compendious words (e.g. 'crippling disability'/'habitual comforts'/ 'financial assumptions') were used to encapsulate longer but essential statements. Useful tips can be learnt by comparing the vocabulary of the summary closely with that of the original passage.
4. An attempt was made to convey the ironical tone of the writing (e.g. 'Lost social status … easily recovered … readily dispensed with …'), though the need to condense inevitably diluted the full flavour.
5. Some rearrangement of the order in which the key points are presented in the passage helped to establish coherence in the summary. For example, 'With money, illness is endurable' encapsulates the meaning of 43 words in the passage ('If we feel … torments.') *and* moves the point to a later stage in the summary than in the passage. Such shifts in the order are often necessary, for the coherence established in a longer piece of writing may be destroyed unless adjustments are made to preserve it in a small-scale version of the essential meaning.

11.11 Work out 3 (with example)

Summarise this passage in clear, concise English, using your own words as far as possible. Write your summary in about 125 words.

Community service used to be something associated primarily with white-collar criminals. But if Maryland's department of education gets its way, it will soon be part of the staple diet of American schoolchildren. The state is trying to ensure that its high-school pupils spend more time working in soup-kitchens and less time hanging around shopping malls [shopping centres]. To that end it has just ratified a plan making graduation from high school conditional on 75 hours of community service.

Maryland started down the road to compulsory community service in 1985, by requiring school districts to make it available to their high-school students. That was not enough for some. Kathleen Kennedy Townsend, the daughter of the late Robert Kennedy, has been working for seven years to win approval for compulsory community service in Maryland's public high schools. Now that her plan has been approved, however, its drawbacks are becoming more apparent.

The president of the Maryland State Teachers' Association has likened the service requirement to slavery. The Baltimore Teachers' Union says that the $10 million cost of the plan might be better spent on more conventional teaching aids – like books. Others worry that the 75 hours of community service will be a burden for poor students, who might otherwise get a part-time job. This last complaint may be the programme's downfall: unlike other proposed public-service plans, Maryland's offer no financial compensation.

Mickey Kaus, the author of *The End of Equality*, an influential new book praising the value of mandatory public service, dismisses these concerns. He says that social benefits derived from public service are a bargain at $10 million, and adds that 75 hours is not too much time to carve out of a student's four years in high school. But public-service programmes are justified, argues Mr. Kaus, only if they overcome social division by mixing people of different backgrounds in a common endeavour. It is not clear that Maryland's programme will do this.

Ms Townsend's dream of mandatory altruism may yet be deferred past its proposed starting date in 1993. The constitutionality of a compulsory-service plan in the high schools of Bethlehem, Pennsylvania, is currently being argued in the courts. Parents there argue that Bethlehem's programme violates their children's free-speech rights as well as the 13th Amendment's prohibition against involuntary servitude.

from *The Economist*

Should American high-school pupils have to undertake community work?

The State of Maryland has recently devised a new requirement for its would-be graduates from high schools – 75 hours of community service. Students have previously been encouraged to take up temporary, unpaid work to help others, but now it could become compulsory.

Some influential supporters claim that compulsory service is an inexpensive way of creating opportunities for social mixing and promoting the common good. Some teachers' leaders would like to see the money spent on more conventional educational equipment.

Fear that the poor will be deprived of part-time, *paid* jobs is likely to be a difficult obstacle. The legal objections to what is seen as a form of slavery are being tested in the courts of Pennsylvania, where another, similar scheme has been proposed.

(125 words)

11.12 Work out 4 (with answer)

The following passage was written by an 83-year-old who, for much of the latter half of the 20th century, has been a household name in matters connected with fashion and the design of clothes. He considers aspects of his life and times during much of the century, uses the first person frequently in order to emphasise his personal involvement with events and changes, and lets his mind wander constructively from subject to subject. When reading this passage, imagine that you are conversing with the author and listening to his views.

In order to test your skills at editing, work your way through the passage and pick out what you consider to be the significant features of change that he recalls. As you write them down, try to gather the specific items into general groups. Look for connections that will help you develop a list of about six important areas.

'MY CENTURY HAS A CLEANER BOTTOM'

*On his 83rd birthday, **Hardy Amies** reminisces about his life and times*

My year, 1909, was in the first decade of the century. Now we are in the last. The 20th is my century. It doesn't seem long. Three times brings us to William and Mary. Six times more to William the Conqueror.

I was just born an Edwardian, and ladies on the District line wore Edwardian dress until 1914. Then we followed my father to his army camps. On 11 November 1918 a thousand day-boys and I cheered our heads off in the playground. War rations were enough to avoid hunger. But there was disgusting marrow jam in brown cardboard cartons.

A Daimler was hired to move us to a farmhouse on rhubarb fields ten miles east of Barking. There was neither gas nor electricity. I boarded at an ancient grammar school just gone public. We were given a bath night once a week. My century has learned to wash. There are more bidets around. My century has a cleaner bottom.

The motor-car became part of our body by the Twenties. My mother died before the second world war without ever having had a refrigerator. My father longed to earn a thousand a year as this was the seal of success. My younger brother was a mongol who did not die until his 60th year. Only in about the last ten years did we have help with the expense of a boy who could never be left alone. My century has learned to look after such things. Whenever I have seen the National Health function, in the countryside especially, it fills me with admiration.

My century has travelled enormously. I was sent to France in 1926 for the last of my summer holidays while at school. Next year I left school to take up an 'au pair' job at the English school in Antibes.

People were just beginning to sunbathe. The big hotels at Cannes and Nice were closed in summer. Winter was the season. Hotels in Juan-les-Pins were opening in the summer. My century has sunbathed too much. Skin cancer in old age is the price we pay for youthful folly. A leather-textured and -coloured skin looks seriously common.

In Paris, I worked in the office of custom agents. The London basket filled with parcels from cloth merchants would arrive next morning at the Court dressmakers in London. I had my foot in the door of a dress house. I travelled home at Christmas, steerage, from Dieppe to Tilbury. The next year I went to a Lutheran parsonage in a small town on the Rhine. I got work at a wall-tile factory. I studied German fiercely and became assistant manager.

I stayed two and a half years in Germany. My 21st birthday was celebrated on 1 August, the same day the French tricolour was lowered on the fortress of Ehrenbreitstein, 1930. The occupation of the Rhineland was over. I went back to England.

My German boss gave me as a parting gift an air ticket from Cologne to Brussels and then on to London. It was Imperial Airways and the seats were wicker armchairs. Several people were discreetly sick into bags.

I wanted to work in Europe but ended up in Birmingham. My mother left the Court dressmaking business in which she had worked for ten years, when war broke out. She kept in touch with the proprietors and several of the staff. I did too. But with never a thought of entering the business.

Suddenly there came an offer to run a fairly recently established bespoke tailors, women's tailoring business, the designer manager of which had left to start his own business. The owners had been my mother's employers.

The shop specialised in tailoring: in what ladies still called 'coats and skirts' but which by the young rich were known as 'suits'. I now see that the 'suit' has truly been the ladies' gear of the century. Based on a man's jacket, Chanel did it in the Twenties: her successor Lagerfeld is still doing it. Hundreds of thousands of women all over the world are wearing versions of men's jackets, made in real or imitation wool, over matching skirts or even printed silk dresses.

Success came to me slowly but steadily. The Coronation of George VI in 1937 brought American buyers to London *en route* for Paris. We made better suits than did the French. I am good at planning tailoring. The placing of buttons and pockets, added to good proportions of the body of the coat, is as important to me as fenestration in a house.

I moved to London. I became friends with fashion journalists and went on into the fringes of the *beau monde*, but slowly – I was intelligent enough not to be pushy. I learned the lingo. But I am surprised to remember that I was invited to a party given in the old Carlton Hotel for the Prince of Wales and Mrs Simpson by Mrs Beatrice Cartwright, an American hostess. 'Molyneux made the dress especially for tonight. It's awful. You should always copy things out of the collection.' I was learning fast.

My century has seen the rise of a huge industry based on ready-to-wear clothes for men and women. Sport has become a bigger influence than elegant living. Taste is not required.

In 1945, I collected some capital from friends. I took a lease of a house built by Lord Burlington in 1735 and badly damaged by a land-mine which fell on Savile Row in the Blitz. I gathered a staff of tailors and seamstresses, and of saleswomen who had treasured their address books from before the war. We had no cloth, so we cut brown paper into what became new models. The war was a long time dying. In February 1946 American buyers came over before we were ready with a collection. They bought everything. New York was hungry for European clothes.

We attempted to make London into a centre of fashion, impertinently comparing it with Paris. By specialising in English suits, we, for a season or two, became part of the European scene. But Paris quickly reformed its industry of cloth merchants, flower-makers, embroiderers and armies of nimble-fingered workers, and drew back into its arms the chic rich and discerning of Europe and later the world. In my century, England lacked financiers who liked and understood fashion. It lacked the support of a scent industry backed by the rose and lavender fields of Grasse.

My century saw long skirts disappear from the streets – not during the 1914-18 war but in the Twenties, culminating in 1926. It was then that they were shorter than they ever had been, just around the knee. They never went above the knee until recently. Women have usually only accepted a difference of an inch from one year to another. I cannot see this, my century, ending with long skirts. I think it will all settle down around the knee rather than round the ankle or the crutch.

The reign of the short skirt was rudely interrupted by that of Dior and his New Look. It was a time of beautiful clothes and plain accessories. It ultimately had to change because it did not take into account the power of sport.

My century is ferociously interested in sport. Young girls dress like sportswomen. Matrons look as if they played tennis or golf. All go to the gym. The Queen, whose custom came to us as early as 1950 when she was still Princess Elizabeth, has always made it clear that she wished to be dressed as correctly as possible, with hat, gloves and handbag. It seemed like a kind of exquisite politeness, but it looked strange next to the hatless Mrs Jackie Kennedy.

I asked my brilliant friend and contemporary, Enoch Powell, at one of his 80th birthday parties, to tell me what was the most exciting thing that had happened to him in his life. 'Flying to Australia,' he said quickly. I have flown there about 20 times. The journey has no fears for me. I am now pretty clear as to the shape and size of the earth.

It is now evident that I think that my century is a pretty stunning one. I do not wish to knock it. But I can't let my fellow inhabitants of the globe get away with everything. We went to the moon. (No one talks any more about that. I can't remember the date.) We created Concorde to fly to New York. Rather feeble arrangements to fly Concorde to Australia quickly petered out. Too expensive.

Travel abroad has brought new tastes into the mouth of my century. With these sensations came an interest in cooking. One of my *Egerias* – ladies I consult about manners they have been brought up to respect – admits that they were not allowed to discuss food at table. They are happy to do so today.

When it isn't food, it's gardening. My century has seen the arrival and the triumph of the garden centre. The Chelsea Flower Show is an annual Great Exhibition. Let us rejoice. Gardens do not make revolutionaries. It would be a good idea to encourage those Serbs and Croats to take to growing roses.

In my century, inflation has truly become inflated. To give examples is to encourage bores. I am fascinated by the statements of politicians that they have plans to control inflation. Looking at my century, I can see that a man now demands for his work many more things than he did when I was born. He requires a centrally heated house, a garden, a television set, a motor-car and holidays abroad. Washing-machines are as common as water-closets. To truly stop inflation you would have to ban all advertising.

I ask my *Egerias* for their favourite developments, in my century. 'The elimination of fog.' In second place they reply, 'Television, the companion of maiden ladies in the country.' Early in my century one snatched a crystal with a cat's whisker. Now television is the voice of my century.

This autumn I shall go to Sydney. At meal-times, listening to the classical music channel, I shall think of the Revd Sydney Smith: 'My idea of heaven is eating pâtés de foie gras to the sound of trumpets.' Only in my century can you do just that at the height of 30,000 feet.

from *The Spectator*

The six areas that seem to incorporate the main points of the passage are:

1 *Care* Hygiene – health – help for brother.
2 *Innovations* Cars – refrigerators – central heating – televisions.
3 *Travel* Work opportunities abroad – holidays – flying.
4 *Activities* Sport – sunbathing – gardening – food.
5 *Clothing* Fashions – mass production and availability – sportswear.
6 *Values* Inflation and spending powers – tastes that change.

Now you should feel confident enough to be able to produce a short survey of this passage in which you present an objective assessment of this century, based on the subjective views of Hardy Amies.

12 Directed writing

LEAG	MEG	SEG	NEAB	WJEC	NICCEA	Topic	Date attempted	Date completed	Self Assessment
✓	✓	✓	✓	✓	✓	Examinations and changes			
✓	✓	✓	✓	✓	✓	Coursework			
✓	✓	✓	✓	✓	✓	'Differentiation'			
✓	✓	✓	✓	✓	✓	An approach to the subject			
✓	✓	✓	✓	✓	✓	Speaking and listening			
✓	✓	✓	✓	✓	✓	Reading			
✓	✓	✓	✓	✓	✓	Ways and means			
✓	✓	✓	✓	✓	✓	Writing			
✓	✓	✓	✓	✓	✓	Practical writing			

12.1 Definition and description

A piece of **directed writing** is a composition of some length written 'to order'. The examiners provide you with **source material** and with detailed instructions which stipulate:

- the *nature* of the material to be used in your answer;
- the *form* your writing must take;
- the *audience* for which it is intended.

Sometimes the length of the piece of writing is strictly and explicitly controlled by a stated **word limit**. More often, the length depends on the time allowed for the question, which may be as little as 30 minutes or as much as one hour. You will, of course, find out what time limits your own examining board sets, and practise accordingly.

A directed writing task may be one question in an examination paper testing understanding, or it may be part of your assessed coursework.

12.2 Some typical instructions for directed writing

1 Passage One gives an account of the meticulous planning of the raid on the bullion van. Passage Two details what happened and how the driver and the security guard rather luckily succeeded in foiling the attempted robbery.

Having studied both passages, write a report of the incident such as the driver might have made to his employers, pointing out weaknesses in the security arrangements and procedures which so nearly allowed the raid to succeed, and making recommendations for improvements.

Use only the material supplied in the two passages, and remember that this is an official report, not a journalistic 'write-up' of a sensational event.

Spend about 15 minutes in studying the two passages and making notes. You will then have 30 minutes in which to plan and write the report, which must be clearly ordered and written in plain, direct English.

2 The following passage (written soon after the events occurred) describes some of the effects of the Blitz on London in 1940.

Imagine that you have been asked to write a 'feature article' for your local paper, commemorating the anniversary of these historic events.

Use only the information supplied in the passage, and do not try to include everything mentioned there. Select those details that you think will be of greatest interest to readers to whom 1940 is a long time ago. Your article should reflect your admiration of Londoners' behaviour as described in the passage.

Use your own words as far as possible. If you do include any expressions from the original passage for their vividness or historical flavour, be sure that they are such as your readers will readily understand.

Write in an appropriate style. Provide a headline for your article. Subheadings may also be used.

You are allowed one hour for this question, and your article should be between 400 and 450 words in length.

3 Look carefully at Map A which shows the start and Map B which shows the route of the Northtown Charity Marathon Run. Then read the official handout following the maps. When you have studied all this material, you must answer both questions which carry equal marks.

Your answers must be based on the information given to you, but you must use and organise the material in your own way and not simply copy from the passage.

Write a letter from the chairperson of the Marathon Run Committee (Mr James Penny) to prospective entrants for this year's run, giving them all the information they need to appreciate the physical demands that the Run will make on competitors. Base the information on the maps and the handout.

Begin the letter 'Dear Enquirer' and end with 'Yours sincerely', followed by the appropriate signature. Provide it with a sensible date.

Before starting to write, study this additional information:

(a) In last year's Run, several entrants who were not physically fit had clearly underestimated the strain involved. Mr Penny wants to ensure that this year's entrants have a medical check before they run.

(b) Learning from last year's experience, the organisers are providing an ample supply of sugar and salt drinks and greatly increased first-aid facilities at regular intervals along the route.

Mr Penny wants to emphasise both these points without frightening prospective (and fit) entrants off.

12.3 What you have to do

The length of the instructions quoted in the previous section is typical of directed writing questions. You have to study them closely, because it is essential to do exactly what you are told to do.

Their length and detail will not seem so frightening once you realise that, whatever the nature of the given source material (maps, diagrams, tables, written passages of various kinds) and whatever the form of writing required of you (reports, letters, articles, diary entries, instructions, and so on) all directed writing questions make the same three basic demands:

1 You must study the source material closely, reading it for full comprehension.

2 You must then extract from the given material all the information required to perform the particular writing tasks you have been set. Go

about this in the methodical way recommended in Chapter 11. The thinking and procedures needed are exactly the same as those needed when you are preparing to write a summary.

3 Finally, you must use the information you have extracted, ensuring that every item you use is relevant to the jobs you have been given. Again, the process is similar to summarising in that you must set the relevant information out in a logical order and reword it to suit the job you are doing. As the instructions quoted in section 12.2 put it: 'Use your own words as far as possible'; 'you must use and organise the material in your own way and not simply copy from the passage'.

12.4 Appropriate style

In section 12.1 it was pointed out that directed writing instructions specify the **form** in which you must write and the **audience** for whom you must write. Those two specifications (form and audience) determine what **style** of writing is appropriate. The examiners provide you with all the guidance you need – if you pay attention, that is.

For example, the first set of instructions in section 12.2 called for a report from the security van driver to his employers. Both the form of the required writing (a report) and the audience (his employers) make it appropriate to write in a formal and objective way. To make sure that candidates did not choose an inappropriate style, they were reminded later in the instructions that 'This is an official report, not a journalistic write-up of a sensational event'.

The second set of instructions stipulated a piece of writing in the form of 'a feature article for your local newspaper'. The audience was not described, because there was no need. The nature of the audience (the readers of a local newspaper) is implicit in the stipulated form. You are expected to draw on your own experience and have a pretty shrewd idea of what such readers would respond to. In any case, key words later in the instructions provided plenty of indications of what would be an appropriate style for this piece of writing: 'interest ... admiration ... vividness ... historical flavour'.

The third set of instructions asked you to write a letter. It was to be an 'open' letter aimed at a public audience. It was to be 'personalised' in its beginning and ending, but it was not truly personal. It was not written to one, individual person. Its content was official and its purpose was to inform and caution. Its style had to match its content, its purpose and its audience while, at the same time, striking a reassuring note. Imagine that you were directed by the examiners to write a second letter, again from James Penny, but this time to a friend. He wants to tell him or her about the work that he is doing to ensure that this year's Marathon Run arrangements will be more successful than those organised last year, when things obviously went wrong. The facts are the same; the style would be somewhat different.

The basic requirement, of course, is to write clear sentences, linked to form a continuous and connected piece of English. But even a correctly written answer that makes accurate use of relevant information cannot be marked highly *unless* its style is appropriate to the form in which it is written and to the audience for whom it is intended.

12.5 Work out 1 (with notes)

The passage below deals with certain aspects of vandalism. Using only the material contained in this passage write an article, in *two* paragraphs, for your local newspaper, setting out:

(a) the serious effects of vandalism;
and
(b) the possible causes of vandalism.

Your two paragraphs should correspond to (a) and (b) above. *Do not add ideas of your own* but select and arrange material from the passage. *Write in good, clear, accurate English and use an appropriate style.* Your article should be in your own words as far as possible; do not copy out whole sentences or expressions.

The editor has told you not to exceed 200 words.

A feature of the last twenty years has been the rapid increase in vandalism in Britain. Vandalism itself, however, is not a new phenomenon, since through the ages there have always been those who preferred to destroy rather than to create; even the word 'vandalism' owes its origin to a race of barbarians who devastated parts of Europe as long ago as the fifth century.

The misspelt graffiti, uprooted newly planted trees, abused train carriages, smashed phone boxes, and bus-stop shelters recklessly destroyed spoil the environment and deprive the public of their amenities for which they have paid. Those who perpetrate such outrages seem to be without any self-discipline and show scant respect for the rights of their fellow-citizens. Moreover, they increase the taxes and the rates that they themselves have to pay.

Some argue that the vandals feel rejected by society with its predominant middle-class standards and have far too much time on their hands. It is conceivable that poor housing and squalid living conditions may lead to this anti-social behaviour, but, if these are the principal causes, it needs to be explained why most of the socially deprived are not vandals. One thing is certain: in order to repair the damage done, local rates have to be increased and national levels of income tax have to take account of the increased expenditure needed to maintain services. Scarce material resources and human skills are unnecessarily wasted in the attempts to reduce the danger to life and property caused by vandalism.

Those who practise vandalism are often of poor education and without parental control. They would defend their behaviour, perhaps, by arguing that society provides them with few youth clubs and recreational activities and that they have nothing better to do with their time. The truth is that they are insecure and feel they must put on a show of bravado in order to impress their peers and members of the gang. Perhaps the growth of gangs and movements, particularly those associated with drugs, has played a major rôle in the increase in vandalism.

It is a pity that the development of new schools and improved health services has been jeopardised because of a lack of financial resources when these very resources are being squandered in repairing the damage and making good the destruction caused by vandalism. The situation poses a real challenge to those responsible for educating the young or maintaining law and order. The evidence everywhere of vandalism demeans the standing of the country in the eyes of foreign visitors who are amazed to read the obscene remarks scrawled illiterately across walls or step through the broken glass of street lamps smashed 'just for a joke'. The pride, too, of local people in their environment is being eroded.

Some of the socially minded politicians give up their efforts to improve the quality of life in the face of such mindless destruction; imaginative designers and developers are reduced to designing amenities which are vandal-proof rather than beautiful and attractive. The older generation, with some justification, blames the younger one and age-groups become even more sharply divided. Some local authorities have become reluctant to improve recreational and social facilities because of vandalism, which is aided and abetted, it is sometimes suggested, by the reduction in police surveillance and an apparently uninterested public which looks the other way when it sees vandals at work. Too many are content to blame the invention of the aerosol can and the felt-tip pen, which make it easy to vandalise buildings and other people's property. Ostrich-like, many ignore what they see and hope that the trail of devastation will cease with the coming of a new generation.

Notes

1. Start work by abstracting the material asked for, listing each key point under one or the other of the headings provided in the instructions: (a) the serious effects of vandalism; *and* (b) the possible causes of vandalism. Use of the given headings ensures that all the material selected is *relevant* to the set task. Restate each point *in your own words* as you note it down. Have an eye to the style required by the assignment (an article for your local newspaper) as you reword the points.

2. In the passage the relevant key points may be divided from each other. For example, the physical damage detailed in lines 6 and 7 is a serious effect of vandalism. So are the reactions of politicians, designers, developers, older people and local authorities described in lines 41–47. Having found one key point bearing on one of the set topics, do not conclude that you have finished with that topic. Keep looking.

3. When you are sure that you have abstracted *all* the relevant material and listed each key point under its correct heading, read through the passage again. Have you included any non-essential material? (For example, nothing in the first paragraph is relevant to the task you have been given; nor is the second sentence of the second paragraph.)

4. You are now ready to plan the article you must write. You know its shape: two paragraphs. As you plan, think out a sensible way of linking the two. Your paragraphs must be connected. Each is part of the *same* article, although each deals with a distinct aspect of the shared subject matter.

5. You must also look for a way of making each paragraph *coherent*. (All the items must 'stick together'.) Perhaps you see that the separate items fall into groups? (For example, paragraph (a): group 1, physical effects; group 2, financial burdens; group 3, less tangible effects – reactions of foreign visitors – erosion of local pride – widening of generation gap; and so on.) If you can hit on coherent groupings, you will be able to present the material in a logical sequence.

6. Now think hard about the style. An article for a local newspaper must be interesting and informative. If you have made an accurate selection of material from the passage, your article will be informative, but unless you present it in an interesting way, the information will not make an impact on your readers. Try to write *plain* and *lively* English. Your language must be *condensed* (or you will exceed the permitted number of words) and it must be easily understood. The *style* in which you write must not get in the way of *what* you write. It must be a smooth-running vehicle to carry information to your readers.

7. Finally, an article must have a *title*. Make it eye-catching (but *not*

'gimmicky'), brief, crisp, accurate. The title *does not count* towards the word limit.

Life in vandalised Britain

The visible effects of vandalism are sickeningly evident in our damaged surroundings. To repair the havoc, council and income taxes are increased and scarce funds switched from limited education and health budgets. Less obvious effects also diminish the quality of life. Foreign visitors think poorly of us. Local pride is worn down and local authorities hesitate to start new projects. Caring people lose heart. New designs and developments must concentrate more on security than on the creation of attractive features.

Conflicting theories try to reveal the causes of this 'damaging disease'. Superficially, some blame the vandals' much-used tools, the aerosol can and the felt-tip pen. Public apathy and police attention to other increasing crimes play their part. The alienation of vandals from a society whose values and advantages they cannot or do not wish to share undoubtedly contributes. Yet that does not explain why most who are poor, badly housed and ill-educated do not turn to vandalism in protest. Certainly, insecurity and its consequent bravado – intended to impress fellow-members of the growing, anti-social gangs – underlie conduct that corrodes our national life.

(190 words)

12.6 Work out 2 (with notes)

Imagine that you have to write for the presenter of a television programme. You have been given the task of preparing an introduction of about 200 words for a documentary film on Professor Stephen Salter, the inventor of a method of producing electricity from sea-waves, and a man whose work has largely been disregarded. All the information that you need has been included in the following article, but you have to select, shape and style your work in order to meet the demands of:

- the spoken voice;
- an audience that probably knows nothing about the topic;
- a presentation that will hold interest.

An inventor making waves

Salter's Duck is a machine to harness the waves to make electricity. Its prospects were sunk in odd circumstances ten years ago. Now the Duck bobs up again. *Bill Cater* met its inventor, Professor Stephen Salter

THE FOUR ELEMENTS, said the ancients, were earth, air, fire and water. Today's world is powered by coal, oil, gas and uranium taken from the Earth to make fire to boil water, to raise steam to drive turbines, to spin generators to make electricity. But such power is finite and its generation is polluting.

Stephen Salter, Professor of Mechanical Engineering at Edinburgh University, chose water – the waves – as a better source of energy; they are clean and will last as long as the world lasts. To use them he invented what has become known as the Duck.

If life were a movie he would have been inspired by the thunder of waves breaking on wild Scottish shores; or an amateur sailor awed but undaunted by mighty seas. In fact, Salter is not much given to striding wild Scottish shorelines, and views sailing as a brave way of being uncomfortable; he says of wave-power experiments in the Solent and Loch Ness: "The people who did the cold wet bits deserve decorations for gallantry, but almost no new knowledge was gained."

No; Salter unromantically declares that laboratory tests are cheaper and better until you've got your sums and your designs right. He puts his own plunge into wave power down to catching 'flu in September, 1973. He joked later: "My wife said to me, with callous indifference to my misery, 'Stop lying there looking sorry for yourself. Why don't you solve the energy crisis?'"

Salter "did a few sums" about the energy in sea waves and was amazed. As later researches showed, the average power over a year in every metre width of Atlantic wave off the Hebrides, for example, is equivalent to 60 kilowatts – enough for 60 one-bar electric fires. How could that power be extracted?

His first idea was something like the float in a cistern which turns the water on and off, a float bobbing up and down in the waves. Experiments on the float's shape – ball, flat flap, kite, tadpole – and position showed that an extraordinary 90 per cent of the power might be extracted from waves by a properly-positioned float shaped like the back end of a duck; pollution-free power everlasting.

It was a good time to be in such research. With an oil crisis approaching, there were many different renewable-energy schemes about and funding was generous, though the government research contracts were often late-paying and always short-term, lasting a year or at most 18 months. (Norwegian researchers pursuing similar goals with the benefit of five-year terms got power from the sea more quickly, *and* export orders.)

Conditions laid down for British teams by the Department of Energy seemed somewhat impractical; not to start with a small unit to test the technology cheaply, but to design one the size of a large modern coal or oil-powered unit, 2,000 megawatts.

"That was like demanding a fleet of transatlantic jets before Bleriot had flown the Channel," says Salter. The size might have been chosen to be too expensive for the Treasury to approve. But the research went ahead, checking wave forces and mooring strains, trying control systems, testing models in tanks, endless calculations and drawings.

The real Duck is designed to be about the same height as a house – 32 feet – and 98 feet long. The nodding movement of such Ducks mounted on a huge hollow spine would provide power, taken to a generator by a hydraulic system, monitored by electronics and controlled by computers.

Joints between sections of spine would allow it to bend. A thousand Ducks, strung on flexible spines nearly 20 miles long, would produce the 2,000 megawatts demanded.

Of all the wave-power devices, the Duck was regarded as the cleverest, most efficient but also the most complicated: "Intellectually elegant but complex to realise," said one engineering journal. Complexity was a black mark against the Duck, though Salter argues that "extra moving parts and extra complexity mean more grey hairs for engineers but more reliable, efficient, easily used machines for everybody else. Complexity of itself is nothing to fear."

What the Edinburgh Duck team found a greater threat was the way that the goal posts seemed to move as they got nearer scoring. If renewable energy worked, it would be a serious rival to nuclear energy, yet the job of assessing the infant renewable energy plans was given to the Energy Technology Support Group (ETSU), based at Harwell and largely recruited from nuclear researchers – King Herod put in charge of Dr Barnardo's, said some wave-power people.

Salter says it wasn't the nuclear engineers he distrusted, but the civil servants and politicians; the ETSU engineer assessing the Duck, Clive Grove-Palmer, became a keen supporter. The aim was to produce electricity for approximately 4p a unit; official estimates for Duck designs reached 5½p and were steadily getting cheaper – approaching the claimed cost of nuclear power generation, itself later found to be vastly underestimated.

But in 1982, after a meeting to which Grove-Palmer wasn't invited, the Department of Energy decided to halt wave-power research in order to save £3 million a year. (Nuclear research was then costing around £200 million.) It wasn't until Department of Energy reports were published, or leaked, that the wave-power groups discovered the apparent reason for the halt, and just how far the goal posts had been moved; new bases for calculating costs had been chosen which said Duck-power costs would be 8p to 12p or more.

Favourable estimates of Duck reliability made by a neutral consultant engineer had without his knowledge been reversed before being presented to the judges. The Department of

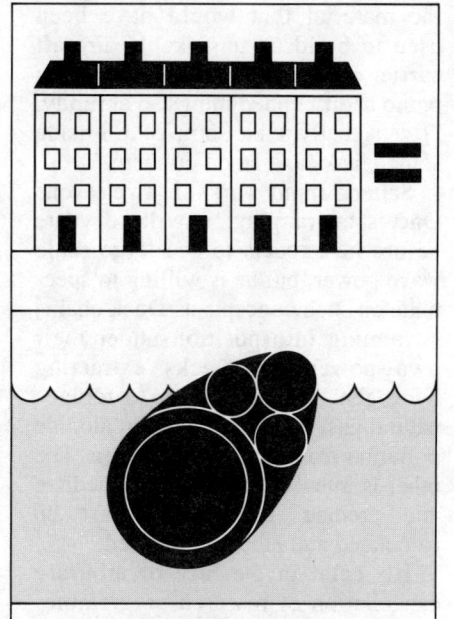

The Duck is shaped like a headless duck. A pair would be roughly the size of a 300-foot terrace of ten houses about 45 feet high

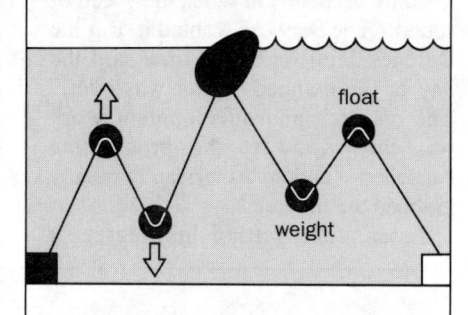

Groups of Ducks would be moored with a weight and a float on each cable making a spring, but keeping the cable tension steady in big waves

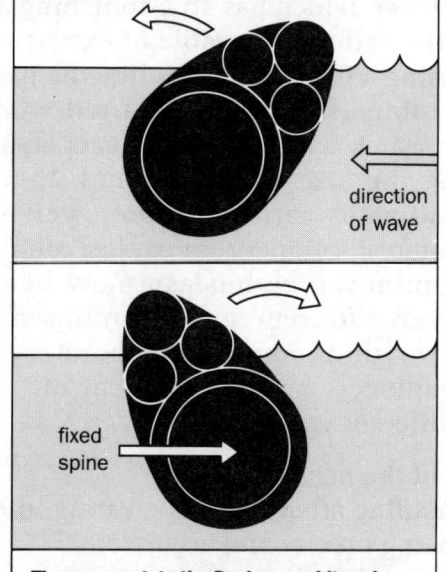

The waves rotate the Duck around its spine, wagging the narrow end to and fro up to about 45 degrees of its resting position; this movement powers the Duck's electricity generators

Energy had replaced detailed quotations for building the Duck by "simplified" new cost rules which upped the cost of some of the heaviest parts from £850 to £10,000 a ton and put nearly £3 million on each Duck.

Finally, Salter's team found official figures of how often cables bringing electricity ashore from the Duck might fail. First estimates predicted failure once every 30 years for a six-mile undersea cable, then in a second report 18 months later at more than twice as often, finally at once a *month*. Yet long undersea cables have been taking power to Scottish islands for half a century without a fault.

Salter fought for the Duck and its research team for nearly 20 years, and has seen ten years wasted, yet shows little sign of bitterness. "We had ten years, then we found ourselves in the political doghouse, now there's another chance," he says. "The baddies are out of the picture now; there's a whole new generation of people at Harwell, and the facts that the nuclear industry managed to conceal for so long are now well known." No point in going over old ground; much more interesting to consider mooring forces, or how a single Duck can take in extra energy, or whether new concrete-and-plastic mixes would make better structures.

Or even ice mixed with woodpulp, the material that would have been used to build an unsinkable aircraft carrier in World War II if the atom bomb hadn't ended things so abruptly. "I've actually made some of it. I made some planks and stood on them."

Salter's mind works on two levels. One is far-ranging; it will be years before he expects to see large-scale wave power, but he is willing to speculate on such concepts as Duck chains swimming into position under their own power; on Ducks extracting hydrogen from sea water to replace natural gas – there's no carbon dioxide pollution from burning hydrogen. The other is intensely practical, immediate and precise. Everything must be calculated and laboratory-tested.

His calm in the face of arbitrary cancellation of research programmes may be because he has seen it all before. He was an apprentice working on a rocket-boosted fighter aircraft able to climb vertically at twice the speed of sound. "The Services wanted it. But the Defence Minister at the time said the day of the manned fighter was over." The research and development work was thrown away, the programme cancelled – and an American company grabbed the market.

Later, after getting his degree at Cambridge, he was involved in robotics and artificial intelligence work at Edinburgh University. Then someone in Whitehall decided Britain really didn't need to know about artificial intelligence or robotics, and cut the funding. So he decided to look into wave energy.

At 53, after 20 years, is he content to go on with it for the rest of his career? "Oh, yes – it's very interesting."

There is a videotape for the instruction of a new generation of young engineers, which shows the tank, a valuable new design in itself, in which models of the Duck have been developed. Miniature waves lift, toss and even overturn the Duck – which always bobs up again. Salter and his team, servants and masters of the machine, cross from tank to control panel to a bank of electronics recording potential power output, while the waves advance this way and that and graphs flick across computer screens.

From something like this will come power for the world of tomorrow, when all the frustrations of Whitehall and Westminster are dead and forgotten. And meanwhile Salter and his team are in their element•

from *World* (the BBC Magazine of Mankind)

Notes

1. Start work by listing the key areas that are considered in this article:
   (a) The need for renewable energy sources.
   (b) A professor invented a 'Duck' – a device for harnessing wave power, which has an astonishing amount of power.
   (c) His method is capable of extracting 90 per cent of that power by using a float that looks like the back end of a duck.
   (d) Problems: time – he started work on the project in 1973, but research was halted ten years later; size – individual floats would be the size of houses and 20-mile lengths required; costs – estimates varied; support – civil servants and politicians lost interest; competition – other countries went ahead with research.
   (e) Optimism: enthusiasm now being shown for the far-reaching needs for energy becoming more evident; realisation that everything must be laboratory-tested; a new generation of engineers and government officials look on the challenges in different ways.

2. Think of the needs of:
   (a) holding attention and creating interest;
   (b) being precise and accurate;
   (c) selecting relevant information.

3. Consider that people are interested in:
   • the continuation of supplies of power at reasonable costs;
   • unusual, simple and effective inventions;

- inventors who have to struggle against 'the authorities';
- political intrigue and alleged inefficiency;
- renewed optimism following apparent failure.

4 Reflect on a good 'angle' to approach this 'story'. The Professor and the Duck? 'Ugly duckling' to successful swan? 20-mile-long monsters offshore? Renewed enthusiasm for renewable energy?

5 Remind yourself of the requirement for plain, condensed, lively English that can be spoken effectively.

Introduction to documentary film on Professor Stephen Salter

As humankind uses more and more energy we are all conscious of the need to explore the ways and means of producing it from different sources. Every moment of the day and night the seas that sweep onto the shores of our island indicate that there is power for ever around us. People have, for centuries, dreamt of harnessing this energy of wave and tidal power. One man's dream turned to reality when his relatively simple invention, a device shaped like the rear end of a duck, could, he claimed, pump electricity onshore from the sea. Yet Professor Stephen Salter's project, on which ten years' work was expended, was shelved by a group of politicians and civil servants. In this programme we examine Professor Salter's apparently remarkable creation, his struggle against bureaucracy, and the new optimism that surrounds his answer to one of our basic needs. Here is a film about a man's energetic work to harness a renewable source of energy for you and me.

(162 words)

13 Expression

LEAG	MEG	SEG	NEAB	WJEC	NICCEA	Topic	Date attempted	Date completed	Self Assessment
✓	✓	✓	✓	✓	✓	Examinations and changes			
✓	✓	✓	✓	✓	✓	Coursework			
✓	✓	✓	✓	✓	✓	'Differentiation'			
✓	✓	✓	✓	✓	✓	An approach to the subject			
✓	✓	✓	✓	✓	✓	Speaking and listening			
✓	✓	✓	✓	✓	✓	Reading			
✓	✓	✓	✓	✓	✓	Ways and means			
✓	✓	✓	✓	✓	✓	Writing			
✓	✓	✓	✓	✓	✓	Practical writing			

13.1 Definition and description

The term **expression** is applied to writing assignments and questions that test your ability to write at some length on a variety of subjects and in different forms. The different kinds of subjects set in these assignments and questions and the different forms of writing that you have to be able to use are explained.

In the case of the 'Practical' or 'Work-based' writing (Chapter 10) and the 'Summary' and 'Directed writing' (Chapters 11 and 12), the content, purpose and audience for whom you are to write will be established by the examiner or employer. The particular tasks are always clearly stated. Although you may find the actual working out of your answer to be a challenge, you will know what is expected of you because the request for a letter, an article, a set of instructions or whatever has been given.

'Expression' covers a wider area of composition, and relies more on your own imagination, inventiveness and judgement, and on your ability to see the *potential* contained in a given subject or title. The same disciplines remain, however, in that you are expected to write well-organised, clear and accurate English. In each case the examiners and moderators are looking for a piece of writing that is:

- carefully planned as an answer to the chosen question;
- soundly constructed and clearly paragraphed;
- written in well-made and varied sentences;
- correct in grammar, punctuation and spelling.

13.2 Different kinds of composition

Classifications

The examiners make it clear that compositions of several different kinds are set. Here is just one typical statement to that effect: 'Dramatic, impressionistic, narrative and discursive subjects will be included.' Study of all the syllabuses and of representative question papers provides the following classifications of composition subjects: (a) narrative; (b) descriptive; (c) discursive; (d) dramatic; (e) impressionistic.

Candidates must learn to identify the category to which their chosen subject belongs, for each kind of subject has its own special features and must be treated accordingly. For example, an impressionistic subject requires a more subjective approach than a discursive subject.

Both the *form* of a composition and the *style* in which it is written must be suited to the kind of subject that has been selected.

The notes that now follow list the distinguishing features of each kind of subject. The work-out sections of this chapter demonstrate how those features affect the planning and writing of compositions of each kind.

Narrative writing

Narrative compositions tell (narrate) a story or give an account of a sequence of events. They are about *action*. For example: 'Write a story entitled *In the Nick of Time*'; 'Give an account of an exciting journey that you once made by land or sea or air'.

A story composition must have plot, characters and atmosphere. A plot is not needed for an account of events, but the narrator must introduce 'human interest' and set it against a realistic background. In both a story and an account of events the narration must move forward. Narrative compositions must not be static.

Descriptive writing

Obviously, **descriptive compositions** describe! They describe a scene or a place or an object or a person. For example: 'Describe either the sights or the sounds at a busy bus station on a winter's day'; 'Describe the appearance, personality and home surroundings of someone well known to you, either of your own age or much older'.

The key to success is the writer's ability to find an imaginative approach to the subject and to shape the composition so that every detail contributes to the overall effect that has been planned. Lacking that creative angle of attack, a descriptive composition is a mere list of details haphazardly strung together. Very boring.

Discursive (argumentative or controversial) writing

A **discursive composition** is one in which the writer presents facts, ideas and opinions about a given topic and *arrives at a conclusion by reasoning*. Typical discursive subjects are: 'What gives popular music its following?'; 'Do you think that smoking should be banned by law?'; 'What are the good and bad points about television?'; 'Consider the arguments for and against fox hunting'.

The alternative names for discursive compositions – **argumentative compositions** and **controversial compositions** – indicate the kind of subjects set and the kind of treatment required.

A genuine interest in and some information about the chosen topic are essential. So, too, are a respect for facts, a balanced attitude to the opinions of others, and a clear presentation of the writer's point of view.

Discursive (argumentative or controversial) subjects are: *discursive*, because they require writers to reason their way to a conclusion; *argumentative*, because they require writers to set out the arguments on both sides and to weigh them fairly; *controversial*, because they require writers to keep cool and think clearly about topics that stir up strong feelings.

Dramatic (conversational) writing

Dramatic compositions must be written in *direct speech*. Hence the alternative name **conversational compositions**. Typical dramatic (conversational) subjects are: 'A lecturer and a student have had a disagreement. Write a dialogue between them in which the circumstances of their quarrel are made plain and in the course of which they come to a friendly resolution of their problem'; 'Write a short play by continuing the dialogue set out below in a manner which develops the dramatic situation'. (The first few lines of the dialogue are provided to introduce the characters and to establish the initial dramatic situation.)

Success in such compositions depends on the ability to write direct speech for two or more characters (dialogue) that sounds convincing and that develops the initial situation in an interesting way.

Impressionistic writing

Impressionistic compositions are highly subjective and imaginative compositions. Several pictures are provided as a starting point. The instructions then read like this: 'Write a composition suggested by one of these pictures. Your composition may be directly about the subject of the picture, or may be based on some suggestion that you take from the picture; but there must be some clear connection between the picture and your writing. You may choose to write in the form of a story or of a description.'

Another kind of impressionistic composition is based on a short poem (or an extract from a poem). Candidates are instructed to describe the ideas or thoughts or feelings that the poem suggests to them (in other words, the *impressions* it makes on their minds). Or they may be told to write – in prose, of course – a description of a place or a person well known to them in circumstances similar to those described in the poem. Or they may be asked to write a story based on the poem.

Whatever the particular form asked for, a successful impressionistic composition requires close observation of the details of the picture (or careful reading of the poem), an imaginative response and a clear link between the given stimulus (picture or poem) and the candidate's writing.

13.3 Examination techniques

Planning your time

Some of your assessed coursework in Expression will be written in your own time. In theory, you can take as long as you like over each piece of writing, for you are not under pressure to finish at a particular time or after writing uninterruptedly for a stipulated period. In practice, however, you need to set yourself a time limit for each piece of writing you do. Other work has to be done and you cannot spend more than a certain amount of your examination preparation in producing expressive pieces for assessment. Also, you will find that a self-imposed time limit is an aid to good work. Writing that can be finished 'any time' has a habit of not getting done or of being rushed through at the last minute. A sensible 'deadline' helps you to concentrate and to write better. A 'tomorrow-or-next-week-will-do' attitude encourages sloppy thinking, poor planning and careless writing.

Some of your assessed coursework (at least one piece – and more than one, for some examining boards) will be written under supervision with a time limit for completion. And, of course, if you have been entered for an examination paper in Expression a time schedule is imposed and you must pace your writing within it. Find out how long the paper is and how many questions you must answer. Then practise answering papers and fitting your answers into the time available.

Sections below give further advice on planning and timing.

Choosing your subjects

In preparing for the examination, you will learn your own strengths as a writer and what kinds of writing you handle best. That experience will help you to reject subjects that are not suited to you. You have to demonstrate that you can write on different kinds of topics and in different forms, so your folder of expressive work must include various kinds of writing. Even so, there will always be the opportunity of selecting subjects that *interest* you. Your best work in composition is done when you can make a *personal* response and write in an individual and fresh way.

Planning your writing

Skimped and careless planning is the commonest cause of poor work in composition. Every piece should be thoroughly *planned* before you start to write it. Three different (but linked) operations are involved: gathering material; selecting material; shaping the composition. Each of these operations is explained and demonstrated in the work-out sections of this chapter.

Length and timing

Each piece of writing that you submit for assessment will be between 400 and 500 words in length. Different examining boards word their requirements in different ways but they do not vary much in what they are looking for.

Reading through and correcting

In *all* your written work, the examiners expect:
- correct grammar;
- accurate spelling;

- clear punctuation;
- appropriate and effective vocabulary.

Always spend a few minutes reading through what you have written and correcting any careless slips you may have made. Valuable marks can be saved in this way. (Section 13.5 provides a demonstration.)

13.4 Summing up

1. 'Expression' tests your ability to write at some length on a variety of subjects and in different forms.
2. The term 'expressive writing' applies to pieces written in the form of *compositions*. It also applies to *practical* (factual and directed) pieces of writing.
3. Subjects for composition may be: narrative; descriptive; discursive; dramatic; impressionistic.
4. When you are writing a composition:
   - Choose a subject on which you can write *interestingly*.
   - *Plan* a piece of writing that suits the *nature* and *form* (narrative, descriptive, and so on) of the subject you have chosen.
   - Write in an *appropriate* style.
   - Take care with *grammar*, *spelling* and *punctuation*.
   - Stick to the *length limits* laid down.

13.5 Work out narrative writing

Getting to grips with narrative subjects

The subjects set for narrative writing are of two distinct kinds:

1. Subjects that require you to write a *story*.
2. Subjects that require you to write an *account of events*.

In each kind of narrative the *action* provides the chief interest, but a story has some special features that are not required in a straightforward narration of events. The following table sets out the characteristic qualities of each:

	A story	*An account of events*
1	Must have a plot. It need not be complicated, but there must be a **story line**. In a story things change. Perhaps a discovery is made or a problem is solved. Perhaps people's attitudes alter or their relationships with one another develop. In some important way a new situation is brought about and the storyteller must plan the events so that they lead to this development.	Does not need a plot, but must progressively relate a sequence of events. The reader's attention is held by a series of incidents. The writer must provide links to connect successive events and to keep the narrative flowing in an interesting way. The action must move steadily forward from the beginning to the end. A successful narrative depends on a clear plan.

2	Needs characters to provide an interesting interplay of personalities and to create tension. There is no need to 'crowd the canvas' with people. Two characters will often be enough. The important thing is to involve people with events. A story is about people doing things.	'Characterisation' (in the story sense) is not required, but some **human interest** makes for a lively narration. Perhaps the personality of the narrator 'comes through' or there are some interesting glimpses of the people taking part in the happenings. The emphasis, however, is on action rather than on character.
3	Description of people and places is essential. The characters are placed against an interesting and convincing background. Much of the interest in a story is generated by the interplay of people, events and setting. A close connection between people and places creates an **atmosphere.**	Description plays an important part in the narration. The emphasis is on action, but action does not take place in a vacuum. Details are needed to help the reader to follow the events. Interest is aroused by lively description of a realistic setting.
4	**Dialogue** (conversation between characters) is essential. People in stories talk to one another (as they do in real life). As they talk, they come alive for the reader and the plot is carried forward. The changing situations of a story (see (1) above) are often brought about by or revealed through dialogue.	Dialogue is not essential, but it can sometimes be introduced to good effect. Speech in a straightforward narrative composition is always directly related to the action. Its purpose is to advance the narrative flow.
5	A story is a piece of fiction. Plot, characters and setting are invented by the writer. Personal experience must be drawn on to create convincing people and places – 'write about what you know' – but a story is essentially made up: imagined.	An account of events must be rooted in the writer's own experience. Firsthand knowledge of the happenings related – or of very similar happenings – is needed. Details may be invented to add life and colour, but this kind of narrative composition is essentially an imaginative treatment of actual events. It is not a piece of fiction, as a story is.

Sometimes the term **anecdote** is used to distinguish between a story and a straightforward narrative. For example:

> Write *either* a story *or* an anecdote based on one of the following: (a) a telephone ringing in an empty house; (b) the non-arrival of an important letter; (c) an ambulance speeding through a city on an icy morning.

An *anecdote* is the narration of an interesting or striking incident or a series of such incidents.

To sum up: if you decide to write a narrative, you must choose between:

A plotted piece of writing
A story. All the events lead up to and help to bring about the situation with which the story ends. This final situation develops out of circumstances and events earlier in the story.

An unplotted piece of writing
An account of events: a description of incidents: a relation of an experience: an anecdote. All these are examples of **reportage**. They are narrations of interesting events happening in succession, one after another.

As this work-out section will show, 'unplotted' does *not* mean 'unplanned'. A clear plan is the basis of successful writing of whatever kind.

Thinking about the subjects on offer

Below is a compilation of some typical examples of subjects for narrative composition as set by the various exam boards.

Story writing

1. 'The Humber, the Menai Straits, the Tay, Sydney Harbour, the Golden Gate – what tales bridges could tell!' Write a story in which a bridge plays an important part.
2. 'It was the weirdest-looking object I'd ever seen.' Write a story in which those words are used at an important moment.
3. 'Even the smartest criminal can make a silly mistake.' Write a story, using those words as its opening.
4. 'I never did discover its hiding place.' Write a story that ends with those words.
5. Write a story entitled *A Broken Promise*.
6. Write a story suggested by the following quotation:

> Hark, they are going: the footsteps shrink,
> And the sea renews her cry.
> The big stars stare and the small stars wink;
> The Plough goes glittering by.
> It was a trick of the turning tide
> That brought those voices near.
> Dead men pummelled the panes outside:
> We caught the breath of the year.
>
> Vernon Watkins

Note that each of those subjects contains a requirement that the writer must observe. Number 1 imposes some control over the contents of the story. Numbers 2, 3 and 4 influence the plot by insisting on the inclusion of given words at a particular point in the story. Number 5 influences both contents and plot by specifying the title of the story. Number 6 is less direct in its controls, but it lays down the condition that the source of the story must be the impressions the writer receives from the poetry. (This kind of assignment, combining narrative and impressionistic subjects, is often set.)

Candidates who can write a good story sometimes miss their opportunity by failing to recognise possible story subjects. When the particular form that a composition must take is not specified, candidates are free to choose whatever form suits them best. For example:

7   Write a composition based on one of the following topics:
    (a) A family gathering.
    (b) Lost property.
    (c) Nightfall.
    (d) A journalistic scoop.
    (e) An unwanted present.

Instructions worded like those permit any of the given topics to be treated as story material. They are, of course, equally available for and suited to straightforward narrative or descriptive treatment.

Straightforward narrative writing

The instructions for the writing of an account of events, a description of incidents, a relation of an experience or an anecdote are worded in various ways. Here are some typical examples:

8   You were one of a crowd waiting for a celebrity to appear. Describe what happened.
9   Describe an experience in the course of which events occurred in a way that contrasted sharply with what you expected.
10 You saw a person knocked off a bicycle by a passing car that did not stop. Tell the story of what happened next.
11 'I shan't do that again', you said. Give an account of the events that led up to that remark.

Only in number 11 are candidates specifically instructed to give an account of events, but the wording of the others is a clear indication that straightforward narrative writing (*not* story telling) is wanted. 'Describe what happened' (1) and 'Describe an experience' (2) instruct the writer to narrate a sequence of happenings. The writing is to take the form of a piece of **reportage:** an account of events that occurred one after another.

Do not be misled by the wording of number 10: 'Tell the story of what happened next'. That is not an invitation to write a story with a plot. It is an instruction to write an anecdote. The key words are: *what happened next.* An anecdote is not a story. It simply unfolds events in a straightforward chronological sequence. It does not bring about those plotted changes of circumstance and situation that are the essence of a story.

All these unplotted forms of narrative compositions – accounts of events, descriptions of incidents, relations of experiences, anecdotes – share the same essential characteristic: they run in a straight line from beginning to end. The writer must keep the narrative flowing. Any break in the continuity is a tiresome interruption at which the reader loses interest.

Making a choice

Most of the varieties of narrative subjects that you are likely to encounter are represented above ('Thinking about the subjects on offer'), so it will be useful to consider them all while demonstrating how a good choice of subject can be made.

Although this book has two authors, this work out is written in the first person singular because choosing a subject is essentially a personal decision. By showing you how *I* go about it, I can illustrate all the points that you will have to consider when you are looking for a subject that suits *you*. In later sections, I shall gather and select material, then plan and write, thus providing a practical demonstration of methods that you can confidently use, whatever your choice of subject.

While steering you through the choice-making process, I do not assume that *my* choice of subject would be right for you. You may be able to write interestingly on a subject that is not for me. You may have ample material for a composition on that subject and the ability to make a good plan for it, whereas I am stuck for ideas and cannot see how to arrange what little material I have. The work out cannot tell you *what* to choose, but it can show you *how* to choose.

If I choose a story composition, I shall have to invent a plot. That is not easy, so I look first at the straightforward narrative subjects on offer, but none of them interests me so much that I feel confident of interesting my reader. I cannot see how I can tap my own experience to find the firsthand material that I need to write a lively composition on any of them.

Turning to the story subjects, I remember to look at those that *may* be written as stories – number 7, (a)–(e) – as well as those that *must* be (numbers 1–6).

At first, I am tempted to have a go at 'A family gathering'. I think that my experiences at my Uncle Henry's house one Christmas provide me with useful material for characters and setting, although I cannot see plot possibilities. Of course, I might treat that topic by straightforward narration, using my imagination to provide some lively and colourful details.

'A family gathering' is a possible subject, but I do not warm to any of the others in that particular list. I cannot at once see plot material in them for stories and I am not very interested in the few ideas that they suggest to me for purely narrative treatment.

Turning to the subjects that are specified for story treatment, I reject the one in which a bridge is to play an important part. I think I *could* write such a story, but it would not come out of my personal experience. My story would be secondhand 'formula' writing; a stale imitation of stories that I have read. So, because I cannot see a way of putting something of myself into this particular story, I decide not to attempt it. Stories ought to be their writers' own creations. Only then can they be fresh and original and, therefore, interesting.

Subjects 2, 3 and 4 put me off by requiring me to include given words at particular points in the story. Many writers have the ability to carry out such instructions without losing their spontaneity. Indeed, the necessity of constructing a story line that brings the given words into the story at the right place seems to stimulate their imagination. But not mine. I know that my story would seem contrived and artificial. The plot would creak.

Again, I am not happy with number 5. I *can* sometimes write a story with a given title, even though that restricts my freedom to invent the contents and the plot; but I cannot recall interesting personal experience on which to base *A Broken Promise*. (Now, if the given title were *A Promise Fulfilled*, I should have lively material ready for use and a good, simple plot needing just a little working up – but that isn't the title!)

I turn to number 6 and, as I read the lines of poetry, I find that I am getting strong impressions. The words are ringing bells in my memory, suggesting exciting possibilities for characters and setting; and I *think* I can see – rather dimly as yet – a possible plot.

At this point I realise that I have spent a lot of time considering possible subjects. My choice must be made. Which shall it be: 'A family gathering' or number 6? I can see good material for characters and setting in the former if I treat it as a story, but I have not had any ideas for a plot. If I treat it as a straightforward narrative, it may lack action. It begins to seem rather a static subject. Nothing much happened. On the whole, I think I see more scope in number 6.

Gathering material

Write a story suggested by the following quotation:

> Hark, they are going: the footsteps shrink,
> And the sea renews her cry.
> The big stars stare and the small stars wink;
> The Plough goes glittering by.
> It was a trick of the turning tide
> That brought those voices near.
> Dead men pummelled the panes outside:
> We caught the breath of the year.

I open my mind to the words. They stir up recollections and imaginings which I jot down as they occur. All that matters at this stage is to capture ideas: selecting and planning come later.

> night – hushed – glittering stars – the sound of the sea – that lonely cottage in Cornwall where we spent a family holiday – a nightmare

The quotation has triggered off a personal recollection and I can link the poet's words with my own experience. This is promising. I explore the possibilities further, reading the words again.

Within the general impressions, certain words seem to be making a particular impact:

> Hark, they are going/footsteps shrink/sea renews her cry/a trick of the turning tide/voices near/Dead men pummelled the panes

I add to the raw material already jotted down, letting memory and imagination work together. Some of my notes are based on fact, some are inventions suggested by the words of the quotation. The distinction between fact and fiction is of no importance when material for a story is being gathered.

> an autumn holiday – starry nights – the sound of the sea – a lamp-lit living-room – my parents downstairs reading – my bedroom very quiet – the sound of footsteps dwindling – along a path? – the 'cry' of the sea again – a rapping at the window – something outside trying to get in – returning to claim something? – what? – 'It's only the sound of the sea' – 'the tide has turned' – the owner of the cottage kept the village shop – talking to him – his stories of days gone by

I can now see exciting possibilities in the material I have gathered. It should give me scope for lively writing and an original treatment, for it springs partly from the quotation and partly from an experience of my own which the poet's words have brought back to me. I must work on the raw material and shape it.

Selecting material and arriving at a plan

There is still a lot to do before I can start writing. The material I have gathered so far could be used in a straightforward narration of events, but I must now think out a plot so that I can turn an anecdote into a story. The connections between the words of the quotation and my raw material are well established, so I am at liberty to invent any details I need to construct a plot; and I am free to adjust the circumstances depicted in the poem to suit my story. I jot down some more notes, building up the material I have already gathered.

I had a nightmare – it frightened me very much – my parents weren't very pleased when I rushed downstairs into the living-room – 'Go back to bed. You've been dreaming.' – that big oak chest in the living-room – black with age – the initials 'I.R.T.' carved on the front – the man we rented the cottage from was called Tressilian – Reuben Tressilian – he kept the village shop and post office – his name over shop door – his family had lived in the cottage for many years – his great-grandfather was lost at sea in a great storm – we went to the shop for groceries the morning after I had my nightmare – he told us about his family that morning

I am beginning to see the bare bones of my story line and I feel confident enough to work on a more detailed plan. I set it out in two columns. The steps in which I shall tell the story are very carefully noted in the left column. In the right, I make notes to help me to work out the details of character, setting and events as I go along. As I work on my plan, I reject some of the material I have already gathered and I alter and add to the rest.

(*Note*: As you study the plan that now follows, bear in mind that I have written it out at greater length than you – or I – would usually do. My purpose is to demonstrate the importance of thinking a subject through and becoming clear about how you are going to treat it *before* you begin to write. If you practise along the lines set out here, you will master the technique of sound planning and learn how to construct a short outline plan on which a good composition can be based.)

The plan

1	Introduce characters and setting – brief description of family, cottage and surroundings.	father, mother, son aged about ten – is story to be told in first or third person? – easier to bring about change in situation if son tells story as it happened – lonely cottage about 2 miles from nearest village – cottage near sea – sound of sea, especially at night
2	Sketch in holiday occupations and pleasures. Build up atmosphere before storm and nightmare.	warm autumn days – walks and picnics – cosy living-room – books and TV – son usually to bed at ten – parents stay up reading for a time – cottage interior described – important to bring old chest to reader's attention because it plays important part in story – initials 'I.R.T.' carved on chest – N.B. chest *not* in living-room – place it on landing outside son's bedroom door
3	The night of the storm. Son's fear. Parents explain it away. They're right, of course – he's been dreaming.	son wakes up – roaring of wind and waves (perhaps earlier?) – sudden hush – tapping at window – footsteps on path – fear – son rushes downstairs – 'someone at my window, trying to get in'/ 'you've been dreaming: it's only the wind rattling the panes – grating of pebbles on seashore'

4	Next morning – to village to shop.	this is a quiet stage of story – storm has died down – his nightmare is over and explained away – bright, calm morning – night fears seem unreal
5	Introduce Reuben Tressilian. He keeps the village shop. Conversation. He tells them about his family.	R.T. owns cottage – rents it to holidaymakers – Tressilians have lived in cottage for years – all fisherfolk – (some of these details to come in earlier? – when cottage is first described?)
6	Climax of story begins here. First mention of Tressilian's great-grandfather.	initials on chest ('I.R.T.') were great-grandfather's – he kept his valuables in it – story told about him – he was lost at sea in great storm – comes back to find chest on anniversary of his death
7	Turning point of story here. Discovery made and situation changes. Son knows date of storm in which 'I.R.T.' was drowned.	care with details here – must be convincing – closely linked together to keep story moving – enough detail to keep reader in picture but don't clutter up the action – best if all told through dialogue? – son and Mr T. talking, but parents silent
8	End of story. Parents were wrong about 'nightmare' and son was right. Final situation follows from and is caused by 7.	don't over-explain – story ends crisply – parents realise what has happened, so does son – suggest this, rather than explaining – they look away – busy themselves in shop – mystery, but no loose ends

Now I can start writing. If I find, as I write the story, that I need to change any details or make minor adjustments to the sequence of events, I am free to do so. The plan is my guide and I shall stick to its main features, but I am not bound to follow it to the letter. I shall almost certainly think of improvements as the act of writing stimulates my imagination; but I shall not make fundamental changes in the structure of my story while I am writing it. I cannot afford to make false starts or leave loose ends in the plot, so it would be dangerous to depart far from this carefully constructed plan.

Writing the composition

When I was ten, my father and mother and I went to a cottage on the Cornish coast for a week's holiday.

It was a lonely place, perched above the sea and not another house near it. There was a village about two miles away where the owner of the cottage lived. His name was Reuben Tressilian. He kept the village post office and shop. ~~He~~ and rented the cottage to holidaymakers.

We had a lovely holiday. The days were warm, and although it went cold at night, we were cosy in the cottage. It was comfortably

There was an open hearth in the living-room furnished with interesting old pieces and pictures. ~~The living room had a big fireplace~~ which made it very cheerful. We had brought books with us and there was a TV set. We spent our days walking, exploring the cliffs and picnicking. In the evenings we sat reading or watching television until they pushed me off to bed at about ten o'clock. I didn't mind. There was a big black oak chest on the landing outside my bedroom door and I often made up stories about it. Some initials were carved on the front and as I lay in bed I used to wonder who 'I.R.T.' was. I guessed that he was the big, bearded man wearing a fisherman's jersey in the old, faded photograph that hung on the wall above the chest.

One night – I shall never forget it – there was a furious ~~big~~ storm. As we sat in the living-room, the wind roared in the chimney and we could hear the waves crashing against the cliffs. I thought it was exciting, but I don't think my parents liked it much.

At ten o'clock my mother looked at the clock on the mantelpiece. ~~mantlepeace~~. 'Off to bed now, Billy,' she said. 'We're going to the village early tomorrow I need some supplies ~~food~~ for the rest of the week.'

'I shan't be able to sleep,' I said. 'Not with all this noise going on.'

'Nonsense! You'll sleep like a log. You've been out in the fresh air all day and you're yawning now.'

'Good night, Billy,' my father said, rather firmly. 'Sleep well.'

As I went past the chest on the landing, I stopped to look at the old photograph. It was swaying ~~moving~~ slightly on its cord in the draught.

'Good night, I.R.T.,' I said. 'Sleep well.'

In spite of the howling wind, I went to sleep at once. I didn't give old 'I.R.T.' another thought before I was off.

And then – I don't know how much later – I woke. I was cold and ~~I~~ scared stiff. ~~was frightened~~. The noise of the storm had stopped. There was a sort of hush, as if the night was holding its breath, and the moon was bright on the window.

Then I heard a crunching sound, like heavy footsteps on the gravel path at the back of the cottage; and – seconds later – 'tap, tap, tap' on the glass. It was as loud as the beating of my heart and there was a shadow on the pane.

Downstairs I ran and into the living-room.

'Quick!' I said. 'Come up to my room. There's something tapping at the window – trying to get in.'

'You've had a nightmare, Billy,' my mother said. 'I'll get you some hot milk and you can drink it by the fire. Then back to bed you go.'

'It's the wind,' my father said. 'And waves beating on the shore. Listen!'

He was right. The storm was raging ~~had started~~ again. The wind was shaking the tiles and the sea roared below the cliffs.

He came up with me and tucked the clothes round me. 'No more dreams, Billy. Sleep well.'

And, strangely enough, I did. No more dreams and no more shadows at the window.

After breakfast we set off for Mr Tressilian's shop. The day was calm and bright and we enjoyed our walk.

'You're having a good time?' Mr Tressilian asked as he reached things off the shelves and loaded up ~~the basket~~ / our baskets.

'Oh, yes.' my mother answered. 'And it's such a lovely cottage. You've got some beautiful furniture there, Mr Tressilian.'

'All family stuff,' he said. 'Tressilians have lived in the cottage for years. They were all fisherfolk, till I gave it up and settled down to shopkeeping.'

'Who was "I.R.T."?' I asked.

He looked a bit surprised, but he answered me.

'He was my great-grandfather – Isaac Reuben Tressilian. That's his photograph that hangs on the wall above the big chest on the landing. He was lost at sea in a great storm, many a year ago.'

'It was his chest, was it?'

'Oh, yes. He had it made the year he was married – the year he built the cottage. He kept his valuables in it. It was always kept locked when I was a boy, though his valuables – such as they were – had long vanished. My father used to tell us a story about that chest. He said that Isaac Reuben always returned on the anniversary of the storm. Looking for his chest, he was. So my father said. He didn't believe it, of course. Nor do I. It was just a story he liked telling us and we liked hearing.'

'He was drowned on the fifteenth of September, wasn't he?' I asked.

'Yes,' Mr Tressilian said. 'He was – on the fifteenth of September 1865. How ~~do~~ / did you know?'

'It was the fifteenth of September yesterday,' I said. 'And I think your great-grandfather came looking for his chest last night.'

I turned to my parents as I said it, but they pretended not to hear. My father was reading a newspaper that he'd taken off the counter and my mother was unusually interested in the label on a bag of sugar.

Reading through and correcting

As you can see, I made some improvements in the couple of minutes that I allowed myself for reading through and correcting. I put right some careless slips of the pen and I was able to tighten up the writing here and there. One or two clumsy expressions jumped out at me as I read through what I had written, and it was easy to find better ways of wording them.

On the whole, however, the writing went smoothly because I had put a lot of thought into gathering and selecting my material and constructing my plan. The *form* of my composition was clear to me before I began to write it, so it was not difficult to find a *style* of expression that was suitable.

A different choice of subject

You may be reluctant to choose a story subject and you are right to be cautious. Never attempt a story unless you can see, quite early on, how you can construct a plot for it. The plot may be very simple, but it must be convincing (no loose ends) and it must bring about an interesting development in the story. In the work out you have just studied I was able to see plot possibilities when the words of the poetry connected with an event that I recalled from my own experience. I had to work on the details, of course, but the outline of my plot began to come through at an early stage.

Like many writers, however, I do not often find it easy to construct a plot, so I usually look for a straightforward narrative subject rather than a story. I hope to find one that interests me and to which I can bring some first-hand experience.

You cannot expect always to find an ideal subject, but things are never as bad as they seem in those first minutes as you read through the set topics and think despairingly, 'I can't write about *any* of these!' You can always find a subject on which you can write competently if you go about choosing and planning in the ways that I am demonstrating in this chapter.

Suppose the subject I chose from page 124 had not been on offer. My second-string subject, you remember, was 'A family gathering', which the instructions permitted me to treat either as a story or as a straightforward (unplotted) narrative. Story treatment was ruled out for me because I could not see plot possibilities in the subject. As I considered it for straightforward narrative, I became less hopeful of success. I knew I could draw on personal experience and write interestingly about people and setting, but I knew also that my potential material lacked the essential ingredient of good narrative – *action*.

When a subject dries up on you like that, you have to look again at subjects that were not immediately attractive as you read through the assignments for the first time. By thinking hard along methodical lines, you will find a topic that you can tackle successfully.

Ask yourself these two questions:

- What are the chief features of a good composition of this kind on this subject?
- What opportunities does this subject offer me to write a composition that contains those features?

The whole purpose of these work-out sections is to help you to find the answers to those questions.

In my own case, looking again at all the composition subjects offered on page 125, I should have to choose number 8: 'You were one of a crowd waiting for a celebrity to appear. Describe what happened.'

For various reasons, that is not my ideal subject for a straightforward narrative composition, but it does bring an item of personal experience to mind and I think I can work that up into a competent piece of writing, fragment though it is.

Faced with subjects that do not look very attractive at first sight, comfort yourself with the old proverb: 'Necessity is the mother of invention.' Necessity is there, without doubt: the necessity to write a composition! Don't panic. Think coolly. Your powers of invention and recall are greater than you realise. Necessity will bring them to your aid and a sound technique will enable you to make use of them.

In the next sections of this chapter I shall describe the qualities of a good narrative and then go on to demonstrate how, bearing them in mind, I feel reasonably confident of writing a successful composition on a subject that I chose because I had to.

Action: the essence of narrative

Any composition that the examiners' instructions identify as an account of events, a description of incidents or the relation of an anecdote must be centred on action. Nothing must distract the reader's attention from the *action*, for it is in the action that the interest lies.

Any other features of such a composition – descriptions of people and places, passages of dialogue, for example – are secondary to the action. Their sole purpose is to make the narrative more vivid and to hold the reader's attention as the action unfolds. Anything that impedes the narrative flow is a tiresome interruption.

Pacing the narrative

Varying the pace of the narrative is a sure way of gaining and holding your reader's interest. Action described at a uniform pace is not very exciting. Your reader will be as bored by a narrative that races breathlessly from start to finish as by one that proceeds throughout at a steady jogtrot.

Try to begin with a striking incident to capture attention. You can then afford a brief description of the circumstances in which the action is taking place and of the people involved. Then be sure to get the action moving again at once. It is often effective to let it run slowly at first, then – at a clearly indicated turning point – to quicken the pace so that the narration carries your reader forward to its climax. Pay special attention to the end. Are you going to finish with the action at its highest point? Or does your treatment of your subject demand a brief rounding-off? Either of these endings can be effective but, if you prolong your composition beyond the highest point of the action, do be *brief*. An anticlimax at the end is a painful letdown.

Narrative links and the narrative thread

To write a successful narrative, you must:

- keep your reader's attention on the action;
- make your reader want to know what happens next.

You cannot achieve those two aims unless your narrative is easy to read.

The provision of narrative links makes for easy reading. These links connect the successive stages of the action and carry the reader along. Without such links, the narrative thread is snapped. Do try to vary their wording. A monotonous succession of 'then ... and then ... next' is boringly obvious. The links should be unobtrusive.

The more carefully you plan before you begin to write, the easier you will find it to provide the essential connections. Once the successive stages of the narrative are clearly set out in your plan, the sequence of events is established and you will be able to carry your reader through the action with only a sparing use of the more explicit verbal links. Incident will follow incident in a natural progression, and you will then not often need to provide obvious 'signals' that the action is moving on.

Narrative details and descriptive details

Some details play an essential part in carrying the action along. These are the narrative details that enable the reader to follow the course of events. For example, if your chosen subject hinges on a street accident and what followed, your reader *may* need to know the colour or make or size of a vehicle involved, or the age and appearance of the driver, or exactly where the accident happened.

You have to judge the relevance of each detail when you are considering whether to include it. Ask yourself: 'Does this detail help my reader to understand what is happening?' Obviously, you must provide the details that play an important part in the action, but be strict in your selection. A narrative cluttered with details is hard to follow. The reader's attention is distracted from the action.

The same considerations apply to descriptive details. Some are needed to make the narrative convincing and lively, but they must be sparingly used or the action will be held up. What matters most in a narrative is what happens. A few carefully chosen details will capture attention and hold interest, but your reader's main concern is with the events themselves.

Human interest

You are not creating 'characters' when you are writing a straightforward narrative, but people usually play the leading parts in the action. Just sketch them in with a few identifying details. It is especially important to do this when the events involve antagonism. Conflict may be present at the outset or it may be generated as the action unfolds. Skilfully revealed by a narrative in which the pace changes, conflict is a source of tension and rising excitement.

Dialogue in narrative

Though always less important than in a story, dialogue can be an effective means of identifying people and indicating that a new stage of the action is beginning. Keep it short. Too much talk interrupts the action. In a straightforward narrative, speech is useful to push the action along while, at the same time, informing the reader about who is doing what.

Narrative style

As we saw in section 13.4, the style of your writing must be appropriate to your subject. A quick-moving style is appropriate to a straightforward narrative. Short sentences, active verbs and a sparing use of adjectives are generally effective when striking and interesting events are being described.

Variations of style, however, are as desirable as variations of pace. A deliberate slowing of the action (to increase tension and lead into a climax) will be marked by a more leisurely style. Descriptive touches are more telling when the language used contrasts with that employed in the purely narrative passages. Quick-fire sentences are an indispensable medium for rapid action, but a narrative that rattles along in staccato bursts from start to finish is no pleasure to read. The writer needs to get his breath from time to time – and so does the reader.

Work out another plan

With all those considerations in mind, I tackle the subject that I have been forced to select. I have no more time left for making a choice and none of the other subjects seems more promising. At least, I can see a way into this one and I must work methodically to make the best use I can of the possibilities that it seems to offer me.

> You were one of a crowd waiting for a celebrity to appear. Describe what happened.

Gathering material

I jot down the material that comes to mind, just as it occurs.

> crowd in square in front of town hall – curiosity led me to join it – gradually discovered what it was all about – local hero expected to appear on balcony – had been given civic dinner and freedom of borough – long wait – crowd patient and good-humoured – gradually turned bad-tempered – I wasn't very keen anyway, so I left – read about events in local paper afterwards – eventual appearance – enthusiastic reception

That is not a lot to write about and it is sadly lacking in action. I shall have to build it up.

Fortunately, the instructions give me some useful pointers: 'You were one of a crowd ... Describe what happened.' I must narrate in the first person singular and I must stay with the crowd longer than I actually did! I can draw on my memories of the night and the crowd up to my departure, and I can reconstruct the later events by using the newspaper report as the basis of my invented material. Although my starting point is an actual event, I can make up any extra material that I need.

Also, I begin to see possibilities for changes of pace to create tension and rising excitement.

> crowd is good-humoured – crowd gets bored – crowd gets angry – celebrity appears – crowd won over at once

And I can see how the action can be presented from various angles.

> observer/narrator (me) – the crowd – the celebrity – the civic dignitaries (especially the mayor) – the police

From some or all of those angles, contrasts and conflicts can be introduced into the narrative to keep it moving and make it lively.

Selecting material and arriving at a plan

First, I shape my composition by mapping out the successive stages through which the narrative will be unfolded. As I work on the outline, I can reject material that does not fit in, adding whatever new material I need.

> (1) I see a crowd. (2) I join in. (3) Eager anticipation – 'X' is to appear. (4) Long wait. (5) Crowd gets bored. (6) Crowd gets restless. (7) Rumours circulate. (8) Crowd gets angry. (9) Ugly mood develops. (10) Police inspector enters town hall. (11) X appears on balcony accompanied by mayor? NO: mayor appears *alone*. (12) Crowd furious. (13) Mayor brings X onto balcony. (14) X talks to crowd, makes flattering speech. (15) Crowd's anger evaporates: happiness all round.

That gives me a satisfactory start. Now I can work out a detailed plan. As I fill in the gaps, I shall get a much firmer grasp of my subject. Some of the proposed incidents will be compressed or omitted; others will be expanded. New ideas will occur. I shall be establishing firmer links, varying the pace, introducing stronger human interest, looking for conflicts and contrasts, placing snatches of speech at strategic points in the narrative. Overall, what I aim to do is to increase the excitement of the narrative without destroying its credibility.

A good plan will firm up the possibilities that I have begun to see: possibilities that were not apparent when I first began to gather my material. I am now confident that, if I can get my plan right, I can write a fluent composition on this subject.

The plan

1 Jump straight into the action. I am part of the crowd when the narrative begins: part of it but detached from it – there's a narrative angle here.

perhaps like this? – 'We want Mel! We want Mel!' There must have been ten thousand people packed into Bursley Town Square that night …

2 *Brief* description of situation. Action has been launched and reader now needs to know what it's all about.

names essential – reader must be helped to believe in narrative – Mel Jones, captain of Bursley football team – Bursley Town Square packed with people waiting for him to appear on balcony after civic dinner and award of freedom of borough – cold dark night – square and town hall floodlit

3 Pick up action again. Crowd has been waiting a long time. Mood is changing.

introduce little old man standing next to me in crowd – he's a useful way of carrying action forward and he's another 'angle' – he provides me with useful details about events – he's not a fan

4 Action quickens. Crowd getting very restless. Jokes rather savagely about mayor and councillors.

'things'll get rough soon' (l.o.m. is talking to me) – 'it's gone ten now and he was due on balcony at nine'

5 Rumours begin to fly through crowd. Action hotter.

'He's not coming out'/ 'mayor's driven away'/ 'it's all over'/ 'dinner's going on till midnight'/ 'toasts and speeches'

6 Crowd angry now. People surge forward. Police on town hall steps look apprehensive.

'We'd best be going, lad.' – but impossible to shove through pushing mob

7 Police inspector enters town hall in a hurry.

8 Mayor appears on balcony. Tries to make himself heard.

groans – jeers – crowd in ugly mood

9 Mayor turns away. Goes back in. Climax of narrative begins here.

fury of crowd – l.o.m. and I in danger of being crushed – trying to get away – perhaps better to go with crowd?

10 Mayor returns. Mel Jones is with him. Some people can see him but most cannot.

confusion reigns – cheers and jeers – scuffles break out

11 Mel Jones begins to speak. Crown gradually calms down. Listens. Cheers. Loves it. Purrs with self-congratulation. Good humour all round.

just hint at his soothing words: a phrase or two will be enough – 'fellow townsfolk … great honour … yours as much as mine' – acid comment from l.o.m.: 'half of them can't hear a word he's saying'

12   We make our escape. Action dies down. Keep this very short. I look back. Balcony is empty but they are still there – happy and singing in the cold dark night.

'Good night, lad. Those idiots'll wait all night for another dose of syrup.'

Obviously, your plan for a composition on that subject would be different from the one that I have just worked out; and I do not claim more for mine than that it provides ample material arranged in an effective order. You might give your narrative a different 'slant', emphasise other aspects of the action, or – of course – write about a completely different series of events occurring in wholly different circumstances. In expressive composition the examiners invite and reward an entirely personal response from candidates.

Even so, we all need the help that comes from a methodical approach to writing. By applying the techniques demonstrated in these work-out sections, you can make a good choice of subject, explore thoroughly the possibilities that it offers you, and then write a composition that does justice to the imaginative thinking that you have put into it.

13.6 Work out descriptive writing

Facing the problem

A descriptive composition seems easy compared with the other kinds. A story demands a plot; an account of events must be securely strung on a narrative thread; a dramatic composition tests the technical skill of writing realistic dialogue; an impressionistic composition exacts an imaginative response to a visual or verbal stimulus. In comparison, a descriptive composition appears to offer the writer much more freedom.

In fact, this apparent freedom can be a trap, for a descriptive composition makes its own special demands. You will probably not have difficulty in finding plenty of material for the descriptive subjects offered to you, but it is not easy to sort that material out and arrange it in an effective order of presentation.

What you must do

A good piece of writing, of whatever kind, has a beginning, a middle and an end. That sounds obvious, but it is a fact that is often overlooked when a descriptive subject has been chosen. Unless the material is presented in a clear progression *from* the beginning, *through* the middle, *to* the end, a descriptive composition is just a ragbag of details. Descriptive items haphazardly thrown together cannot hold the reader's interest, however vivid and telling they are in themselves.

A descriptive composition must have *unity*. In other words, it must be a complete and self-contained piece of writing, all the *parts* of which contribute to the *whole*. To impose unity on your material, you have to do a lot of imaginative thinking and careful planning before you begin to write.

Some typical descriptive subjects

1. Write a description of a scene that you know well, bringing out its special character.
2. Write a descriptive composition entitled *either* (a) 'A lonely place' *or* (b) 'A night scene'.
3. My best friend.
4. Overheard remarks.
5. Breakfast.
6. A room of my own.
7. Describe the scene *either* at a railway station *or* at a public swimming-pool.
8. The river.
9. The street market.
10. Closing time at the supermarket.

Making a choice

A good choice depends on two factors: your interest in and personal experience of the subject; your ability to 'see into' the material that you gather and to find an 'angle of attack'.

Your material will not ring true unless you have some personal experience of what you are describing. For example, do not choose subject 10 in the above list if you have never been in a supermarket at closing time. Again, you will certainly have abundant personal experience from which to draw your material for subject 5, but what a very dull catalogue of details your composition will be unless you can find an 'angle' on it. A subject such as that demands a fresh and lively approach.

The wording of the first subject on that list sums up two very important points about descriptive writing. It instructs you to describe something that you know well (a scene in that case) and to bring out its special character. Whatever its particular subject, a **descriptive composition** must be about something (or somebody) you know well *and* bring out the special character or significance that it has for you.

Working out a descriptive subject

I have chosen subject 5, 'Breakfast', for the purposes of this work out. As a candidate in the examination I should probably choose subject 2(a), 'A lonely place', because there is one particular moorland scene that I know especially well and I feel confident that I could describe it in a way that would bring out the very special character that it has for me. But the subject 'Breakfast' gives me a better chance of demonstrating two important techniques:

1. How to gather fresh and interesting material for a descriptive subject that could easily seem stale and secondhand.
2. How to find a personal angle of attack from which to plan a descriptive composition that is lively and original.

Gathering material

Think in particular terms, not in general terms. Not breakfasts in general, but breakfasts (or a breakfast) that *you* have taken part in. Open your mind to the subject and gather personal, not abstract, material.

bacon and eggs – toast and marmalade – tea or coffee – a bowl of cornflakes and a rush – snatched piece of bread and butter – the bus leaves in 5 minutes – what a lovely day it's going to be! – what shall we do? – oh, lord, it's snowing! – where's Jean – not out of bed yet – she'll be late again – breakfast/*break* fast – first meal of the day – new life – lovely – smells – toast's burning – no hurry – pass the butter – milk's boiled over – can't stop – what a start to the day! – why is everyone so grumpy? – yawn – switch that noise off – oh, this sun!

Looking for an angle of attack

Because I have been thinking about the subject in personal and particular terms – in other words, finding my material in my own experience – I am becoming aware of a pattern. My ideas have been jotted down just as they occurred, but I can see a way of shaping them:

rush/leisure
good humour/bad temper
enjoying food/bolting food
fine weather/bad weather
zest/apathy

A strong contrast underlies the apparently haphazard collection of ideas. That contrast provides me with an angle of attack.

Finding a theme

Following up this way of looking at my subject matter, I see that a theme is emerging: 'Breakfast as it *can* be, contrasted with breakfast as it usually *is*'. This emerging theme will now direct all my thinking and planning because, with it in mind, I can see how to describe breakfast in a purposeful way. For me, the subject now has a particular character and significance that I am aiming to express through my description. With that theme I can give my writing unity. Every descriptive detail that I include will bear on the theme.

Again, I can now make a plan that has a clear-cut shape. I can find a good beginning, link each paragraph to the others, arrive at an effective ending, because I have found a central idea to shape my writing. I know what I want to say.

Finding 'the idea behind the description' is the hardest job when you are writing a descriptive piece: the hardest and most important, for a composition without a theme is a mere catalogue of descriptive details, lacking unity, plan and purpose.

Some more descriptive subjects

Sometimes the examiners' instructions draw your attention to the importance of providing a theme and implicitly warn you against producing a mere catalogue of details. Note the wording of this writing assignment:

Treasured possessions.
(You may wish to describe some of the things you value most and show why you would hate to lose them.)

By including the words *and show why you would hate to lose them*, the examiners are saying, in effect, 'A mere catalogue is *not* what we want. We want to read descriptions of the things you treasure that shows us *why* you treasure them.'

If you were tackling that question, you would have to take that theme as your guide as you gathered and selected your material and arrived at your plan. Here are some of the considerations that I would bear in mind.

1. Personal and particular thinking – *my* treasured possessions. I'll make a list.
2. How many? I can't find time or space for more than three or four. In any case, although I don't want to lose any, there aren't more than a few that I'd *hate* to lose. If I include too many, I can't bring out the significance of those that really matter.
3. Which shall I include? The *most* treasured, of course; but it's not easy to say which they are. Think hard about this, by going on to 4.
4. *Why* would I hate to lose each one? Let's have another look at the list I've made and start sorting them out by asking that question: my copper ring, because it was given to me by a very special person/my radio, because I get so much pleasure from it/my tool kit, because it's so useful/my post office savings book, because it's worth money ...
5. I'll choose four possessions, each of which I'd hate to lose for a different reason. That will give my composition variety and, therefore, added interest.
6. Order of presentation? I must think ahead. How to arrive at an interesting *sequence* is problem. I mustn't make it a simple list of one thing following another. I know: start with the most *valuable* one (in money terms, that is); go on to the most *useful* one; go on to the one that gives me most pleasure; end with the one that isn't worth very much in money terms but means most *to me* because of the person who gave it to me.
7. That's the outline settled. Now I can work out a detailed plan. I've got to know *before* I begin to write exactly how I'm going to tackle the descriptions. Take the radio, for example. What sort of description can I give of that? What details are relevant? The theme gives me my way in. I'd hate to lose it because of the pleasure it gives me. How does it do that? Because of its splendid tone? Because of its worldwide wavelength coverage? Because it's small and portable? Whichever of its features are the ones that make it most treasured are the ones to describe in detail.

Directed thinking of that kind is the basis of a successful plan.

Getting the order right was a problem when dealing with that subject, but many descriptive subjects are so worded that the order of writing is plain. For example:

> Describe the changing activities of your street from dawn to dusk of a summer's day.

If I choose that subject, I know where to begin (at dawn) and I know where to end (at dusk); but I must put more thought into it than that. The structure will be loose unless I can link the beginning and the end to round it off. If I can find a way of doing that, I shall be able to impose a unity on my composition, making each detail and each part contribute something important to the whole. Descriptive writing that is full of unrelated bits and pieces is very boring.

I try out several ideas and, in the end, decide on this as a unifying link:

dawn – day beginning – light   both are quiet times – the day
dusk – day ending – dark   begins and ends in silence

I think again. It's not as good as I thought it was! My street isn't very quiet at dusk! So I try for a unifying idea by working along different lines: the street is long; shops and houses on both sides; trees, street lamps, pavements, doorsteps; people walking, talking, laughing, shouting; cars moving, cars parked. I must take up a viewpoint – present the scene from an angle. Where? From a particular window? – whose? Downstairs window or upstairs? Or see the scene from a flight of steps? – church steps? – a memorial? – a monument? – a statue? (possibilities here: bustle of street contrasting with quietness).

Whichever angle I select, I can unify my composition by seeing and hearing everything from it. It is *my* street, after all, so I should be able to communicate its changing activities and personality as time passes over it on a summer's day.

Again, inside the dawn-to-dusk limits, I must select particular descriptive moments. I can't describe everything that happens at every successive minute of the day. Even if I could, it would be a rather boring and long-winded progression of 'then ... and then ... and then'!

Something like this might work: (1) dawn; (2) nine o'clock; (3) lunchtime; (4) mid-afternoon; (5) dusk. I see the possibility of a three-part structure there. Beginning: (1). Middle: (2), (3) and (4). End: (5).

I suggest that you now work on some of the descriptive subjects on page 138, gathering, selecting and arranging your material in the ways I have demonstrated. Find your angle of attack and establish your theme for each subject. Then make a detailed plan for one and write about it.

13.7 Work out discursive writing

What the examiners are looking for

The special features of discursive (argumentative or controversial) compositions were described in section 13.2. The subjects set are concerned with facts, ideas, opinions, and the examiners are looking for:

- a genuine interest in the subject and an adequate fund of information about it;
- the ability to give due weight to a contrary opinion, while coolly and reasonably rejecting it;
- the ability to set out an argument step by step and to arrive at a sensible conclusion.

To satisfy those requirements, discursive writing must be carefully planned and clearly expressed.

Some typical discursive subjects

1. Do you agree with the view that at a time of high unemployment women should give up their jobs so that unemployed men can get work?
2. 'We are squandering the natural resources of the planet and future generations will have to pay for our selfishness.' Put the case for three or four practical

measures that you think we could and should take to safeguard the future of our children.
3   Do you agree that watching television is a waste of time?
4   Argue the case *for* or *against* the reintroduction in Britain of *either* capital punishment *or* corporal punishment.
5   'Since alcohol causes as much suffering as any of the illegal drugs, the sale and consumption of alcoholic drinks should be banned.' What are your views on that statement?
6   'No subject should be compulsory at school or college, for we never learn well what we learn unwillingly.' Suppose that you sympathise with that point of view but, even so, believe that *one* particular subject should be compulsory. Make out your case.
7   Present your case for *either* believing *or* not believing in *one* of the following: (a) extraterrestrial life; (b) the Loch Ness monster, or any other monster; (c) ghosts; (d) fortune-telling.
8   Do you agree with those who argue that everyone at the age of 18 should be conscripted into the armed forces for a period of military service?
9   'We live in a world of which one half is affluent and the other half is poverty-stricken.' What are your views and what remedies would you advocate?
10 'To derive pleasure from the death of living creatures is an abominable thing. I'd abolish hunting and all other kinds of blood sports.' What are your opinions on this contentious subject?

Making a choice

First, ask yourself whether you have enough knowledge of a particular subject to be able to write a composition of the required length. You do not have to be an expert to write well on any of the subjects offered, but you are expected to have the general information that a thoughtful person interested in the subject would have picked up from reading and talking about it and/or from discussions on television or radio. As you have seen, ideas for story, narrative and descriptive compositions are often generated as you gather and plan your material, but you will not obtain the material you need for a discursive composition by that method. Again, if you are short of information, this probably means that you are not very interested in the subject; and interest in your chosen subject is a prerequisite for successful writing.

This is not to say that a discursive composition must be crammed with facts. The examiners are less concerned with the quantity of your information than with the use you make of it in setting out your argument. Even so, to be able to deploy an argument and arrive at a sensible conclusion, you must have some knowledge of the subject.

Read the question carefully

Consider very carefully the particular 'line' that the examiners are asking you to pursue. Are you being asked to put a case *for*? Are you being asked to consider both sides? Are you being asked to propose improvements? Marks are often thrown away because the candidate does not obey the instructions. For example, subject 7 in the list above instructs you to present your case for *either* believing in *or* not believing in ...'. There, you are not invited to consider both sides but to argue for or against belief. Because balanced views are wanted, it is always sensible to show an awareness of the opposing case, but a full exposition of it in this composition would be a waste of time. You would be marked on the part of the composition that obeyed the instructions. The other part would be ignored.

Look at subject 6: 'Suppose that you sympathise with that point of view …'. In other words, do not debate that point of view. Take it for granted and deal with the meat of the question, which comes later.

Planning and style

A well-developed argument is required. It must be reasoned, balanced, thoughtful and interesting. It must, therefore, be based on a careful plan in which your ideas are arranged in a logical sequence. When you are planning, think in terms of a three-part structure: (1) introduction; (2) body of argument; (3) conclusion.

The introduction is best confined to one paragraph. Four or five paragraphs will suffice for the body of the argument. The conclusion is the destination towards which you have led your reader throughout the composition. It knits up the strands of your case and expresses your final opinion. Make it pithy. One paragraph should be enough if your argument in the body of the composition has been thoughtfully directed.

A clear, easily read style is essential. Your reader's attention should be concentrated on *what* you are writing, not distracted by *how* you are writing it. Firm, varied sentences and a crisp, accurate choice of words will sustain interest in and win agreement with the argument you are putting forward.

Never get carried away by the strength of your feelings. You are expected to have opinions and to express them, but in a reasoned manner. The point is well illustrated by subject 10 in the list above. '"To derive pleasure from the death of living creatures is an abominable thing. I'd abolish hunting and all other kinds of blood sports." What are your opinions on this contentious subject?' The quotation used as a 'subject trigger' expresses strong feelings, but the examiners are asking you to give your *opinions* on the controversial topic fired off by the quotation. What they want is a reasoned discussion of the question raised by the vehement words of the quotation. They expect you to have a decided point of view, but your conclusion must be reached by thoughtful argument. Your use of language should reflect your cool and reasoning approach to the subject. A discussion conducted in emotional terms – 'abominable', for example – would not be appropriate.

Work out a plan

As a rule, you know what your conclusion is before you begin to plan. The subject interests you. You have some information about it and you know what you think about it. Your problem is how to use your information in a developing and reasoned argument that justifies your opinions on the subject. In a sense, you are planning backwards from your conclusion and it is often helpful to do your preliminary thinking in this order:

1. This is what I think about this subject.
2. What are the facts and what are the arguments that lead me to this conclusion?
3. How can I best set out those facts and those arguments to show that I have good reasons for coming to my conclusion?

I shall now work out a plan for subject 5 on the list.

'Since alcohol causes as much suffering as any of the illegal drugs, the sale and consumption of alcoholic drinks should be banned.' What are your views on that statement?

I know that I do not agree that the sale and consumption of alcoholic drinks should be banned. What are my reasons? What facts am I relying on?

(1) Alcoholic drinks need not be harmful. (2) There is some medical evidence to suggest that *moderate* drinking is beneficial. (3) Moderate social drinking is a source of pleasure. (4) Banning harmless pleasure can never be right. (5) In any case, a legal ban leads to law-breaking (e.g. the crime that accompanied prohibition in America; the evasions and severe punishments in some countries today).

Having jotted down my own positive reasons for the opinion I hold, I look at the arguments that underlie the proposition with which I am disagreeing. I must take opposing views into consideration if my argument is to stand up.

(1) Yes, alcohol *can* cause suffering. (2) Whether it causes *as much* suffering as the illegal drugs, I do not know; and nor does the author of the statement. The proposition is very sweeping. (3) I suppose that cocaine and heroin – the so-called 'hard drugs' – are meant by 'the illegal drugs'. Their sale to and use by the general public should certainly be banned (even though they have their proper and beneficial *medical* uses). (4) The proposition makes no distinction between 'the illegal drugs', the general use of which *must* be harmful, and alcohol, the use of which *may* be harmful – but only when it is *misused*.

I have now sorted out my ideas. I know *where* my argument is going. I know, roughly, *how* it will get there. As I work out my plan, I have two remaining problems to sort out: (a) Where do I begin? (b) In what order shall I develop my argument?

Plan (with notes)

1 Introduction
Must be 'punchy' to gain reader's attention. Must make it plain that I am beginning a thoughtful discussion of the subject. *One* paragraph along these lines: the statement quoted is an assertion, not a reasoned opinion – it ignores the distinction between alcoholic drinks, which may be harmful, and hard drugs, which must be – on this dubious basis, it calls for an indiscriminate ban.

2 Body of argument
Here I must do three things: (1) demonstrate weakness of proposition; (2) deploy my positive arguments for permitting sale and consumption of alcoholic drinks; (3) lead reader step by step towards agreement with my conclusion. Thinking about those three tasks suggests the following sequence of paragraphs.

Paragraph 1: Cannot be denied that immoderate drinking causes mental and physical suffering – many alcoholics – families distressed – hospitals burdened – but this is misuse, abuse, of alcohol.

Paragraph 2: Benefits of alcohol that statement ignores – social pleasure – medical evidence in favour of moderate use.

Paragraph 3: Dangers of prohibition – the American experience – modern examples – law evasion and law enforcement – crime inevitably accompanies prohibition.

Paragraph 4: Some habits are so vicious, some substances so dangerous as to warrant banning – for reasons given, not alcoholic drinks – most people use them as source of harmless pleasure – cannot justifiably take away the pleasure of a majority because a minority misuses it.

3 Conclusion
One pithy paragraph, knitting together strands of argument. Banning pleasure always dangerous and rarely justified. Considering the inevitable harmful consequences of a legal ban, the case against alcoholic drinks is too weak to support their prohibition.

A note on appropriate language

As you already know, emotional terms and excited writing must be avoided. You will not convince your reader by shouting. The cool, thoughtful tone of good discursive writing calls for a degree of formality in its style, but do not confuse formality with pomposity. Long-winded sentences and 'big', would-be important words will not impress your reader. An easy, plain style is best, but do not use slang or colloquialisms (see Chapters 15 and 16).

13.8 Work out dramatic writing

Remember that a dramatic (or conversational) composition must be written in direct speech, but – as you will see from the work out – you can use 'stage directions' to help to develop the action and to suggest the emotions and attitudes of the characters. A dramatic situation is tense and exciting because the characters are in some sort of confusion or conflict. The action rises to a climax and then ends with a quick clearing up of the confusion or resolution of the conflict.

A typical question

> *David McKenzie, a young man of eighteen, is sitting at the table of a living-room making a model from a kit; his sister, Jacky, a bright-eyed nervous teenager, is curled up in an armchair watching television. Their father, who has just returned from work, is recovering his spirits by trying to read the evening newspaper.*
>
> *There is an insistent ringing of the doorbell. Mrs McKenzie is heard going to answer it, and there are muffled sounds of a serious conversation outside. The door of the living-room opens violently. She appears, disturbed and shaking.*

MR MCKENZIE [*casually looking up*]: What is it, dear?
MRS MCKENZIE [*breathlessly*]: There's a policeman at the door.
DAVID: Oh, no!

Jacky quickly unrolls herself from the chair and switches off the television; she looks anxiously at her father and bursts into tears.

Write a short play by continuing the dialogue in a manner which develops the dramatic situation. (You are advised to continue the method of setting out the dialogue, but *do not copy out the extract*. If you wish, you may introduce one or two more characters or add a further scene.)

Work out: stage 1

Analyse the given dramatic situation out of which you must develop a short play.

1. Peaceful domestic scene suddenly interrupted by arrival of policeman.
2. Four characters briefly introduced:
   (a) David McKenzie (brother) – sitting working at model – quiet – eighteen.
   (b) Jacky McKenzie (sister) – bright-eyed, nervous – watching TV – curled up – teenager.
   (c) Mr McKenzie (father) – tired after work – trying to read newspaper.
   (d) Mrs McKenzie (mother) – disturbed – shaking – opens door violently.
3. Another character – policeman – as yet an unknown quantity.

Work out: stage 2

Identify possible dramatic 'growth points'.

1. Jacky's reaction – looks anxiously at father – bursts into tears – frightened of father's reaction – thinks she knows why policeman has called – nervous person, so assumes that policeman's visit means trouble for her.
2. David's exclamation ('Oh, no!') – is that caused by annoyance at interruption or does he think something is catching up with him? – quiet character, so has possibilities for surprising dramatic development.
3. Father – no reaction given, so can be used in any way that develops drama – father-figure, so give him authority and some control over events – remember, he's tired and wants to read his paper in peace.
4. Mother – upset – bewildered – worried – not so much an actor in the drama as a reactor to events?
5. Policeman – why has he called? – obviously the mainspring of the action – provide a harmless reason for his visit but do not reveal it at once – in meantime, let other characters react in confused, nervous or angry way.

Work out: stage 3

Outline development of dramatic situation.

Suppose the policeman has called to interest the McKenzies in a police/public co-operation in a 'neighbourhood watch' scheme.

Suppose David thinks he wants information about his motor bike. The licence is due for renewal.

Suppose Jacky thinks he saw her and her friends leaving a disco late the previous evening. They were happy and excited and making a lot of noise. Perhaps there has been a complaint? What will her father say?

Leave Mr and Mrs McKenzie in bewilderment. He's fed up because he's tired and wants to relax. She's anxious about her children. Give Mr McKenzie an active role. Give Mrs McKenzie a passive role.

Thinking it out has provided: (a) a development of the given dramatic situation; (b) action that rises to a climax; (c) an ending that untwists the strands of the action and resolves the tension.

Work out: stage 4

Write the dramatic composition in accordance with the instructions supplied.

MR MCKENZIE [*wearily*]: What on earth does he want? You'd better bring him in. Oh, do be quiet, Jacky! What's the matter?
JACKY [*between sobs*]: We didn't mean ... it was only fun ...
DAVID [*searching through his wallet*]: I filled it in the other day. Don't say I didn't post the blessed thing.
  By this time, Mrs McKenzie has brought the policeman into the living-room. He is a young man, with a pleasant smile.
POLICEMAN: I'm sorry to disturb you, but I'd like to have a talk.
  Jacky and her mother speak at the same time and nobody hears what they are saying. The policeman looks enquiringly at Mr McKenzie, whose patience is wearing thin.
MR MCKENZIE: I wish somebody would tell me what this is all about. Jacky, keep quiet until you have something sensible to say. Don't upset yourself, Alice. There's nothing wrong – as far as I know.
DAVID [*waving an envelope*]: It's here! All filled in and signed – and the money's inside. If I catch the last post, they'll get it tomorrow.
  David makes for the door, smiling happily, but the policeman speaks to him before he can reach it.
POLICEMAN [*firmly*]: If you could just give me a moment ... I'm particularly anxious to talk to young people, like you and your sister.
JACKY [*tearfully*]: I'm sorry, but – honestly – I don't know how to ...
MR MCKENZIE: Where d'you think you're going, David? Sit down. [*He turns to the policeman.*] Perhaps if you sat down too, we'd get somewhere. I think my two children have gone out of their minds.
MRS MCKENZIE: Oh, yes, do sit down. I'll go and get us all a cup of tea. I'm sure you'd like one?
  She turns towards the kitchen door, pleased to have something practical to do.
POLICEMAN: Well, that's very kind of you, but perhaps you'd just listen to me first. You are all concerned in this.
JACKY: No! You've got it wrong. It wasn't *their* fault. They weren't there. They were here, at home, when ...
MR MCKENZIE: Jacky, if I have to tell you to shut up once more, I'll go as barmy as you. [*He turns to the policeman.*] Now, young man, I think I can guarantee you a few minutes of silence. What's it all about?
POLICEMAN: We're trying to start a neighbourhood watch scheme. Each station in our division is contacting the households in its area. There's to be a public meeting in the Town Hall at 7.30 next

Tuesday and I'm here to invite you all to it.
DAVID [*putting the envelope back in his wallet*]: So that's it! Oh, what a pity! I can't go on Tuesday – it's my training night.
JACKY [*very enthusiastically*]: Oh, what a good idea! I'll be there and I'll bring some of my friends.
MRS MCKENZIE: Tuesday, you say? I'm afraid I can't. I always spend the evening with Gran on a Tuesday. She's getting on, you know, and she looks forward to Tuesdays.
MR MCKENZIE [*very firmly*]: I think we shall be well represented at the meeting, officer. Jacky's very keen – you can see that. And I'm sure David will put off his training for once. He takes a lot of interest in legal matters, don't you, David?

David is about to answer, but he looks again at his father's expression and changes his mind.

POLICEMAN: I'll leave these leaflets for you to read before the meeting. [*He hands one to David and one to Jacky.*] Thank you for your interest and I'll look forward to seeing you next Tuesday evening. I don't think I'd better have that cup of tea, thank you, Mrs McKenzie. I've got several more houses to visit.

Mrs McKenzie shows the policeman out. David returns to his modelling. Jacky reaches for the television switch.

MR MCKENZIE [*picking up his newspaper*]: Now, David, you'd better go and post that letter. And don't tell me it doesn't matter. If a policeman's visit reminded you of it, it matters all right. And, Jacky, you can forget about television for half an hour. Celebrate your lucky escape – whatever it was – by helping your mother in the kitchen. *I'm* going to read my paper.

13.9 Work out impressionistic writing

The examiners' instructions

As you saw in section 13.5, a composition on an impressionistic subject may be written in the form of a story. It may also be written as an unplotted narrative or a description, or in *any form that the particular instructions permit*.

Whether the provided stimulus is verbal (a few lines of poetry) or visual (a picture or a series of pictures), the examiners usually invite candidates to respond by writing *one* of several different forms of composition which they stipulate. Which form of composition you choose is entirely up to you, provided that it is one of the forms permitted by the question.

Instructions for impressionistic writing are worded in many different ways. You may be told to write a story based on a picture or a poem. You may be told to write a descriptive piece suggested by several pictures (or just one). You may be told to give an account of the thoughts and feelings that a picture or a poem suggests to you. (An instruction such as that calls for a very carefully planned piece of writing.)

To familiarise yourself with the range of instructions, study the list of typical assignments given in the next section. Before doing so, however, remind yourself of the stipulation that applies to *all* impressionistic compositions of whatever form: your writing must be directly and clearly connected with the given poetry or picture. That is its starting point.

Some typical impressionistic assignments

1. Using the picture as a starting point, write a story or compose a descriptive piece.
2. Write a story or a description or an account of your thoughts and feelings suggested by *one* of the pictures on the accompanying sheet. Your composition should be directly about the subject of the picture or take some central suggestion(s) from it: *there must be some clear connection between the picture and what you write.*
3. Using the following lines of poetry as a starting point, write a story or describe your personal response.
4. Write a composition based on the accompanying picture postcard.
5. Write a composition suggested by the following quotation.
6. Write on an idea suggested by the picture below.
7. Write on an idea, *or* on places, *or* on persons, suggested by the following lines.
8. Look at the photograph printed below and then do *one* of the following:
   (a) Write a story in which the driver of the car in the picture plays an important part.
   (b) Write a story entitled 'The car that broke down'.
   (c) Write about the thoughts and feelings that the picture suggests to you.
   (d) Describe what you imagine may have happened just *after* the photograph was taken.

Work out your methods

Revise section 13.5, where a sound method of writing an impressionistic composition is demonstrated in full detail.

In that work out the stimulus was poetry and the form chosen for the composition was a story. Here are some notes on how to use a pictorial stimulus to write compositions of various kinds.

Picture subjects

The picture material may be a photograph of a dramatic scene, or a 'still' from a television play or a film. It may be a news picture from a paper or a magazine, or it may be a landscape or townscape. It may be a photographic reproduction of a work of art. It may be a strip cartoon. It may be comic or serious; strictly realistic or imaginatively suggestive. The range of possibilities is large, but whatever the subject or the nature of the picture, your writing must spring out of a close and imaginative response to it.

A story based on a picture

Imagine that you are one of the people in the picture, or imagine that you took the photograph or that you painted the picture. This way, you involve yourself in the possibilities of action, get to know the people, find an angle from which to tell your story.

Having identified with one of the people in the picture or with the photographer or artist, let your thoughts play on possible relationships (enmity, love, rivalry, support, and so on) between your 'angle character' and other people in the picture. The seeds of your plot lie here.

Study facial expressions, gestures, clothes, ages, postures, and so on, as shown in the picture. Sharp observation of such details will provide descriptive material and plot development for your story.

Only when you have 'interpreted' the picture in this way, by an imaginative exploration of *what* is happening and *why* it is happening, can you use it as the springboard for a story.

Descriptive writing based on a picture

Study the picture closely, with a sharp eye for its details. You will find yourself responding imaginatively to some particular item. A frowning face, an open window, a shadow on a doorstep, a child's smile, a car without a number plate, a smart hat worn at a rakish angle ... such are the pictorial hints that will start you off.

Look for your 'angle of attack' (see page 149) in the interaction of a detail with the overall impression that the picture makes. That crucial angle of attack may be discovered either by narrowing down your focus from the picture as a whole to a particular detail, or by focusing first on a detail and then widening your view to take in the whole picture. Try both ways of searching for your viewpoint.

Once you have established your angle of attack, move in an ordered sequence from your starting point to your planned ending. Unless you consistently maintain your chosen angle, you will let in irrelevant details and weaken the structure of your composition. Unity (each detail and each part contributes to the impact of the *whole*) is vital. Remember: 'No false starts and no loose ends.'

Impressionistic writing based on a picture

Instructions such as 'Write about the impressions you receive from this picture' or 'What thoughts (and/or feelings) does this picture suggest to you?' require a different kind of answer from those we have been considering earlier. They limit you by excluding narrative or descriptive forms of composition, but they offer you great freedom of imaginative response to the picture. Provided that your subject matter is triggered off by something in the picture (and is clearly seen by the reader to be so evoked) you can allow your imagination to journey beyond the picture's bounds.

Model structure

Many candidates find that the following model structure provides a sound basis for picture compositions of the kind we are discussing here:

1   Introduction

Brief but vivid description of the 'trigger detail' in the picture and of your immediate response to it. One paragraph.

2   Body of composition

Three or four paragraphs describing the associated ideas, thoughts and/or feelings that the 'trigger' has set off in your mind. It is essential to link these paragraphs so that each leads your reader on to the next. You must establish a clear forward flow of ideas, thoughts, feelings.

3 Conclusion

A final paragraph, rounding off the imaginative journey on which you have taken your reader. It is structurally effective and imaginatively satisfying to return to the trigger detail from which the essay began.

14 Personal writing

LEAG	MEG	SEG	NEAB	WJEC	NICCEA	Topic	Date attempted	Date completed	Self Assessment
✓	✓	✓	✓	✓	✓	Examinations and changes			
✓	✓	✓	✓	✓	✓	Coursework			
✓	✓	✓	✓	✓	✓	'Differentiation'			
✓	✓	✓	✓	✓	✓	An approach to the subject			
✓	✓	✓	✓	✓	✓	Speaking and listening			
✓	✓	✓	✓	✓	✓	Reading			
✓	✓	✓	✓	✓	✓	Ways and means			
✓	✓	✓	✓	✓	✓	Writing			
✓	✓	✓	✓	✓	✓	Practical writing			

14.1 Personal letters

When we write to our relatives and friends we are not bound by conventions. 'Do as you wish' is sound advice. Yet there are some expectations connected with these matters and as we all need guidelines to achieve anything in life, the few observations that are made below may be of some help.

Of course we *know* our own *friends*, what *interests* us and how we are *impressed* and *amused* by *experiences* that involve us. Really that goes without saying ... and yet much of it does go, it goes without our being able to express it readily, especially in writing. Mastering this depends upon our acquisition of the skills being encouraged in this book. It also means that we must have a high regard for the words in italics:

- *know* – be aware of your own insights into life, for they are unique;
- *friends* – they matter, need to be kept and deserve something 'special';
- *interests* – beware that these topics can become self-centred;
- *impressed* – avoid the solemn, but have an eye for the serious insight;
- *amused* – humour may be the core of many letters, but don't overdo it;
- *experiences* – think before you write, for more happens than you recall at first.

14.2 Matters to bear in mind

People like receiving letters. Market researchers tell us that so-called 'junk mail' is preferred to having the postman pass by. Consequently when you write, it's worth making it a memorable treat for someone.

Postcards have their advantages – the limited space available imposes the discipline of being brief. Evelyn Waugh once maintained that if you could not write what you wanted to express within the space provided on a postcard then it was not worth writing at all!

You are the centre of the letter that you write – its inspiration and subject. Avoid being completely self-centred. There are topics that you can be objective about.

Humour is vital, but it's attained by more than the extensive use of exclamation marks. Subtle insights, shrewd observations, distinctive contrasts, conversational snippets, unusual incidents and aspects of human behaviour need to be noted and expressed. Tend to be restrained rather than brash in your style of expression.

The well-worn tracks of letter-writing (clichés and hackneyed phrases) should be avoided. 'Wish you were here', 'the weather is ...' and 'the food is ...' need to be restructured. Jot down your ideas on the back of an old envelope before you start writing the letter. You will be surprised how you will overcome those repetitive patterns of words that are often caused by trying to think of things to say as you write. A little preparation works wonders.

To help overcome the 'commitment' problem, write and stamp the envelope first. Consider it as a contract to make you complete the task in hand.

15 Using words

LEAG	MEG	SEG	NEAB	WJEC	NICCEA	Topic	Date attempted	Date completed	Self Assessment
✓	✓	✓	✓	✓	✓	Examinations and changes			
✓	✓	✓	✓	✓	✓	Coursework			
✓	✓	✓	✓	✓	✓	'Differentiation'			
✓	✓	✓	✓	✓	✓	An approach to the subject			
✓	✓	✓	✓	✓	✓	Speaking and listening			
✓	✓	✓	✓	✓	✓	Reading			
✓	✓	✓	✓	✓	✓	Ways and means			
✓	✓	✓	✓	✓	✓	Writing			
✓	✓	✓	✓	✓	✓	Practical writing			

15.1 Basic skills

Chapters 15–19 concentrate on word choice (vocabulary), grammar, punctuation and spelling. Used together with Chapter 22, which provides varied practice in solving all sorts of common problems, they give you help with your written English.

The explanations, advice and work outs in each of the earlier chapters have referred to a particular area of the work tested by the GCSE examination in English: expression (both composition of various kinds and practical writing in various forms), understanding and response, summary and directed writing. However, you have been given frequent reminders that your performance in all these tests finally depends on your competence in the basic skills of written English. As a rule, examination papers include similar reminders. For example:

> You are reminded of the importance of orderly presentation and clear English in your answers.

In all your coursework you will certainly be encouraged to pay careful attention to the clarity and correctness of your written English.

A caution about the need for 'clear and correct English' may be a useful reminder, but it is worded too generally to be of much practical help. You may feel that it does not throw a great deal of light on what is expected of you – and unless you have learnt beforehand what is meant by 'clear and correct English' (and practised writing it), it won't!

The fact is that, in issuing their reminder, the examiners assume that you have learnt the ground rules of written English and know how to apply them. What they are saying, in effect, is this: no matter what kind of question they are answering, all GCSE candidates are expected to be competent in the basic skills of written English. Those who are not will lose marks.

The various examining boards phrase their requirements in their own way, but they all have common aims and apply the same standards. Careful study of their syllabuses and grading criteria makes it possible to draw up a list of the qualities of written English looked for in the work of all candidates.

Paragraphing

Every piece of writing you do must be carefully organised. Its subject must be introduced, developed and carried onwards to its conclusion. (In other words, it must have a thought-out beginning, middle and end.) The firm overall structure required cannot be achieved unless it is based on a linked and logical sequence of paragraphs, each of which deals with one (and only one) main topic.

Sentences

Your sentences must be grammatically correct. In their construction and their tone they should be appropriate to the particular ideas and feelings you are trying to express. Your awareness that you are attempting to achieve a particular effect in one sentence and a different effect in another will be reflected in the variety and range of sentence structures that you employ.

Choice of words

You must choose your words carefully and sensitively. You can do this only if you have a large vocabulary on which to draw, and some feeling for the way words work. Evidence that you have tried to suit the expression to the particular sense you want to convey and to the tone of voice you consider to be fitting will be a very strong point when your work is assessed. 'Correct', 'varied' and 'appropriate' are the terms used by the examining boards when describing the qualities they hope to find in candidates' use of words.

Punctuation

Correct grammar and appropriate word choice must be supported by well-judged punctuation consistently applied. Clear, accurate use of the basic punctuation marks in one of the most important ways you have of getting your meaning across and avoiding ambiguity and misunderstanding. Punctuation and sense go hand in hand.

Spelling

Although you are not expected to be faultless, you *are* expected to spell all commonly used words correctly. Ignorance and/or carelessness will cost you marks – and rightly so. As in grammar and punctuation, so in spelling, the examination demands a standard of literacy below which you must not fall.

The importance of structuring your answers – both overall and in paragraphs – has been demonstrated frequently and in detail.
    The basic skills of written English described above in the list of the examiners' requirements are dealt with in this and subsequent chapters. Do not fail to study them closely. Then work through the exercises and tests in Chapter 22. The benefits will be apparent in all your written work in English – and in all your other subjects too.

15.2 Enlarging your vocabulary

Your **vocabulary** is the range of words that you can use. The larger that range, the better your work in all the English questions – and the better your performance in all your other subjects.

To enlarge your vocabulary you must be interested in words: their meaning, derivation, pronunciation and spelling. While preparing for your examination (and afterwards, we hope) pay attention to every new word you meet: words that you have not heard or seen before; *and* familiar words used in ways that are new to you.

Get the dictionary habit. First, you must learn the 'signalling' system of abbreviations, different typefaces, brackets, and so on, that your dictionary uses to convey a lot of information in a small space. Different dictionaries use different 'codes', so, to get full help from the entries, you must study the 'preliminary matter' in your own dictionary. As this example shows, 'knowing' a word involves more than simple definition, although that is the essential starting point:

> **summary**, a. & n. Compendious, brief, dispensing with needless details, done with dispatch, (*a s. account*; *s. methods, jurisdiction*, etc.); hence **summarily**, adv. (N.) brief account, abridgement, epitome. [n. f. L. *summarium*.]

To build up a vocabulary that will be adequate for your examination, you must make frequent and proper use of your dictionary.

15.3 Meaning and context

Examination questions, especially in tests of understanding, often draw your attention to the fact that the meaning of a word depends very largely on the context in which it is used. A typical instruction reads like this:

> Explain the meaning of the following words and expressions *as they are used in the passage*.

Remember that a word can have several meanings and can act as different parts of speech, *according to the context in which it is used*.

For example, my dictionary tells me that the word *pat* can be used as a noun, as a verb, as an adjective or as an adverb. It can mean (among other things): a stroke or tap; a small mass formed by patting; to strike gently; opportune(ly); apposite(ly). In all the following sentences, *pat* is correctly used but it means something different in each:

1 Get me a pat of butter.
2 Don't pat yourself on the back.
3 The startling news came pat to their purpose.
4 Question him again if you like, but he has his story pat.

Context must always be considered before meaning can be established. Your dictionary gives you as many meanings as it has space for and indicates the common ways of using a word, but it cannot tell you which particular meaning and which particular usage you need. Your study of the context provides the solution.

15.4 Prefixes and suffixes

A **prefix** is a letter or a group of letters joined on at the *beginning* of a word to change its meaning and to make a new word (*un* + 'happy' = unhappy). A **suffix** is a letter or a group of letters joined on at the *end* of a word to change its meaning and to make a new word ('friend' + *ship* = friendship).

You must learn to recognise the meaning and the function of the prefixes and suffixes most frequently found in English. For example, you must know the difference between *ante*date and *anti*dote; between *ab*ject, *in*ject, *ob*ject, *pro*ject, *re*ject and *sub*ject; between occup*ancy* and occup*ant*; between wood*ed* and wood*en*.

15.5 Synonyms, antonyms, homophones

Synonyms

Synonyms are words having the same (or very nearly the same) meaning. For example: *blend/mixture; change/alteration; start/begin*.

But when you need to substitute one word for another, as so often in directed writing and summary, you must remember that words are *not* lifeless counters, instantly interchangeable. You have to consider whether the proposed substitute carries the required *shade* of meaning. The following points must be borne in mind.

1. Words often convey feelings as well as ideas; and the feelings associated with a word are an important part of its meaning. For example, *evil* 'means' *bad* (and *bad* 'means' *evil*) but *evil* carries with it different (and much stronger) feelings than *bad*. The two words cannot simply be interchanged. You could not sensibly write (or say), 'Travelling overnight was an evil decision, for we were tired out when we arrived.' (See section 15.8.)

2. Very rarely do two words mean exactly the same thing, although they may be close enough in meaning to be interchangeable. You have to be satisfied that the word you choose is precisely right for the particular meaning you want to express. For example, *end* and *finish* are very close in meaning and they may be interchangeable in some contexts, but they may convey quite different senses in other contexts. Compare: 'There was a dead heat at the finish of the Tadcaster Hurdle' with 'The loss of sponsorship funds means the end of the Tadcaster Hurdle'.

3. Words must be appropriate to their context. You have to consider not only the sentence in which a word is to be used, but also the paragraph in which that sentence occurs and – often – the passage as a whole. You have already seen that a particular use of language demands a fitting (appropriate) choice of words and you must bear this in mind when selecting synonyms. For example, *respire* 'means' *breathe*, but the two words cannot be freely switched around. There are many contexts in which *breathe* is appropriate but in which *respire* would be inappropriate. Similar considerations apply to *buy/purchase, live/reside, house/residence*, and to many other synonyms.

Antonyms

Antonyms are words of opposite meaning: *difficult/easy*; *happy/unhappy*; *strong/weak*.

The considerations that apply to the selection of synonyms apply equally to the selection of antonyms. In respect of length, a long journey is the opposite of a short journey. Opposite moral judgements are expressed in the two sentences: 'He is a good man'/'He is a bad man'. *But* is the meaning of 'Those sausages were bad' the opposite of 'Those sausages were good'?

Homophones

Homophones are words that sound the same or nearly the same, but are spelt differently and have different meanings: *complement/compliment*; *fair/fare*; *gait/gate*; *sail/sale*.

There are a great many of these 'confusables' – a name that epitomises the danger they present to a careless writer.

15.6 Compendious words

The need to know (and to know how to use) these 'space-savers' was demonstrated in Chapter 11. Essential when summarising, they are invaluable in all uses of written (and spoken) language. They pack a tremendous punch. With a wide range of compendious words in your vocabulary, you can write and speak plain, forceful English, and steer clear of verbosity and the pretentious fluffiness that is death to the language. Many of the tests in Chapter 22 provide practice in substituting compendious words for long-winded expressions. (See also sections 16.3–16.7.)

15.7 Literal and figurative uses of language

Figurative use of language is a frequent, useful, colourful element of everyday speech and writing. We are not usually confused by it. When we hear that somebody has been 'spurred on', we do not suppose that a sharp instrument has been applied to his or her sides. We understand that he or she has been impelled to make additional efforts. If 'the books were cooked', we do not suppose that they were boiled in a saucepan or baked in an oven. We understand that the accounts have been falsified.

A common mistake is to employ language figuratively and to make nonsense of it by inserting the word *literally*. ('How did you feel when you heard that you had been selected?' 'Astonished! You could literally have knocked me down with a feather.') Of course, *you* would not make that silly mistake, but many people do – and it's catching! The example illustrates too the danger of **cliché** inherent in many popular figurative expressions. (See section 16.8.)

Tests of understanding frequently require you to distinguish between these two uses of language, for the passages set often include vivid and emotive figurative expressions. (See section 15.8.) When summarising, any figurative expressions that are essential to the key points must be reworded as literal statements.

You are not as a rule questioned directly about **figures of speech**, but you should learn to recognise the following: **alliteration**; **metaphor**; **paradox**; **onomatopoeia**; **personification**; **simile**. They are in common use, and failure to recognise them causes misunderstanding of content and purpose. Figures of speech often play a major part in conveying the **nuances** of meaning which you must be able to detect in passages set as tests of understanding.

15.8 The language of fact and the language of feeling

Words may be used primarily to convey facts and ideas. They may be used primarily to communicate feelings or emotions. The former is described as a *referential* use of words. The latter is described as an *emotive* use of words.

- **Referential use of language** Words are used as 'labels'. They name and describe things and their attributes. They are used factually and *objectively*. The writer (or speaker) says, in effect, 'I am using language to deal with things as they are.'
- **Emotive use of language** Words are used to communicate feelings and emotional attitudes. They are used *subjectively*. The writer (or speaker) says, in effect, 'I am using language to communicate my feelings about these matters and I want to persuade you to share those feelings.'

Many words have both a denotation and a connotation. The **denotation** is the 'labelling function' of the word – what the word 'actually means' (to put it very crudely). The **connotation** is the feelings and emotions associated with the word – the 'emotional tones' that it carries with it. For example:

1. They chose a *blue* car last time. (*denotation* of 'blue' uppermost)
2. We felt very *blue* when they left. (*connotation* of 'blue' uppermost)

Denotation is uppermost when words are used literally. Connotation is uppermost when words are used figuratively.

Referential language (stressing *denotation*) is the appropriate language for scientific, factual, practical and discursive writing.

Emotive language (stressing *connotation*) plays a large part in creative, persuasive, impressionistic writing.

Your recognition that language is being used in one or the other of these two ways helps you to determine the writers' intentions when you are studying passages set for understanding and response. Your own pieces of directed writing and composition are, of course, proof that you can (or cannot!) use words in ways that are suitable to a particular kind of writing. The explicit instruction 'Write in an appropriate style' is the key to successful directed writing. A composition the style of which is not appropriate to the kind of subject chosen falls at the first hurdle.

15.9 Idiomatic and proverbial expressions

An **idiom** is a form of expression (or of grammatical usage) peculiar to a particular language. For example, English idioms using the word *heart* include: 'a person/cause after one's own heart'; 'with all one's heart'; 'from the bottom of one's heart'; 'break one's heart'; 'by heart'; 'go to one's heart'; 'in good heart'; 'with a heavy heart'; 'know by heart'; 'learn by heart'; 'lose heart'; 'lose one's heart'; 'not find it in one's heart to' … . And that is only a selection of 'heart' idioms.

Mastery of its idioms is a sure mark of proficiency in the use of a language. That is why it is so difficult to speak or write a foreign language 'like a native'. We may have the vocabulary we need and know the grammar, but the idioms often defeat us.

Mishandled idioms cost marks in an English examination and, although nobody can sit down to learn all the idioms of English just like that, you can prepare yourself for the examination by checking the accuracy of the idioms you hear and read *and* of those you habitually use. Careful listening and reading and the use of reference books (such as Roget's *Thesaurus* and Brewer's *Dictionary of Phrase and Fable*) will increase your range and fluency and help you to guard against blunders such as confusing 'lose heart' with 'lose one's heart' – an increasingly common mistake.

Proverbial expressions, like idioms, are part and parcel (an idiom!) of everyday speech and are frequently used in written English. Many are centuries old and some, with constant use, have degenerated into clichés (see section 16.8). Many retain their freshness and vigour and the stock is continually renewed. Again, you have to rely on your sense of style to guide you when writing. Is the expression that you are about to use stale and overworked? (No self-respecting writer could use 'over the moon' or 'sick as a parrot'!) Can you find words *of your own* to say what *you* want to say? If so, use them.

However, you must acquaint yourself with the meaning of the commonest proverbs, any of which may be encountered in a passage set for understanding or summary. In answering those questions, you may be required to rewrite sentences containing idiomatic and proverbial expressions so that their sense is unchanged.

15.10 Good writing

Chapter 16 discusses and illustrates the faults most commonly committed when using words. You will find that each offends against one or more of these basic rules of good writing:

- be plain;
- be direct;
- use no more words than are necessary;
- think hard to find the right word;
- use active verbs rather than passive verbs where you have a choice.

Your written English will reach the standard that the examiners expect if you make a consistent effort to apply those rules every time you write.

16 Misusing words

LEAG	MEG	SEG	NEAB	WJEC	NICCEA	Topic	Date attempted	Date completed	Self Assessment
✓	✓	✓	✓	✓	✓	Examinations and changes			
✓	✓	✓	✓	✓	✓	Coursework			
✓	✓	✓	✓	✓	✓	'Differentiation'			
✓	✓	✓	✓	✓	✓	An approach to the subject			
✓	✓	✓	✓	✓	✓	Speaking and listening			
✓	✓	✓	✓	✓	✓	Reading			
✓	✓	✓	✓	✓	✓	Ways and means			
✓	✓	✓	✓	✓	✓	Writing			
✓	✓	✓	✓	✓	✓	Practical writing			

The mistakes of style and vocabulary listed in this chapter are those most frequently made in written English.

Each mistake is defined and discussed in a separate section, but it is helpful to think about their causes before looking at each of them in turn. They all arise from one or more of these bad habits:

- carelessly or ignorantly using the wrong word;
- using more words than are needed;
- using pompous expressions to sound important;
- using stale, tired words and expressions;
- using language that does not fit the occasion.

Because they have common origins, the faults overlap. For example, writers who use more words than are needed will probably be guilty of *tautology* or *circumlocution*, or both at once. *Verbosity* (see Section 16.7) manifests itself in different ways, all of which break the rules of good writing.

16.1 Malapropisms

A **malapropism** is a word used in mistake for one that resembles it, often resulting in an unintended comic effect; *always* resulting in nonsense:

1. All newly elected members of the society must attend the *propitiation* ceremony to be held at 6 p.m. next Friday.
2. The interviewer lost his temper and accused the shifty politician of *invading* his questions.
3. As the excise duty has increased, so have deaths caused by drinking *implicitly* distilled spirits.

Comments

The mistake is as old as language itself, but it takes its name from Mrs Malaprop, a character in R. B. Sheridan's play *The Rivals* (1775). One of her most famous 'malapropisms' neatly demonstrates the mistake: 'a nice derangement (*arrangement*) of epitaphs (*epithets*)'. Shakespeare's character Dogberry (*Much Ado About Nothing*) was a specialist in malapropisms nearly two hundred years earlier than Mrs Malaprop herself: 'You are thought to be the most *senseless* and fit man for the constable of the watch.'

16.2 Tautology

Tautology is the practice of needlessly saying the same thing more than once in different words (*tauto-* = 'the same'):

1 The guests arrived *in succession, one after the other*.
2 I have arranged to be called at *6 a.m. in the morning*.
3 Brown then bought out his partner and so became the *sole* and *only* proprietor of a *thriving* business *that was doing well*.

Comments

Think hard about the sense and you will avoid tautologies. We all seem to have an itch to write (and say) more words than are needed, as if a plain statement is somehow not sufficient on its own. As a result, we use superfluous words which add nothing to the meaning but clog up the sense of what we want to say.

16.3 Circumlocution

Circumlocution is a roundabout way of speaking and writing:

1 Candidates who scored low marks in summary *in many cases* exceeded the word limit.
2 Your application is *under active consideration* by the Board.
3 Pensioners *received a disappointment in the shape of the fact that* their pensions were not increased.

Comments

Spotlighted, the fault is so obvious that we wonder how we can ever commit it; but we all do. Each of those examples needs just a little thought to turn it into good English:

1 Candidates who scored low marks in summary often exceeded the word limit. (Or, and better: Many candidates who scored low marks in summary exceeded the word limit.)
2 Your application is being considered by the Board. (Or, and better: The Board is considering your application.)
3 Pensioners were disappointed because their pensions were not increased.

16.4 Pomposity

Pomposity is the use of self-important and inflated language: using out-of-the-way words and expressions to impress, and avoiding the shorter, simpler and more familiar terms that would express the same meaning. Pompous language conceals the sense – and it is often meant to. Jargon (see section 16.5) is usually present also.

1. The *counterproductive trends* in the industrial *production situation* are *escalating* to a *serious degree*.
2. Candidates must *operate* within the *time parameters obtaining*.
3. The *prolonged state of belligerency occasioned severe financial stresses. Governmental fiscal imposts* were increased *prior to its termination*.

Comments

Circumlocution usually goes with a pompous choice of words (*to a serious degree* = 'seriously'). In themselves, there is nothing wrong with long words or words outside an everyday vocabulary; but there is no justification for far-fetched language when there are simple and familiar terms to do the job. The examples just given can be rewritten in plain, direct English, without changing the intended sense and with greatly increased clarity and force:

1. Industrial production is falling seriously.
2. Candidates must keep to the time limit.
3. The long war cost a lot of money. Taxes had to be raised before it ended.

Plain English is crisp and means what it says. Pomposity is woolly and often does not mean what it appears to say. The **vogue words** of pompous people are loosely used. Examples are: *parameters; syndrome; ambivalent; liquidate; interface; approximate; optimum; orientate; viable*. All those words (and dozens more) are fashionable today. They *can* be used accurately and precisely, but only in appropriate contexts.

16.5 Jargon

Jargon comprises technical terms used in an inappropriate context. **Technical terms** are words and expressions that are used in particular arts, sciences, professions and occupations: there are technical terms in acting, for example; in physics, in psychology, in law, in medicine, in politics. In their appropriate contexts, they are accurate, intelligible, indispensable tools of communication. They become 'jargon' *only* when they are transplanted. Each of the vogue words listed above has an important job to do on its home ground. For example, *syndrome* is a technical term in medicine; *parameter* in mathematics; *viable* in biology.

Some technical terms have passed into general use without losing their accuracy and plain, honest dealing: *altering tack* (from sailing) is one such expression, used figuratively, as many of them are. The label 'jargon' (which means 'twittering'!) cannot be stuck on them.

Examples of and comments on jargon are included in the next section, which deals with a fault that is closely related to it.

16.6 Gobbledegook

Gobbledegook is pompous official writing, stuffed with the jargon of government departments: 'officialese'. Unfortunately, it has found its way out of the offices in which it first flourished and it is now one of the commonest faults in written English. The word *gobbledegook* is onomatopoeic, imitating the sound made by a turkey-cock.

1. The district surveyor has arrived at the conclusion that the physical properties and configuration of the terrain of the site make the proposal to erect habitations thereon a proposition of dubious viability.
2. Throughout a long period of time extending over several years there have been considerable and recurring variations in personnel in the establishments of this manufacturing agglomeration.
3. It has been decided by the minister that the incidence of the levying of prescription charges under the new regulations shall remain under active consideration and that, pending a decision being formulated, the current practice shall apply to such classifications of exemptees as would have remained exempt had the new regulations not been promulgated.

Comments

Many of the faults already discussed come together in those examples. Jargon and gobbledegook (the jargon of officialdom) are usually accompanied by tautology, circumlocutions and pomposity.

The meanings of examples 1 and 2 can be expressed plainly and directly:

1. The district surveyor has decided that the shape and surface of the site make it unsuitable for house-building.
2. For several years, the number of workers in this group of factories has varied considerably.

It is not so easy to turn the third example into plain, sensible English. Either the writer did not know what he wanted to say or he did not want his readers to know. The meaning seems to be:

3. The minister is still considering how the new prescription charges will be levied. Until he or she makes a decision, people who were exempt under the old regulations will remain exempt.

16.7 Verbosity

Verbosity is using more words than are needed. The symptoms of the disease include tautology, circumlocution and pomposity. Writers who use jargon and gobbledegook always suffer from verbosity and – be warned – the sickness is highly infectious. We are all in danger of catching it.

16.8 Clichés

A **cliché** is an expression that has been used so often that it has lost its freshness and vigour. Some clichés have become so worn out that they no longer add meaning. They have degenerated into verbal lumber, not worth the space that they take up:

1 *To all intents and purposes* the government appears to have changed its policies without telling the electors.
2 As was only *right and proper*, the insurance company settled the claim *then and there*.
3 After so many disappointments, we cannot rationally hope that he will *turn over a new leaf* at his *time of life*.

Comments

In example 1 the cliché adds nothing to the meaning of the sentence. Rewrite:

1 The government appears to have changed its policies without telling the electors.

What does *to all intents and purposes* say that *appears* does not?

In example 2 the cliché *right and proper* is not a tautology, though it sounds like one (*right* = 'correct' and *proper* = 'seemly'). But are the two senses needed? In this context the only relevant point is the legal correctness with which the insurance company behaved. The second cliché, *then and there*, means 'at once', 'promptly':

2 As they were obliged to do, the insurance company settled the claim immediately.

The clichés take up space without doing enough work to justify their presence.

3 After so many disappointments, we cannot rationally hope that he will reform at his age.

Clichés are usually verbose and they are *always* a sign of a stale mind. Whenever you are about to use a well-worn expression, stop. Then ask yourself, 'Do I need this formula? Can I find another – a more direct – way of putting my meaning across, in my own words?' Remember George Orwell's advice: 'Cut out all prefabricated phrases.'

16.9 Colloquialisms

Colloquialisms are expressions and grammatical forms used in familiar speech, but are not appropriate in formal writing:

1 'Come on, Bill! We're going to be late.'
   'Can't hurry. Breathless this morning.'
   'You smoke too much.'
   'I know. Shouldn't smoke at all, the doctor says.'
   'Give it up, then.'
2 'As I see it, there's a simple answer.'
   'Show me.'
   'Cut this para – this one. Begins, "Everyone has an active vocabulary and a passive vocabulary." Save six lines if we lost the last two sentences.'
   'Yes, I see – but hold on. Let's see – better: take it back. Whole para, I mean. Back to – "yes, that's it". Not happy about cutting it. There's a

short page on proof 67 – see? Slot it in there – no damage done if we reword "connectives".'

Comments

The following characteristics of colloquial English, illustrated in those two examples, are inappropriate in formal written English:

1 free and easy expressions (*hold on*);
2 contractions (*we're*; *there's*; *that's*);
3 abbreviations (*para*);
4 verbless sentences (*Breathless this morning*);
5 omission of subjects, especially pronouns (*Save six lines ...*);
6 rapid leaping about from one topic to another (the second speaker's last utterances in example 2);
7 reliance on tones and gestures to fill out the meaning of the spoken words ('act out' the dialogue in example 2).

Naturally, when you are writing dialogue (in a story composition, for example), colloquialisms are appropriate. Nobody will believe in your characters if they talk like a book.

16.10 Slang

The *Concise Oxford Dictionary* defines slang as: 'words and phrases in common colloquial use, but generally considered in all or some of their senses to be outside of standard English':

1 There's this *geezer* standing at the corner.
2 I gave him *the old one-two*.
3 They *hopped it pretty smartish*.

Comments

In example 1 the slang word *geezer* is preceded by a characteristic construction of present-day slang: *There's this ...* . In example 3, *pretty smartish* is also a slang construction. Such non-standard uses of grammar are often associated with slang vocabulary.

It is not always possible to make a clear distinction between colloquial English and slang. Slang is often, but by no means always, a feature of familiar speech. You would certainly use colloquial English in conversation with your grandmother or an old family friend, but you would probably not use slang; at least, not as frequently as you would use it in conversation with people of your own age.

It is helpful to think of language as being in 'levels of appropriateness'. Taking that view, *man* is the word for formal written English; *chap* for colloquial English; *bloke, guy, geezer* (or whatever word happens to be 'in') for slang.

Slang is a matter of fashion. Slang expressions originate in the specialised vocabularies of particular occupations, hobbies, social groups. (In this, slang resembles jargon.) These expressions are taken up by other users of English and are the 'in thing' for a time. Then they fall out of use and are forgotten. Today's slang is old-fashioned and unintelligible tomorrow.

It is wrong to use slang expressions in formal written English because: (a) their meaning may not be understood outside the comparatively small circle in which they happen to be used; (b) they go out of date very quickly; and (c) like jargon, they are 'prefabricated phrases', used by writers who are too lazy to find their own ways of expressing their own thoughts.

17 Correct grammar

LEAG	MEG	SEG	NEAB	WJEC	NICCEA	Topic	Date attempted	Date completed	Self Assessment
✓	✓	✓	✓	✓	✓	Examinations and changes			
✓	✓	✓	✓	✓	✓	Coursework			
✓	✓	✓	✓	✓	✓	'Differentiation'			
✓	✓	✓	✓	✓	✓	An approach to the subject			
✓	✓	✓	✓	✓	✓	Speaking and listening			
✓	✓	✓	✓	✓	✓	Reading			
✓	✓	✓	✓	✓	✓	Ways and means			
✓	✓	✓	✓	✓	✓	Writing			
✓	✓	✓	✓	✓	✓	Practical writing			

Faulty grammar in your written English will cost you marks. This chapter will help you to reach the grammatical standard required by the examiners. (You must also work through the follow-up exercises in Chapter 22.) It sets out the basic grammar that all candidates are expected both to know and to be able to use when writing. Then it lists and gives examples of all the common mistakes, supplying the corrections needed to turn them into good English. It is not a complete account of English grammar. Much information that would appear in a full study of the subject is deliberately omitted. It concentrates on the grammatical points that you can put to use to avoid some very common errors.

Candidates are not sufficiently aware that poor grammar is a frequent cause of failure in English examinations. A large vocabulary is important, but a knowledge of words alone is not enough. We may know all the words that we need to express a particular meaning, but unless we use those words grammatically, we cannot get their meaning across. If our handling of grammar is very poor indeed, we can hardly make ourselves understood at all; but *any* misuse of grammar is enough to slow communication down and cause misunderstanding. That is why your examiners require you to show them that you can write grammatical English.

Your ability to handle grammar correctly depends on your understanding of:

- the work that words do in sentences – words as *parts of speech*;
- the changes that must be made to word-forms according to the work that they are doing – *inflexions*;
- the grouping together and positioning of words in sentences – *syntax*.

17.1 Words as parts of speech

Words

First, you must remember that a **word** is a particular part of speech *by reason of the particular work that it does in a sentence*. It is not useful to look at a word in isolation and say, 'This word is a noun'; but it helps our understanding of grammar to look at a word in a sentence and say, 'This word is doing the work of a noun in this sentence'.

The same word may do different work – and, therefore, function as a different part of speech – in different sentences. For example:

1 A child's *top* lay on the floor. (noun)
2 We shall easily *top* last year's results. (verb)
3 He seems to be their *top* man. (adjective)

There are eight parts of speech: *nouns, pronouns, adjectives, verbs, adverbs, prepositions, conjunctions,* and *interjections.*

Nouns

A **noun** is a word used in a sentence to name someone or something. For example: '*Jane* was sitting in that *chair.*' 'They all showed great *loyalty* to their *team.*'

- A **common noun** names a member of, or an item in, a whole class of people or things. For example: 'It was a huge *book* of six hundred *pages.*' A common noun is the name *common to* all the members of or all the items in the class.

- A **proper noun** names a particular person, place or thing. For example: '*Jean* is the best swimmer in *London.*' The name 'Jean' is *proper to* (belongs to) Jean: it distinguishes her from the others. The name 'London' is proper to one particular place: it distinguishes it from the others. Proper nouns begin with capital letters.

- An **abstract noun** names a quality or a state of mind or feeling. For example: 'Marks will be be awarded for *accuracy* and *neatness.*' Abstract nouns name non-physical things, concepts that exist only in the mind: loyalty, honour, jealousy, anger, welfare.

- A **collective noun** names a group or collection of people or things: *crew, team, library, flock* are words that are often used as collective nouns.

Pronouns

A **pronoun** is a word used in a sentence to stand for (or in place of) a noun. For example: 'The plate was so hot that *it* burnt the table.'

- A **personal pronoun** stands for (or in place of) a person or thing. For example: 'Pass the ticket on to Robert if *you* don't want *it.*'

- A **demonstrative pronoun** points to or at a person or a thing. For example: 'I like *these* but they would not be as useful as *those.*'

- A **relative pronoun** relates to (refers to) a noun or pronoun used earlier in the sentence. That noun or pronoun is called its **antecedent**. For example: 'My purse was in the bag *that* I left on the counter.' (The antecedent of *that* is 'bag'.)

- An **interrogative pronoun** is used in some questions. For example: '*What* were you going to say?'

- A **pronoun of number or quantity** indicates how many or how much. For example: 'Customers are restricted to *three* because we have *few* left.'

Adjectives

An **adjective** is a word used in a sentence to describe ('qualify') the person or thing named by a noun or a pronoun. For example: 'The *little* boy was used to crossing *busy* streets.'

- A **descriptive adjective** qualifies a noun or a pronoun by describing its qualities. For example: 'Shall I wear my *green* dress?' A descriptive adjective may be separated from the noun or pronoun that it qualifies. For example: 'I think her dress was *green*.'

- A **possessive adjective** indicates possession or ownership. For example: 'Was *her* dress green?'

- A **demonstrative adjective** points to or at the noun or pronoun that it qualifies. For example: '*That* dress was hardly suitable for *this* occasion.'

- A **relative adjective** introduces a subordinate (or dependent) clause (see section 17.4) and links it to another clause. For example: 'We let them have *what* money we could spare.'

- An **interrogative adjective** is used in some questions. For example: '*What* train did you catch?'

- An **adjective of number or quantity** indicates how many or how much. For example: '*Few* customers showed *any* interest and we sold only *ten* books that day.'

Do not confuse adjectives with pronouns. An adjective is always used to *qualify* a noun or a pronoun. A pronoun always stands *in place of* a noun. For example: '*My* car [possessive adjective] is for sale and I want to put in a bid for *yours* [possessive pronoun].' 'Is *this* hat [demonstrative adjective] the right size?' 'No, but I think *that* [demonstrative pronoun] is.')

Verbs

A **verb** is a word used in a sentence to indicate action or being. For example: 'We *ran* for the train but we *were* too late.'

Person and number

There are three **persons** and two **numbers**. For example:

	Singular	*Plural*
1st person	I laugh	we laugh
2nd person	you laugh	you laugh
3rd person	he/she/it laughs	they laugh

Tense

The **tense** indicates the time in which the action takes place or the state of being exists: *present*, *past* or *future*. For example: 'I ride' (present); 'I rode' (past); 'I shall ride' (future).

Voice

There are two **voices**: *active* and *passive*. For example:

	Active	*Passive*
1	The mechanic repaired the car.	The car was repaired by the mechanic.
2	The expert is studying the evidence.	The evidence is being studied by the expert.

Transitive and intransitive

A verb is used **transitively** when it has an object. It is used **intransitively** when it does not have an object. For example:

	Transitive	*Intransitive*
1	She sang an aria.	She sang.
2	The government is negotiating a new treaty.	The government is negotiating.
3	They fought a good fight.	They fought hard.

When a verb is used transitively, the action is carried across (*trans-*) from the subject of the verb to the object of the verb. Many verbs can be used either transitively or intransitively.

Finite and non-finite verbs

A **finite verb** has a subject. Because it has a subject, it is 'limited' (made finite) by having person, number and tense. A **non-finite verb** does not have a subject; therefore, it does not have person, number or tense. The non-finite forms of the verb are: the *infinitive*, the *present participle*, the *past participle* and the *gerund*.

- The **infinitive** The verb-form containing the word 'to'. For example: *to walk; to read; to sing.*

- The **present participle** The verb-form ending with *-ing* and functioning as an adjective. For example: 'This is a *teasing* problem.' The present participle is also used with the verb 'to be' to form the **continuous**, or **imperfect**, tenses of verbs. For example: 'We *were waiting* for the bus.'

- The **past participle** Like the present participle, it functions as an adjective, but it does not end with *-ing*. It takes many different forms. For example: 'A *beaten* and unhappy team flew home.' '*Bought* bread does not taste like home-*baked* loaves.' 'The election resulted in a *hung* parliament.' The past participle is also used to combine with **auxiliary** (helping) verbs to form the **perfect** (completed) tenses and the passive voice of verbs. For example: 'Those greedy children *have finished* the cake.' 'Their offices *were raided* last week.'

- The **gerund** Like the present participle, it is a verb-form ending with *-ing* but, whereas the present participle functions as an *adjective*, the gerund functions as a *noun*. For example: 'The *dripping* tap kept us awake' (*dripping* is a present participle, functioning as an adjective qualifying the noun 'tap'); 'The steady *dripping* kept us awake' (*dripping* is a gerund, functioning as the noun subject of the verb 'kept').

Mood

- The **infinitive** has already been noted. For example: '*To be asked* for my ticket again annoyed me.'

- The **indicative** is the 'mood' in which statements are made or questions are asked. For example: 'He *was* quite angry, *wasn't* he?'

- The **imperative** is the 'mood' in which orders are given or requests are made. For example: '*Go* away!'

- The **subjunctive** has few uses in modern English and, in any case, since most verbs have the same form for both the subjunctive and the indicative, the question of its use hardly arises. However, it is still correct to use the subjunctive mood of the verb 'to be' when expressing a wish or stating a condition that is very unlikely to be fulfilled. For example: 'If I *were* a millionaire, I would endow a research centre for peace studies.' 'She would still be champion if she *were* a few years younger.'

Adverbs

An **adverb** is a word used in a sentence to add to the meaning of (to 'modify') a verb, an adverb, or an adjective. For example: 'We made the journey *quickly*.' 'We travelled *quite* comfortably.' 'It was not a *very* crowded train.'

Adverbs often, but by no means always, end with *-ly*. You cannot safely identify a part of speech by its form. Its *function in the sentence* is the decisive factor.

Simple adverbs

These may be classified as follows:

- **Adverb of time** For example: 'They always arrive *late*.' (arrive *when*? – late)
- **Adverb of place** For example: 'Stop *there*.' (stop *where*? – there)
- **Adverb of manner** For example: 'He works *well*.' (works *how*? – well)
- **Adverb of quantity, extent or degree** For example: 'I have eaten *enough*.' (eaten *how much*? – enough)
- **Adverb of number** For example: 'We wrote *twice*.' (wrote *how often*? – twice)

Interrogative adverbs

These are used to ask questions. For example: '*When* are you going?' '*Why* are you leaving?'

Relative adverbs

These connect two clauses (see section 17.4). A relative adverb *relates* the clause that it introduces to a word in another clause which it modifies. For example: 'May is the month *when* Paris looks its best.' (The relative adverb *when* joins the two clauses and it relates its own clause to and modifies the verb 'is'.)

Prepositions

A **preposition** is a 'relating' word. It introduces a phrase (see section 17.3) that contains a noun or a pronoun. It relates that noun or pronoun to a word elsewhere in the sentence. For example: 'I backed the car *into* the garage.' (The preposition *into* relates the noun 'garage' to the verb 'backed'.) 'We chose the house *at* the end.' (The preposition *at* relates the noun 'end' to the noun 'house'.)

Note that the preposition introduces a phrase: 'into the garage' functions as an adverb; 'at the end' functions as an adjective. The word *preposition* means 'placed before'. A preposition is always placed before a noun or a pronoun in the phrase that it introduces and it relates that noun or pronoun to another word. For example: 'There was a present *for* me.'

Many words can be used either as prepositions or as adverbs. For example: 'Leave the parcel *inside* the porch.' (The preposition *inside* relates the noun 'porch' to the verb 'leave'.) 'Leave the parcel *inside*.' (The adverb *inside* modifies the verb 'leave'.)

Conjunctions

A **conjunction** is a joining word. It joins two separate items in a sentence. It may be used to join one word to another. For example: 'Toast *and* marmalade, please.' It may be used to join one phrase to another. For example: 'It is a bad journey by rail *or* by road.' It may be used to join one clause to another. For example: 'The old man left a lot of money *but* his son soon spent it.'

- **Co-ordinating conjunctions** connect items that do the same work in the sentence. They are 'of equal standing'. In the three examples just given, the items are linked by a co-ordinating conjunction.
- **Subordinating conjunctions** connect subordinate clauses to main clauses (see section 17.4). For example: 'He went on working *although* he was tired.' 'The government lost support *because* it ran out of energy.'

Interjections

An **interjection** is a word or a group of words 'thrown into' a sentence to express a feeling (of surprise, boredom, tiredness, etc.). It has no grammatical connection with or function in the rest of the sentence. For example: '*Oh dear*, he is going to be late again.' '*Hello!* who's that?'

17.2 Inflexions

The grammar of some languages requires many changes of word-forms, or **inflexions**. For example, in German – a 'highly inflected' language – adjectives change their word-forms according to the person, gender, number and case of the nouns that they qualify. In this respect, English is an uncomplicated language. Adjectives do not change their forms. ('A *red* dress was hanging in the cupboard.' 'She always wore *red* dresses.')

Nevertheless, correct grammar demands *some* changes in word-forms, the chief of which occur in the use of:

- **Personal pronouns** For example: Kate and *I* were invited. They invited Kate and *me*.
- **Verb-forms** For example: The cause of many grammatical errors *is* [not 'are'] carelessly used inflexions.
- **Plural noun-forms** For example: *baby/babies*, but *donkey/donkeys*.
- **Comparative and superlative word-forms** For example: *sad/sadder/saddest; little/less/least; favourable/more favourable/most favourable*.

As you will see in section 17.5, inflectional errors crop up time and time again.

17.3 Phrases and sentences

Written English makes clear sense only when words are grouped together and positioned in sentences in grammatically correct ways. The rules that govern the arrangement of words in sentences are the rules of **syntax**. (*Syntax* = 'marshalling', 'setting out in order'.)

Phrases

A **phrase** is a group of words that does not make *complete* sense by itself:

1. in that photograph
2. sitting at the back
3. scorched by the sun

Each of those word groups makes some sense, but not complete sense. They are unfinished utterances.

Sentences

A **sentence** is a group of words that makes complete sense: it can stand on its own without the addition of other words. It is an *independent*, self-contained, finished utterance:

1. She smiled.
2. People could not hear.
3. The plants wilted.

Each of those word-groups makes an independent, self-contained, *finished* utterance. It does not need additional words to make sense, although its meaning can be *expanded* by the addition of a phrase:

1. She smiled in that photograph.
2. People sitting at the back could not hear.
3. Scorched by the sun, the plants wilted.

Subject and predicate

A sentence makes complete sense because it contains two parts: a *subject* and a *predicate*. The **subject** of a sentence is the part that *names* (identifies or announces) the person, idea or thing about which the sentence is saying something. The **predicate** of a sentence is the part that *says something* about the subject.

	Subject	*Predicate*
1	She	smiled.
2	People	could not hear.
3	The plants	wilted.

Every sentence must contain both of those parts. Take either away and it ceases to be a sentence, because it is no longer able to make an independent, self-contained, *finished* utterance.

How phrases work

A phrase does the work of an adjective *or* an adverb *or* a noun (see section 17.1):

1 That chair *by the fireplace* is his. (The adjective-phrase qualifies the noun 'chair'.)
2 They have gone *on holiday*. (The adverb-phrase modifies the verb 'have gone'.)
3 He hoped *to win*. (The noun-phrase is the object of the verb 'hoped'. It answers the question *what*? They hoped *what*? – to win.)

Many common errors in written English are caused by incorrect positioning of phrases. If you are clear about the work that a particular phase is doing, you will position it correctly.

Phrase structures

Phrases are classified according to the work they do (adjective-phrase; adverb-phrase; noun-phrase) *and* according to their structures.

Prepositional phrases

A **prepositional phrase** begins with a preposition:

1 The crowd pressed *against the barriers*. (The prepositional phrase functions as an adverb modifying the verb 'pressed'.)
2 A man *with a gun* was arrested. (The prepositional phrase functions as an adjective qualifying the noun 'man'.)

Participial phrases

A **participial phrase** begins with a present participle or with a past participle:

1 *Living in the country*, we were not used to crowds. (The participial phrase functions as an adjective qualifying the pronoun 'we'.)
2 *Bought at a sale*, the car was a bargain. (The participial phrase functions as an adjective qualifying the noun 'car'.)

Gerundive phrases

A **gerundive phrase** begins with a gerund:

1 *Practising daily* perfected his skill. (The gerundive phrase functions as a noun. It is the subject of the verb 'perfected'.)
2 She started *having nightmares*. (The gerundive phrase functions as a noun. It is the object of the verb 'started'.)

The gerund and the present participle both end with *-ing*, but they have different grammatical functions – and so do the phrases that they introduce. In the sentence 'Practising daily perfected his skill' the gerundive phrase functions as a noun. In the sentence 'Practising daily, he perfected his skill', *practising daily* functions as an adjective qualifying the pronoun 'he'.

A gerundive phrase always functions as a noun. A participial phrase always functions as an adjective. This is far from being a mere quibble.

Failure to recognise those two different functions is the cause of a great many errors in sentence construction.

Infinitive phrases

An **infinitive phrase** begins with an infinitive:

1 *To sit and mope* is no answer to the problem. (The infinitive phrase functions as a noun. It is the subject of the verb 'is'.)
2 They were ready *to go out*. (The infinitive phrase functions as adverb modifying the adjective 'ready'.)

Accurate and fluent written English depends on correct structuring of phrases and their correct positioning in sentences.

17.4 Kinds of sentences

The simple sentence

In the subject of a sentence the most important word is the subject-word. In the predicate of a sentence the most important word is the verb. Provided that those two words are present, you have a sentence:

1 Stunned by explosions, fish rise to the surface of a river.
2 Having spent too long on comprehension, candidates often hurry their summaries, with disastrous consequences.

	Subject	*Predicate*
1	Stunned by explosions, fish	rise to the surface of a river.
2	Having spent too long on comprehension, candidates	often hurry their summaries, with disastrous consequences.

	Subject-word	*Verb*
1	fish	rise
2	candidates	hurry

Each of the original sentences can be stripped down to its two essential components (the verb and its subject-word) and *remain a sentence*: 'Fish swim.' 'Candidates hurry.'

The term *simple* does not refer to the length of the sentence or to its intellectual content. It is a grammatical term, referring solely to the structure of the sentence: a structure that is built on *one* finite verb.

The simple sentence is the bedrock construction on which the writing of good English rests. All the other kinds of sentences are based on the simple sentence. They extend its framework, but they do not alter its fundamental structure.

The simple sentence provides the backbone of written English and, as you will see in section 17.5, many of the common errors arise because that backbone is broken; as happens when, for example, a writer splits a participial adjective-phrase away from the noun to which it refers, or separates a subject-word so far from its verb that he forgets to make them 'agree'.

Clauses and sentences

Many sentences contain *more than one* finite verb:

1. He *started* the car and *drove* down the street.
2. She *opened* her bag and *looked* in her purse, but it *was* empty.

There are two finite verbs in example 1 and three finite verbs in example 2. Put the same fact in different words: there are two *clauses* in example 1 and three *clauses* in example 2. A **clause** is a group of words containing a finite verb and forming part of a sentence.

Main (or independent) clauses

Each of the clauses in examples 1 and 2 above can stand on its own and make complete sense without the help of the others:

1. He started the car./He drove down the street.
2. She opened her bag./She looked in her purse./It was empty.

Clauses of that kind are called *main* (or *independent*) clauses. A **main clause** makes a self-contained, *finished* utterance. It can stand alone without needing help from another clause.

Subordinate (or dependent) clauses

Some clauses need help from other clauses to make complete sense. They cannot stand alone:

1. They rewarded the boy *who found the wallet*.
2. *When I feel tired*, I relax in the garden.
3. They were certain *that he would be elected*.

On their own, the italicised clauses cannot make complete sense. Clauses of that kind are subordinate (or dependent) clauses. A **subordinate clause** does not make a self-contained, finished utterance. It cannot stand alone. It needs help from the main clause. Such a clause is *subordinate* because it is 'lower in rank' than a main clause. It is *dependent* because its meaning depends on a main clause.

Subordinate clauses function as: adjective-equivalents (example 1 above); adverb-equivalents (example 2 above); noun-equivalents (example 3 above).

Sentences: simple; complex; double; multiple

Classified by grammatical structure, there are four kinds of sentences. Here is a checklist.

	Sentence class	*Grammatical structure*
1	**Simple**	*one* finite verb
2	**Complex**	*one* main clause AND *one or more* subordinate clauses
3	**Double**	*two* main clauses WITH OR WITHOUT subordinate clauses

4 Multiple   *more than two* **main clauses**
                        WITH OR WITHOUT **subordinate clauses**

Examples:

1 *Simple sentence (one finite verb)* Finding their hotel comfortable and welcoming, the travellers decided to rest in Melbourne for a few more days before continuing their long journey.

2 *Complex sentence (one main clause with, in this example, two subordinate clauses)* Because their hotel was comfortable and welcoming, the travellers decided that they would rest in Melbourne for a few more days before continuing their long journey.

3 *Double sentence (two main clauses without, in this example, subordinate clauses)* Their hotel was comfortable and welcoming and the travellers decided to rest in Melbourne for a few more days before continuing their long journey.

4 *Double sentence (two main clauses with, in this example, one subordinate clause)* Their hotel was comfortable and welcoming and the travellers, who had a long journey ahead, decided to rest in Melbourne for a few more days.

5 *Multiple sentence (in this example, three main clauses and no subordinate clauses)* Their hotel was comfortable and welcoming and the travellers decided to rest in Melbourne for a few more days, but their long journey lay ahead.

6 *Multiple sentence (in this example, three main clauses with two subordinate clauses)* Their hotel was comfortable and welcoming and the travellers decided to rest in Melbourne for a few more days but they knew that their journey, which was a long one, lay ahead.

The content of each of the six sentences is the same, but the simple sentence expresses it more directly and plainly than any of the others. Its greater effectiveness does not come solely from its verbal economy. It is, in fact, only one word shorter than the next most economical sentence (3), though nine words shorter than the wordiest (6). It is the best sentence because it is the most *sinewy*, all its parts held firmly together and in place. Even its nearest 'rival' (3) is looser ('... and ... and ...'). The rest are sprawling in comparison.

    This is not to argue that a simple sentence is always the best. For some purposes and on some occasions, one of the other structures will be more suitable. What the comparison does prove is that good written English depends very greatly on the care and skill with which sentence structures are selected and handled.

17.5 Common errors

Errors in 'agreement'

The verb must **agree with** its subject in number and in person. This is the rule of *subject/verb concord*.

Faults caused by 'attraction'

When the subject-word (noun or pronoun) is separated from its verb by nouns or pronouns of a different number, the verb may be 'attracted' to agree with a noun or a pronoun that is not its subject-word:

Wrong
1 A crate of empty bottles were left at the back door.
2 Recent technological developments of that long-known material, glass, has influenced industrial design.
3 A new computerised system controlling the stock and despatch of thousands of spare parts were installed at the factory.

Right
A crate of empty bottles *was* left at the back door.
Recent technological developments of that long-known material, glass, *have* influenced industrial design.
A new computerised system controlling the stock and despatch of thousands of spare parts *was* installed at the factory.

Collective noun subjects and their verbs

Treat a collective noun as a singular subject when the group or collection is thought of as a *whole* – as *one*. Treat it as a plural when the sense stresses that it comprises *separate members or items* and that they are being thought of as *individuals*:

Wrong
1 The government have lost support.
2 My family have lived in this house for a hundred years.
3 The crew was inoculated against various tropical diseases.

Right
The government *has* lost support.
My family *has* lived in this house for a hundred years.
The crew *were* inoculated against various tropical diseases.

This particular subject/verb problem spills over to pronouns and possessive adjectives referring to the collective noun subject. They must be made to agree with it. Be consistent and stick to the number you first settled on. A haphazard mixture of singulars and plurals is confusing:

Wrong
1 The government is being harried by their opponents.
2 The BBC has announced that they will not increase the fees that it has offered for racing coverage.
3 After a poor season, the Midlands club informs our sports editor that their new manager has its full confidence.

Right
The government is being harried by *its* opponents.
The BBC has announced that *it* will not increase the fees that *it* has offered for racing coverage.
After a poor season, the Midlands club informs our sports editor that *its* new manager has *its* full confidence.

Relative pronoun subjects

A relative pronoun is the subject of the verb in the subordinate clause that it introduces. The relative pronoun must agree with its antecedent, and the verb in the subordinate clause must agree with the relative pronoun:

	Wrong	Right
1	This is one of the best books that has been published by this enterprising firm.	This is one of the best books [plural antecedent of *that*] that *have* been published by this enterprising firm.
2	She is among those talented minor stars who has received consistently poor publicity.	She is among those talented minor stars [plural antecedent of *who*] who *have* received consistently poor publicity.
3	Scholarship is still indebted to research into the derivations and meanings of English placenames that were pioneered by Sir Frank Stenton.	Scholarship is still indebted to research [singular antecedent of *that*] into the derivations and meanings of English placenames that *was* pioneered by Sir Frank Stenton.

Other troublesome pronoun subjects

Difficulties arise with these pronouns: *anybody, anyone, each, either, everybody, everyone, neither, none*. Generally, they are treated as singulars:

	Wrong	Right
1	Anybody hoping to win a fortune on the pools are almost certain to be disappointed.	Anybody hoping to win a fortune on the pools *is* almost certain to be disappointed.
2	Neither of those proposals seem practical.	Neither of those proposals *seems* practical.
3	We do not impose decisions on our members, each of whom have a personal contract.	We do not impose decisions on our members, each of whom *has* a personal contract.

However, there are times when *none* is used in a plural sense to mean 'not any' rather than the clearly singular sense of 'not one'. The verb should then be plural. Many writers would prefer the latter of these versions: 'Although the box of eggs hit the floor from a considerable height, none was broken.'/'Although the box of eggs hit the floor from a considerable height, none were broken.'

The problem of the 'follow-up' pronouns and possessive adjectives is more acute. According to the rule, this sentence is correct; but is it sensible? 'When the victorious team arrived at the station, everybody rushed forward, shouting his head off in the excitement of the moment.' Surely 'shouting their heads off' would make better sense?

Again, the absence of 'common gender' personal pronouns and possessive adjectives makes for clumsiness or inaccuracy or both. The sentence 'Each UK citizen must show his passport at the barrier' is grammatically correct, but carries the nonsensical implication that all UK citizens are males! The 'official explanation' that, in such uses, 'he' means 'he or she' is pretty thin. Often *he or she* (*his or her*) will get us out of the difficulty, but repetition of the formula is clumsy. Often, plurals can perfectly well be substituted for singulars. Instead of 'Everyone wanting to pay by cheque must provide evidence of his identity', we can write 'People wanting ... of their identity.' Here, as always, hard and clear thinking is needed.

'Either ... or'/'neither ... nor' subjects

The construction involves two separate subjects and one verb. When both subjects are of the same person and number there is no difficulty. 'Either

Joan or Freda *is* certain to call.' 'Neither the children nor their grandparents *want* to go out.' When the two subjects are of different persons and/or number, the verb must agree with the *nearer* subject. 'Neither the pupils nor their teacher *welcomes* Monday morning.' 'Either one of my assistants or, in an emergency, I *am* available after closing hours.'

Parenthesis in subjects

The punctuation of what appears to be a double (and, therefore, a plural) subject may throw all the stress onto the first part of the subject. The verb then agrees with it. 'Truth-telling, and all its attendant inconveniences, seldom *attracts* a politician.' 'The new weapon, with its technicians, *was* flown out in great secrecy.' The punctuation is all-important. Remove the parenthetical commas and the subject is clearly plural.

Appositional words in subjects

Words in apposition to the subject-word must not be allowed to break subject/verb concord:

	Wrong	*Right*
1	The treasure-trove – coins, medals, precious stones – were sold.	The treasure-trove – coins, medals, precious stones – *was* sold.
2	Two wretched companies, the ill-fed and despairing residue of the rebel army, was captured.	Two wretched companies, the ill-fed and despairing residue of the rebel army, *were* captured.

'It' as a 'provisional' subject

Always singular, however 'attractive' the plurals that it may introduce. 'There seems little doubt that it *was* those blocked culverts that caused the flooding.'

'Here' and 'there'

Used as introductory adverbs, these are often mistaken for the subject of the verb:

	Wrong	*Right*
1	Here, in remarkably good condition, is the chancel, the altar and the east window of this great ruin.	Here, in remarkably good condition, *are* the chancel, the altar and the east window of this great ruin.
2	After the quiet introduction, there follows energetic and near-dissonant passages of great power.	After the quiet introduction, there *follow* energetic and near-dissonant passages of great power.

Wrong case

Nominative, accusative, genitive cases

- **Nominative case** The case of the subject-word.
- **Accusative (or objective) case** The case of the object-word *and* of the noun or pronoun following ('governed by') a preposition.
- **Genitive case** The case of a 'possessing' word.

Case in nouns

The genitive case is signalled by an **apostrophe**. (The rules are given in Chapter 18.) English nouns do not have special word-forms for the other cases. The commonest trouble spots in the use of genitive nouns are pinpointed and corrected in these examples:

	Wrong	*Right*
1	The tomatoe's on that stall are too dear.	The *tomatoes* on that stall are too dear.
2	That boys' handwriting is illegible.	That *boy's* handwriting is illegible.
3	Victorian girl's clothes look very odd to us.	Victorian *girls'* clothes look very odd to us.
4	He was knocked out in the third round of the mens' competition.	He was knocked out in the third round of the *men's* competition.
5	Several of Dicken's novels have been filmed.	Several of *Dickens'* (or *Dickens's*) novels have been filmed.

Personal pronouns

Nominative and accusative case forms are often misused:

	Wrong	*Right*
1	They are making an exception of you and I.	They are making an exception of you and *me*.
2	It is a good crop in warm areas, but not practicable for we who garden in the north.	It is a good crop in warm areas, but not practicable for *us* who garden in the north.
3	This group – it includes Jane, Rosie and I – moves off after they.	This group – it includes Jane, Rose and *me* – moves off after *them*.

Relative pronouns: 'who' (nominative) and 'whom' (accusative)

	Wrong	*Right*
1	We have appointed a principal whom we think will give leadership.	We have appointed a principal *who* we think will give leadership.
2	We have appointed a principal who we think the staff will support.	We have appointed a principal *whom* we think the staff will support.
3	We have appointed a principal to who we think the staff will respond.	We have appointed a principal to *whom* we think the staff will respond.

Personal pronouns in comparisons

Note the difference between these two sentences: (a) 'That firm is offering you a bigger salary than I.' (b) 'That firm is offering you a bigger salary than me.' The meaning of (a) is: 'That firm is offering you a bigger salary than I am offering you.' The meaning of (b) is: 'That firm is offering you a bigger salary than it is offering me.'

The genitive case of personal pronouns

Never use an apostrophe to mark the genitive of personal pronouns. The correct word-forms are: *mine, yours, his, hers, its, ours, yours, theirs.*

Note: *it's* is the contracted form of *it is.*

Wrong verb-forms

The verbs 'to lay' and 'to lie'

The verb 'to lay' must be used transitively; the verb 'to lie' must be used intransitively:

Wrong	*Right*
1 I was laying down when the door bell rang.	I was *lying* down when the door bell rang.
2 Lie the material on a flat surface.	*Lay* the material on a flat surface.
3 They have lain six courses of bricks.	They have *laid* six courses of bricks.

The verbs 'to raise' and 'to rise'

The verb 'to raise' must be used transitively; the verb 'to rise' must be used intransitively:

Wrong	*Right*
1 Rise the girder another foot.	*Raise* the girder another foot.
2 As the sun was raising, we rose the flag.	As the sun was *rising*, we *raised* the flag.

If you want an increase of pay, ask for a *rise* not a *raise,* or you may find yourself being hoisted off the floor!

'May' and 'can'

These are **defective verbs**, so called because they lack the full range of tenses and forms. (For example, there is not an infinitive 'to may', nor is there a future simple tense, 'I shall can'!) The other defective verbs are: *must, ought, shall, will.*

May and *can* have different meanings. Correct usage is illustrated by these examples:

1. *May* I go out?
2. You *may*, if you *can* afford the time.
3. He *can* play a good game but his form is erratic.
4. He *may* play a good game but he must be calm.
5. The Act says that we *may* not import livestock without a licence.

Phrases in the wrong places

This is a very common fault and one of the most serious that a writer can commit. Remember that a phrase does the work of an adjective *or* an adverb *or* a noun. (See pages 175–6.) A phrase cannot do its proper work unless it is put in its right place in the sentence:

	Wrong	*Right*
1	Old books are always in demand by collectors with coloured plates.	Old books with coloured plates are always in demand by collectors.
2	A rabbit is wanted for a little boy with floppy ears.	A rabbit with floppy ears is wanted for a little boy.
3	I remembered that I had not switched off the electric fire while running for the bus.	While running for the bus, I remembered that I had not switched off the electric fire.
4	Arriving at the ground late, the seats we wanted had been sold we found.	Arriving at the ground late, we found that the seats we wanted had been sold.
5	Alarmed by falling sales, millions were spent on advertising by the brewers.	Alarmed by falling sales, the brewers spent millions on advertising.

Pronouns used with vague or wrong reference

A pronoun must always be seen to refer clearly and accurately to the noun (or noun-phrase) that is its antecedent. Woolly use of pronouns – particularly *this*, *that*, *these*, *those* and *it* – is a frequent cause of poor communication in writing.

For example: The team's record had not been inspiring despite a splendid month in mid-season. *This* was a cause for concern, but *it* should be remedied shortly, our reporter was told. *This* accounted for falling gates, but the setback was temporary and *it* was improving. Supporters, the club said, should bear *this* in mind when reading the results and forming an opinion. *These* would improve drastically if *it* was given time.

Sudden shifts of voice, tense and person

	Wrong	*Right*
1	Once the plumber had found the leak it was able to be repaired quickly by him.	Once the plumber had found the leak *he was able to repair* it quickly.
2	The examiners referred to poor handwriting, reporting that you had difficulty in reading many scripts.	The examiners referred to poor handwriting, reporting that *they* had difficulty in reading many scripts.
3	Unfortunately, many people were bored by the sermon and lose interest in the message.	Unfortunately, many people were bored by the sermon and *lost* interest in the message.

18 Punctuation

LEAG	MEG	SEG	NEAB	WJEC	NICCEA	Topic	Date attempted	Date completed	Self Assessment
✓	✓	✓	✓	✓	✓	**Examinations and changes**			
✓	✓	✓	✓	✓	✓	**Coursework**			
✓	✓	✓	✓	✓	✓	**'Differentiation'**			
✓	✓	✓	✓	✓	✓	**An approach to the subject**			
✓	✓	✓	✓	✓	✓	**Speaking and listening**			
✓	✓	✓	✓	✓	✓	**Reading**			
✓	✓	✓	✓	✓	✓	**Ways and means**			
✓	✓	✓	✓	✓	✓	**Writing**			
✓	✓	✓	✓	✓	✓	**Practical writing**			

Correct **punctuation** plays a crucial part in the writing of clear English. The various marks are used to indicate:

1 *a stop or pause* – full stop, question mark, exclamation mark, comma, semicolon, dash;
2 *possession and omission* – apostrophe, ellipsis marks;
3 *direct speech or quotation* – inverted commas or quotation marks;
4 *apposition, bracketing, parenthesis* – pairs of commas, pairs of dashes, round brackets, square brackets;
5 *joining up* – hyphen.

18.1 Full stop .

The **full stop** is used:

1 *To mark the end of a statement sentence* This is its most important function. It is the sign that a self-contained utterance has been completed. It marks off a finished, independent statement from the one that follows. Every statement sentence must begin with a capital letter and end with a full stop. The full stop is also known as the **period** because it 'puts a period to' a sentence (brings it to an end).

2 *To mark an abbreviation* For example, *Oct.* = October. Note the difference between an **abbreviation** (*Nov.* = November) and a **contraction** (*Dr* = D(octo)r). Most writers use a full stop to mark an abbreviation but not to mark a contraction. However, many well-known and commonly used abbreviations (such as BBC) are *not* punctuated. **Acronyms** – abbreviations which can be pronounced as words, such as NATO and UNESCO – are never punctuated.

3 *To mark an omission (three full stops)* The three full stops marking an omission are called **ellipsis marks**. When they occur at the end of a sentence, they are followed by a full stop. Study these examples:

(a) Read the sentence 'Good written English ... clearly punctuated' and express its full meaning in your own words.
(b) Express the full meaning in your own words of the sentence beginning 'Good written English ...'.

18.2 Question mark ?

The **question mark** is used *to mark the end of a question sentence*. Do not use a full stop as well:

- Have you heard the news?

Do not use a question mark at the end of an *indirect* question:

- I asked whether you had heard the news.

18.3 Exclamation mark !

The **exclamation mark** is used *to mark the end of an exclamation, interjection or sharp command*. Do not use a full stop as well.

- He's dropped it!
- Oh dear! I shall be late.
- Hand it over!

Use an exclamation mark only when strictly necessary. Do not try to add emphasis or to draw attention to the point that you are making by using this overworked punctuation mark.

18.4 Comma ,

The **comma** is used in a variety of ways:

To separate words used in a series or list

- She bought tea, jam, milk and flour.

To separate phrases used in a series

- She walked quickly down the street, round the corner and into the main road.

To separate clauses used in a series

- She found the bus stop, waited a few minutes, got on the first bus and took an upstairs seat.

In general, when the last item in a series is joined on by *and* a comma is not used before the conjunction. (Conjunctions *join*, but commas *separate*.) However, the sense may sometimes require a final comma:

- She bought tea, jam, milk, bread, and butter.

The final comma may also be useful in making the sentence structure clearer, or to improve the rhythm of the sentence:

- The journey begins by bus, continues by ferry, and concludes by train.

Do not put a comma after the last word in a list:

- Nuts, ginger, cloves are the ingredients. (*Not* Nuts, ginger, cloves, are the ingredients.)
- Nuts, ginger and cloves are the ingredients. (*Not* Nuts, ginger and cloves, are the ingredients.)

In pairs, to mark off words in parenthesis

- Some candidates, it was clear, had misread the question.
- He is upset, I know, but he will get over it.

In pairs, to mark off words in apposition

- Jones, the man responsible, is to be relied on.
- They sent their senior representative, the district inspector, the next day.

To mark off the beginning of direct speech or a quotation

- The witness replied, 'I have no knowledge of that.'
- Look at the line beginning, 'Now the setting sun …'.

Remember that the presence or absence of a comma (or of a pair of commas) can change – or even destroy – the meaning of a sentence. For example, these two sentences are worded identically, but their meanings are different:

- The language questions, which are compulsory, must be answered on the special sheet provided. (*All* the language questions are compulsory.)
- The language questions which are compulsory must be answered on the special sheet provided. (*Some* of the language questions are compulsory.)

Which of the two sentences is correctly punctuated depends on what the writer meant to say.

The use of a comma to separate main clauses is often a matter of choice. I chose to use a comma to separate the two main clauses in this sentence because I wanted to bring out a contrast:

- These two sentences are worded identically, but their meanings are different.

It would not have been wrong to omit the comma after 'identically'.

Generally, a comma is not needed between two main clauses having the same subject.

- They were nearly home when they ran out of fuel.

However, there will be occasions when a pause (marked by a comma) will add something to the sense or make it clearer:

- They were nearly home and they were confident of winning, when they ran out of fuel.

Most writers would argue for the comma in that sentence.

18.5 Semicolon ;

The **semicolon** is used in two ways:

To separate items in a list when the items themselves contain commas

- Accessories for this model include: supplementary lenses, ranging from 28 mm to 400 mm; dedicated electronic flash; filters, for both colour and black-and-white film; an aluminium-framed hold-all.

To separate clauses the sense of which would be weakened if they were split off into new sentences

- When we started, we hoped to complete the cataloguing in six months; but, after a year, we had not made much progress.
- Baffled by the absence of clues, the investigators were looking for a new lead; they suspected that one might have been overlooked in the initial confusion.

18.6 Colon :

The **colon** is used in these ways:

To introduce a list

- The following items will be sold on Tuesday: livestock, hay, implements, gates and fencing.

To introduce a quotation or lengthy items of direct speech

- Keats wrote: 'A thing of beauty is a joy for ever'; and critics have been arguing about its meaning ever since.
- The precise words in the agreement are: 'We shall waive our customary practice in your case and free you from the obligation to maintain the paths.'

To mark a dramatic break between two main clauses

- Man proposes: God disposes.
- They cannot win: we cannot lose.
- We do not know: we have faith.

To introduce a clause that explains or expands on a statement made in an earlier clause

- The seedlings are in a bad way: there has been no rain for a month.
- I received a rebate from the Inland Revenue: a great surprise.

18.7 Apostrophe '

The **apostrophe** is used in two ways:

To mark the genitive case of a noun

1. Singular noun: add *'s*
   - *book* The *book's* pages were defaced.

2. Plural noun ending with *s*: add *'*
   - *books* The *books'* previous owner was at the sale.
   - *fairies* The *fairies'* wings came off in the amateur pantomime.

   Remember: it is the number of the genitive (possessing) noun that matters, not the number of the possessed noun. Compare the following: 'Those are my boy's books.'/'He played for the boys' under-11 team'.

3. Plural noun not ending with *s*: add *'s*
   - *men* Use the *men's* entrance.
   - *mice* There are *mice's* nests in the attic.

4. Proper noun ending with *s*: add *'* or *'s*
   - *Marks*   Marks' (or *Marks's*) bowling has improved.
   - *Dickens* Which of *Dickens'* (or *Dickens's*) novels have you read?

   Generally, add *'s*; but you may think that 'Ulysses' bow' *sounds* better than 'Ulysses's bow'. Either word-form is correct.

5. When two (or more) proper nouns share the ownership, mark the one nearer (or nearest) to the 'possessed' noun:
   - Pete and Dud*'s* comic act delighted us.

To mark the omission of a letter or letters

- They *can't* (cannot) pay.
- *He'll* (He will) write soon.
- Ten *o'clock* (of the clock).

18.8 Inverted commas ' ' " "

Inverted commas are also called **quotation marks** or **speech marks**. Either single marks (' ') or double marks (" ") may be used. Inverted commas are used as follows:

In direct speech to indicate the words actually spoken

- 'I can hear a noise in the basement,' Bill said.
- Bill said, 'I can hear a noise in the basement.'

- 'I can hear a noise,' Bill said, 'in the basement.'

Note that *only the words actually spoken* are enclosed in the quotation marks.

In quotations within quotations

- The policeman asked Bill, 'Did you say, "I heard a noise in the basement"?'

In that example double quotation marks were used inside single quotation marks. It is also correct to use single marks inside double:

- The policeman asked Bill, "Did you say, 'I heard a noise in the basement'?"

Note that the question mark was included with the words actually spoken by the *policeman*, who was asking Bill a question. But *Bill's* quoted words did not include a question mark, since they took the form of a statement not a question.

To indicate the title of a film, book, play, poem, newspaper

- Have you seen 'Stars Wars'?
- Do you read 'The Trumpet'?
- I learnt Keats's poem 'Ode to Autumn' by heart.

Titles are sometimes underlined or italicised instead of being enclosed within quotation marks:

- There is an excellent account in *Racing Times*.

Remember that quotation marks are never used in reported speech (nor are question marks):

- *Direct speech* Their lawyers asked, 'Are you ready to sign the contract?'
- *Reported speech* Their lawyers enquired whether we were ready to sign the contract.

18.9 Dash –

The dash is used in four ways:

As a pause mark before an explanation

- They sold their heirlooms – furniture, pictures, books.

To separate a 'summing up' from the items preceding it

- The gearbox, transmission, suspension – all constitute a revolutionary design concept.

To enclose a parenthesis, instead of paired commas or round brackets

- If this parenthesis – the part between the dashes – were left out, the remainder would still constitute a meaningful sentence.

To show a range
- Monday–Friday
- 1939–45

Be on your guard. The dash is often overworked. Do not use it carelessly as a substitute for a full stop or a comma.

18.10 Round brackets ( )

Round brackets are used in two ways:

To enclose additional information or explanations
- Hardy's long life (1840–1928) spanned the reigns of three monarchs.

To enclose apposition or parenthesis
- After his death, his impoverished widow sold his finest painting (the portrait of Sir Digby Wood) to a scoundrelly dealer for £25.

A pair of dashes may be used for this purpose instead of round brackets. Both dashes and brackets should be reserved for occasions when a pair of commas does not provide a strong enough effect.

18.11 Square brackets [ ]

Square brackets are used to indicate that a word or words included in quoted matter are not part of the original material:
- Johnson answered, 'I have no doubt that they [the poems of Ossian] are forgeries.'

18.12 Hyphen -

The hyphen is used in these ways:

To join up two (or more) words that are regarded as a compound word
- mother-in-law; twenty-two; self-contained

Many expressions begin as hyphenated words and lose the hyphen with continued use:
- sea-plane/seaplane; look-out/lookout

Remember that the presence or absence of a hyphen can change the meaning of a word:
- They hope to recover that valuable chair.
- They hope to re-cover that valuable chair.

To indicate that an unfinished word at the end of a line is completed at the beginning of the next line

- The scientists are still looking for the answer.

Remember that the unfinished word must be split at the end of a syllable; and that the hyphen must be placed at the *end* of the line, not at the beginning of the next.

Spelling 19

LEAG	MEG	SEG	NEAB	WJEC	NICCEA	Topic	Date attempted	Date completed	Self Assessment
✓	✓	✓	✓	✓	✓	Examinations and changes			
✓	✓	✓	✓	✓	✓	Coursework			
✓	✓	✓	✓	✓	✓	'Differentiation'			
✓	✓	✓	✓	✓	✓	An approach to the subject			
✓	✓	✓	✓	✓	✓	Speaking and listening			
✓	✓	✓	✓	✓	✓	Reading			
✓	✓	✓	✓	✓	✓	Ways and means			
✓	✓	✓	✓	✓	✓	Writing			
✓	✓	✓	✓	✓	✓	Practical writing			

19.1 Self-help

English spelling does present some difficulties, but not nearly so many as people like to believe when they are excusing themselves for being bad spellers. The main causes of bad spelling are inattention and laziness – not the problems inherent in English orthography. Tackle your spelling difficulties on the lines suggested here and you will reach the required standard by the time you take your examination.

Visualise and syllabise

Pay attention to the look of words as you read and when you use your dictionary: *observe* their spelling. Look at and remember their *syllables*; not all of which may be sounded in their correct pronunciation, but all of which are present in their correct spelling (*vet/er/in/ary*). Look at and remember **silent letters**, too. Some seem to be silent because they are not pronounced in sloppy speech (Feb*r*uary; arc*t*ic). Some *are* silent because they are not pronounced in correct speech (de*b*t; vic*t*ualler).

Prefixes and suffixes

The commonest of all spelling errors occur at word joints, where a prefix is affixed at the beginning of a word or a suffix is affixed at the end (see section 15.4). There is no excuse for misspelling (mi*s* + *s*pelling) 'disappoint' (di*s* + appoint), 'dissatisfy' (di*s* + *s*atisfy) or 'keenness' (kee*n* + *n*ess), to give just a few examples of the kind of words that are frequently the cause of lost marks.

Pinpoint your mistakes

When you misspell a word, you do not get all of it wrong. You make the mistake at a particular point. Look it up. Write it out, underlining your trouble spot(s) – to<u>bacc</u>o, ac<u>comm</u>odation, pa<u>rall</u>el. Learn it.

Donkey work

There is only one way to get better at spelling: work at it. The advice given here will help you to approach spelling intelligently, but it cannot remove the hard labour.

1. Resolve not to repeat your mistakes.
2. Make a list of the words you get wrong – and *learn* them.
3. Invent your own ways of avoiding your besetting errors. I used to have trouble with *mantelpiece*. I put it right by working out this **mnemonic**: 'You don't put a mant*le* on a mant*el*piece'. It may sound silly to you, but it cured me of misspelling *mantelpiece*.
4. Face the fact that you will simply have to memorise the correct spelling of some words by repeating it over and over again. It is a long time now since I went wrong with 'ono-mato-p-o-e-i-a' (= *onomatopeia*); but it took hard work to fix it in my memory. I did it partly by the syllables, partly by individual letters – and mostly by sheer determination to get it right.

19.2 Trouble spots

Study these examples. Whenever you misspell a word in one of these categories, add it to the list and learn it.

Silent-letter words
- Silent *b*: bom*b*, clim*b*, lam*b*
- Silent *g*: desi*g*n, *g*nash, si*g*n
- Silent *k*: *k*nife, *k*nob, *k*nuckle
- Silent *p*: *p*neumonia, *p*sychic, recei*p*t
- Silent *w*: *w*rap, *w*restle, *w*rist

Words containing *au*
- *au*ction, g*au*ge, somers*au*lt

Words containing *ua*
- eq*ua*l, q*ua*lify, q*ua*y

Words spelt with *gh*
- silent *gh*: bou*gh*, fou*gh*t, thorou*gh*
- *gh* = *f*: cou*gh*ing, lau*gh*ter, trou*gh*
- *gh* = *g*: *gh*astly, *gh*etto, *gh*ost

Words spelt with *ph*
- Beginning *ph*: *ph*easant, *ph*ysical, *ph*ysics
- Ending *ph*: autogra*ph*, paragra*ph*, trium*ph*
- Containing *ph*: em*ph*atic, ne*ph*ew, sym*ph*ony

Words spelt with *ch*
- *ch* = *k*: a*ch*ing, *ch*emist, s*ch*eme
- 'soft' *ch*: ba*ch*elor, ma*ch*inery, whi*ch*

Words spelt with *tch*

- bu*tch*er, ma*tch*, wre*tch*

Double-letter words

- *bb*: a*bb*reviate, ra*bb*it, ru*bb*ish
- *cc*: a*cc*elerate, a*cc*ording, o*cc*ur
- *dd*: a*dd*ress, mu*dd*le, su*dd*en
- *ff*: a*ff*ord, para*ff*in, to*ff*ee
- *gg*: a*gg*ravate, lu*gg*age, su*gg*est
- *ll*: co*ll*ision, exce*ll*ent, pi*ll*ar
- *mm*: co*mm*and, co*mm*on, gra*mm*ar
- *nn*: begi*nn*ing, cha*nn*el, tyra*nn*y
- *pp*: a*pp*arent, a*pp*oint, su*pp*ort
- *rr*: ba*rr*el, ca*rr*iage, qua*rr*el
- *ss*: dismi*ss*, hara*ss*ed, profe*ss*ion
- *tt*: a*tt*itude, le*tt*uce, ma*tt*ress

19.3 Word groups

Grouping words by their beginnings or endings is a useful way of remembering how to spell them. Bear these classifications in mind and add to the examples provided.

Beginning *des-*

- *des*cribe, *des*erve, *des*troy

Beginning *dis-*

- *dis*astrous, *dis*cipline, *dis*solve

Ending *-ance* or *-ant*

- assist*ance*, nuis*ance*, ten*ant*

Ending *-ence* and *-ent*

- abs*ence*, pres*ent*, promin*ence*

Ending *-al*

- education*al*, horizont*al*, municip*al*

Ending *-el*

- chap*el*, chis*el*, parc*el*

Ending *-le*

- ax*le*, musc*le*, vehic*le*

Ending -sion

- colli*sion*, occa*sion*, transmis*sion*

Ending -tion

- ambi*tion*, parti*tion*, voli*tion*

Ending -ar

- calend*ar*, irregul*ar*, simil*ar*

Ending -er

- cylind*er*, travell*er*, surrend*er*

Ending -or

- corrid*or*, govern*or*, interi*or*

Ending -our

- col*our*, harb*our*, vig*our*

Note that when a noun ending with *-our* adds *-ous* (to form an adjective), *u* is dropped from *-our*:

- glam*our* but glam*or*ous
- hum*our* but hum*or*ous
- vig*our* but vig*or*ous

19.4 Common confusables

Homophones and near-homophones (see section 15.5) are often confused. Take care when using the words in this list:

- accept/except;
- access/excess;
- affect/effect;
- allusion/illusion;
- altar/alter;
- ascent/assent;
- capital/capitol;
- choose/chose;
- clothes/cloth;
- coarse/course;
- complement/compliment;
- conscience/conscious;
- council/counsel;
- dairy/diary;
- descent/decent;
- desert/dessert;
- dual/duel;
- dyeing/dying;
- formally/formerly;
- later/latter;
- lead/led;
- loose/lose;
- peace/piece;
- personal/personnel;
- principal/principle;
- quiet/quite;

- respectfully/respectively;
- stationary/stationery;
- their/there;
- to/too/two;
- weather/whether.

19.5 Some spelling rules

Some of the traditional spelling rules are complicated and riddled with exceptions. The donkey work recommended earlier in this chapter yields much better results. However, there are a few comparatively simple rules to which there are not many exceptions.

Rule 1

The prefix/suffix rule (see section 19.1). Never add or subtract a letter at the 'joint' in a word:

- dis*s*ervice, mis*u*nderstand, under*r*ate

Rule 2

With *suc(c)-*, *ex-* and *pro-*, double *e* must go. By applying that rule, you can remember how to spell prec*ee*ding and proc*ee*ding and similar words:

- exc*ee*d, succ*ee*d, proc*ee*d (but proc*e*dure)
- conc*e*de, prec*e*de, rec*e*de

Rule 3

i before *e* when the sound is *e*, except after *c*. Thus, when the sound is *e*:

- *ie* ach*ie*ve, gr*ie*f, p*ie*ce
- *ei* conc*ei*t, dec*ei*ve, rec*ei*ve

Here, though, is an exception:

- *seize* breaks the rule – *e* sound; no *c*; but *ei*

When the sound is not *e*:

- *ie* cr*ie*d, f*ie*rce, fr*ie*nd
- *ei* *ei*ght, r*ei*n, th*ei*r

Rule 4

When a word ends with *-e* and you add to it, drop the *e* when the addition begins with a vowel or *y*:

- acquir*e*/acquiring; bon*e*/bony; hat*e*/hating

Note that words ending with *-ce* or *-ge* keep the *e* when the addition is *-able* or *-ous*:

- courage/courag*eous*; notice/notic*eable*

Rule 5

When a word ends with *e* and you add to it, keep the *e* when the addition begins with a consonant:

- advance/advancement; hate/hateful; like/likewise

Some exceptions:

- argue/argument; awe/awful; due/duly; true/truly

Rule 6

Most words ending with a single consonant double that consonant when an addition beginning with a vowel is made:

- blot/blotting/blotted; mat/matting/matted
- begin/beginning; transmit/transmitted; propel/propelling
- refer/referring; signal/signalled; travel/traveller

Some exceptions:

- develop/developing/developed
- limit/limiting/limited
- profit/profiting/profited

Rule 7

When *-full* is joined to another word, it loses one *l*:

- boast + full → boastful
- fear + full → fearful

Rule 8

When *-full* is joined to another word ending with double *l*, each word loses one *l*:

- full + fill → fulfil (*but* fulfilled)
- skill + full → skilful (*but* skilfully)
- will + full → wilful (*but* wilfully)

Rule 9

A word that ends with double *l* loses one *l* when it is joined to another word:

- all + so → also
- well + fare → welfare

Rule 10

Words ending with *-our* drop the *u* when *-ous* is added:

- humour/humorous; valour/valorous; vigour/vigorous

Rules for plurals

1. Most words add -s: lamp/lamps.

2. Most words ending with -o add -es:
   - tomato/tomatoes

   Some exceptions:
   - cuckoo/cuckoos; piano/pianos; solo/solos; studio/studios

3. Words ending with *consonant* + *y* change the *y* into *i* and add -es:
   - memory/memories; lady/ladies

4. Words ending with *vowel* + *y* keep the *y* and add -s:
   - donkey/donkeys; toy/toys

5. Words ending with -f or -fe change the *f* or *fe* into *v* and add -es:
   - calf/calves; half/halves; loaf/loaves

   An exception:
   - roof/roofs

6. A few words change their vowels:
   - foot/feet; goose/geese; man/men; tooth/teeth

7. A very few make no change:
   - deer/deer; salmon/salmon; sheep/sheep

20 Presentation and handwriting

LEAG	MEG	SEG	NEAB	WJEC	NICCEA	Topic	Date attempted	Date completed	Self Assessment
✓	✓	✓	✓	✓	✓	**Examinations and changes**			
✓	✓	✓	✓	✓	✓	**Coursework**			
✓	✓	✓	✓	✓	✓	**'Differentiation'**			
✓	✓	✓	✓	✓	✓	**An approach to the subject**			
✓	✓	✓	✓	✓	✓	**Speaking and listening**			
✓	✓	✓	✓	✓	✓	**Reading**			
✓	✓	✓	✓	✓	✓	**Ways and means**			
✓	✓	✓	✓	✓	✓	**Writing**			
✓	✓	✓	✓	✓	✓	**Practical writing**			

20.1 Purpose

'The case against a man accused of a drink-driving offence was adjourned by Huddersfield magistrates because no one could read the handwriting of the doctor asked to give a medical report.' This newspaper report of an occurrence in a north of England court suggests an irony. A man had been arrested on a charge of being unfit to control a vehicle. Part of the evidence submitted to the court suggested that a certain doctor was unfit to control a writing implement! As a result of the driver's alleged behaviour, life and property could well have been at risk. In the case of the doctor's actions, time and effort were wasted.

People throughout the world spend billions of hours a day communicating with one another. Mistakes happen; misunderstandings occur. The attempted elimination of the irritating, troublesome, and sometimes tragic, consequences of these lapses in effective communication should be one of our personal aims in life. As individuals we have a moral duty to be clear and straightforward in our dealings with others.

The ways in which we present our ideas – whether in speech or on paper – are partly determined by the technical skills we possess and partly by our determination to succeed. Some people have a gift for good presentation. They may speak in apparently effortlessly or they may be able to write in a style that is attractive. Others have to strive to succeed. Yet technological advances mean that assistance is readily available. Recent generations have been the first in history to see and hear themselves on film and tape. Individuals can carefully scrutinise their own manner of speaking *without* asking for the opinions of others. Typewriters, word-processors and desk-top publishing have become standard equipment for those who 'trade in the written word'. The sophisticated elements of these machines promote clever and reliable features of layout and presentation. Even the humble pen, with its relatively modern features of constant ink supply, all-purpose point or nib and low cost, is no longer an instrument to torture the user.

The National Curriculum has required the examination boards to take **presentation** and **handwriting** into account when assessing scripts. This is part of an attempt to raise standards, to make candidates conscious of their responsibility to produce clear and legible work, and to establish some sort of quality control. The attempted elimination of wasted time and effort is part of any management reform ... and this is no exception.

20.2 Ways of looking

Clarity, euphony (having an attractive sound) and simplicity are said to be the three qualities necessary for a good style of expression for both the written and spoken word. When it comes to the actual features of handwriting, then these need to be amended slightly. Judgement is primarily made on how *clear* it is to read. *Attractiveness* matters, especially when there are pages of script. *Simplicity* is important because complicated styles need working out – and that can take unnecessary time and effort.

Yet it would be misleading to suggest that good presentation can be determined by improved handwriting alone. The necessary steps to achieve high standards in this area are threefold and involve ways of looking at the overall effects:

- consider the disciplines that are vital;
- think of the elements that require attention;
- formulate the strategy that is needed.

1. The *disciplines* required are order and consistency.
2. The *elements* are letters, words, sentences and paragraphs.
3. The *strategy* involves structure, size, space and shape.

20.3 The disciplines

Although human beings have ways of creating chaos, waste and devastation, one of the attributes of humankind is the ability to impose order and uniformity on what appears to be disorganised. Some people are particularly good at this – literally, in a big way. They can see how global and space projects can be formulated, or political movements inspired, or religious creeds spread. Many people see things on a smaller scale and have tidy minds that can make day-to-day living relatively easy. A common feature is this ability to place objects or ideas in some sort of manageable order and to see that this is consistently maintained.

There are problems with a mental state that is *exclusively* devoted to imposing orderliness. A person can become obsessed with quantity, rank and sequence to the detriment of quality and beauty. Imaginative powers can be inhibited and irritation caused by unnecessary factors. Yet in such specialised matters as examinations we have to be able to recollect what we have studied, collect the relevant topics into significant groups, and present them in an orderly way. Examiners complain that many candidates fail to put their thoughts into meaningful sequences.

Imagine that you have presented an examiner with a script that is neatly written, with clear sentence constructions. Add to this that you have divided your topics into paragraphs and contained them within the demands of the question. What is his or her reaction going to be to the inevitable errors that you have made in areas of your compositions? The answer is – a sympathetic response. You will not be passed on the strength of your presentation, but you will gain respect. This can be a decisive matter.

So do concentrate on imposing order on all aspects of your writing and be consistent in maintaining it throughout each task.

20.4 The elements

Let us look for a moment at the four elements that require this disciplined approach.

Letters

At least ten years have probably been spent developing the style of handwriting you were taught at school. You may not consider that the time has come for a radical change, but look carefully at the ways in which you produce individual letters of the alphabet. Could they be clearer? Ask someone whose opinion you value to make a judgement. If you then feel that the time has come for you to develop a new style, make a study of it. Go to your library and borrow a book on handwriting or calligraphy. Study the next section of this book and see how by the application of the four 'S' words – structure, size, space, shape – you can make crucial alterations which will give a new dynamic to your handwriting.

Words

The effective linking of your letters makes words, which are the most vital units for instant recognition. Their construction as well as choice is important. Construction is dealt with in the next section, while vocabulary-building in order to promote choice is something that you have been encouraged to do throughout this book. A wide vocabulary, which you can call upon for accuracy, variation and interest, is a great help in the presentation of ideas.

Sentences

The ability to construct a sentence that has the right proportions and which contains sufficient information is a skill to be prized. It gives the reader the confidence that you are in charge of your subject, and keen to present your ideas in an orderly manner with a logical development. If in doubt, return to section 17.4 and study the relevant examples.

Paragraphs

A balance is necessary between the presentation of a short paragraph, consisting of one or two sentences in which the subject is not developed, and a long paragraph where the reader's attention span is tested. The secret of success is to have one topic in mind that is to be dealt with by the paragraph; by and large, the paragraph should not consist of more than six sentences. The first sentence should refer to the topic that is being introduced. The second and subsequent sentences should define, expand and illustrate that topic. The final sentence should conclude the topic, and perhaps anticipate the subject of the following paragraph. The creation of a page in which the paragraphs are decisively produced is a great asset in the business of presentation.

20.5 The four 'S' words

Structure your letters of the alphabet so that they take into account the needs of those who are reading them. They can have flourishes and twists, tails and squiggles – that choice will reflect your style – but when examinations are involved then they must be **legible**. Legibility depends upon clarity. So above all, be clear.

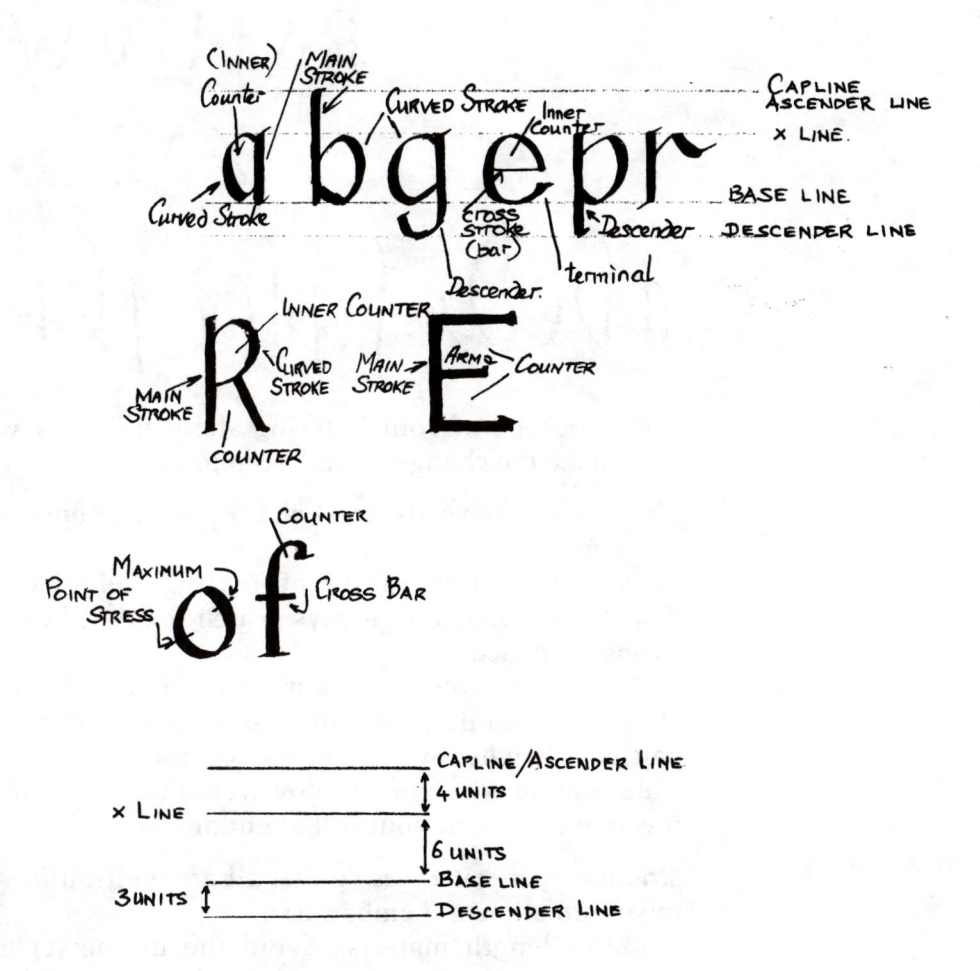

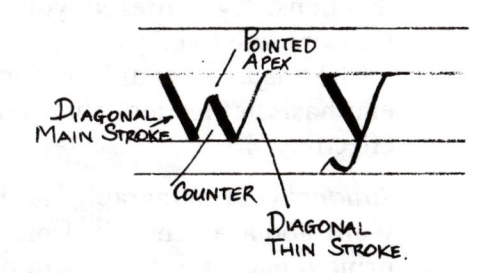

The *size* of your lettering matters. Look at the lines that are available on the paper that you normally use, and resolve to keep within them. The diagram shows you that letters are made within a grid that is ten units high from the **base line** to the **cap. line**. The **x line** is six units above the base; the descender line is three units beneath it. Use the guidelines and keep within the confines!

Look closely at the individual letters and consciously observe where the so-called 'counters' are to be found. Make a note of your counters as you create them and allow enough space within each.

a b c d e f g h i j k l m n o p q r s t u v w
x y z

A B C D E F G H I J K L M N O P Q
R S T U V W
X Y Z

a b c d e f g h i j k l m n o p

If the shape of your lettering alters and your writing becomes clearer, then make the change ... and keep to it.

Structure your words so that they vary. Repetition deadens; variation enlivens.

The *size* of words can be off-putting. Being accurate is more important than being brief, but always search for the shorter word. It may make a stronger impact.

The *space* between words must be enough to signal that the division is absolute. Reading is done at speed and misunderstandings occur particularly when words are run together.

Be conscious as you employ words that you are *shaping* ideas. They are precious and merit your full attention.

Structure your sentences so that all are well-built. Avoid flaws and so save misinformation and embarrassment.

Size or length matters. Avoid the undue terseness that results from repeatedly using short sentences or the feeling of breathlessness that results from employing too many words.

The same rule about visual *spacing* between words applies to sentence divisions. Try to present your subject within one sentence and do not allow it to straddle two.

The *shape* of your sentences should fit neatly into the paragraph. If emphasis is needed, then end the paragraph with a short sentence. It's effective.

Structure your paragraphs so that they stand out on the page. Insert the first word about an inch in from the margin. This is not always done on the printed page, but it helps to present the handwritten paragraph.

The *size* of the paragraph should usually be between three and six sentences. Longer blocks of writing or print tend to weary the eye.

Effective *spacing* can be achieved by leaving a line between each paragraph.

In fact, the *shape* of the layout of an article, advertisement or essay is partly determined by the use of the space rather than by the impact of the written or printed word.

Train yourself to stand back and look at the outlines made by your handiwork. If it's to read well, it should be good to look at.

21 Reference material

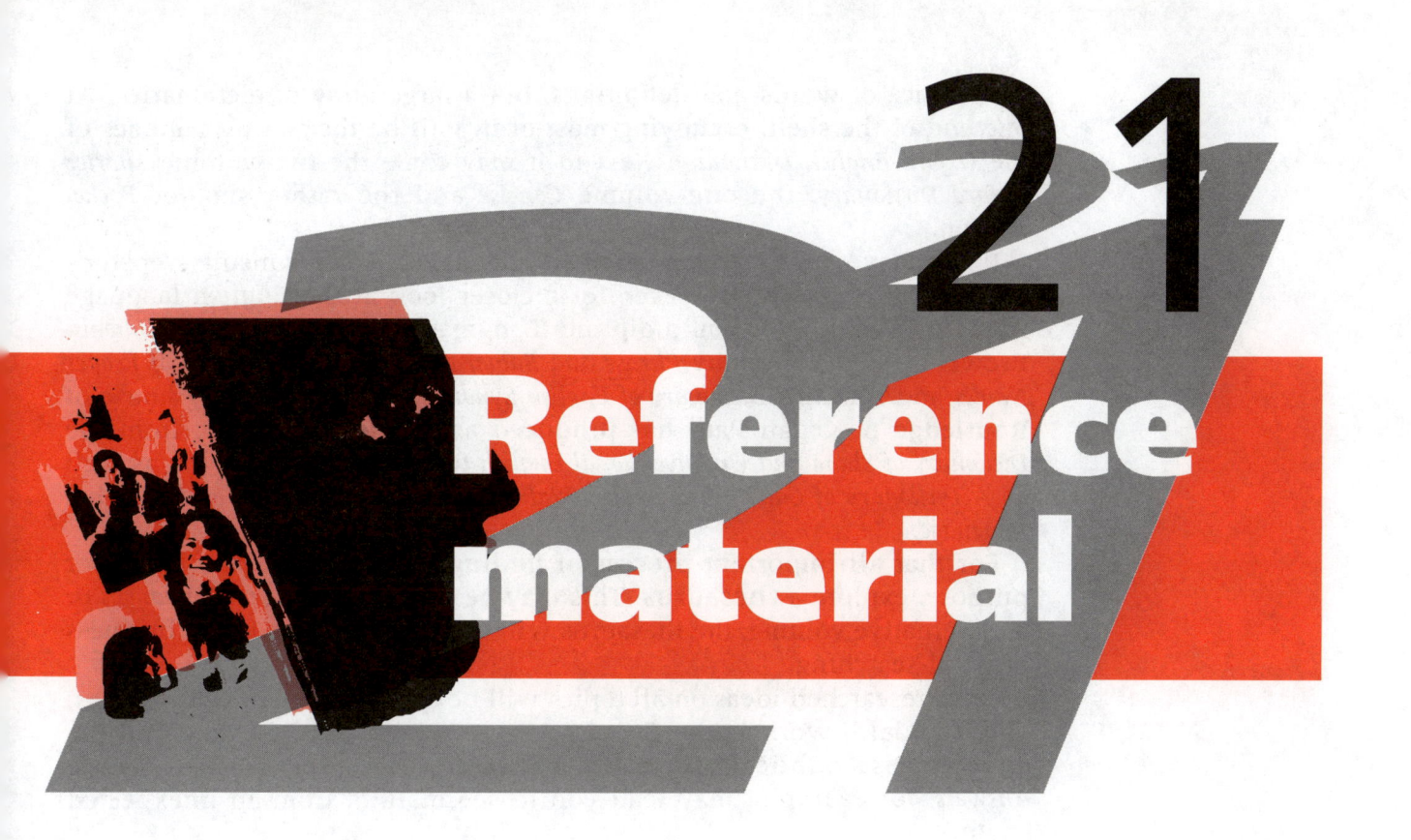

Much of this book has been devoted to directives about ways of speaking, reading, writing, making sense of words and putting them in sensible constructions.

Now is the time to invite you to look a little wider. References to the complete range of human activities are to be found, stored conveniently, on the open shelves of any medium-sized public **library**. These **reference sections** have been developed throughout the 20th century, but in the past few years they have reflected the dynamic growth of recorded information. 'All human life is there' – at least written material on:

- people;
- places;
- ideas;
- events;
- trends;
- activities;
- words.

These resources are often overlooked by people as they may appear to have the 'specialist' tag about them. Yet the information here is immensely useful for everyday needs, especially when it comes to matters of success in examinations of all kinds. Here there are:

- *knowledge* – pure, simple … as well as complex;
- *answers* – to questions posed in the school, the college and the company;
- *stimulus* – for coursework and essay responses;
- *interest* – topics that might appeal to you and which might even lead to your promotion.

Let us begin with words. They are stored by the million, even in a relatively small reference library. A number of prominent publishers produce **dictionaries**; each has its merits. The 'standard' work in this area is published by the Oxford University Press and you will find not just a vast choice of words and definitions, but a large array of dictionaries. At one end of the shelf, occupying most of it, will be the twenty volumes of the *Oxford English Dictionary*. Next to it may come the two-volume *Shorter Oxford Dictionary*, the one-volume *Concise* and the rather smaller *Pocket* edition.

If you have an American interest you may wish to consult Webster's range of dictionaries. However, for a closer look at the English language from other angles you could dip into Longman's *Dictionary of English Idioms*, Brewer's *Twentieth Century Phrase and Fable*, the *Penguin Dictionary of Proper Names* and Harrap's *Dictionary of English Synonyms*. The publishing house of Routledge & Kegan Paul has produced an interesting range, from the *Dictionary of Slang and Unconventional English* to *A Dictionary of Jargon*, as well as *A Dictionary of Catch Phrases* and *Walker's Rhyming Dictionary of the English Language*.

For that all-important process of finding the right word to suit your purpose, explore a **thesaurus**. This may be the famous *Roget's Thesaurus* or an alternative volume: the thesaurus will greatly assist you in the business of word-searching.

Fully-researched ideas on all topics will be there in the **encyclopaedias**. The 'standard' work is the *Encyclopaedia Brittanica*, but you may find the more concise publications to be of greater value. The *Guinness Book of Answers*, for example, may lead you to see matters from an unexpected angle.

Events and important current facts are recorded and listed in an annual publication called *Whitaker's Almanac*. Likewise, the Central Statistics Office produces *Social Trends* once a year: here is a 'window of insight' into the ways in which we live in the UK, with information about population and households, education and employment, income and wealth, leisure and the environment, housing and transport.

Places are not neglected. The *Ordnance Survey* **maps** cover Britain in intricate detail and **gazetteers** will give you details of even the smallest place. **Road atlases** show the patterns of roads throughout the British Isles and *The Times Atlases* look at the world from an astonishing variety of projections and perspectives and according to various specialised interests.

Shelves are devoted to individual activities – from literature and music to sport and pastimes. No sooner has someone produced, written, composed, invented, played or devised anything of significance then someone else will collect the relevant material, distil it and bring out a **compendium** of information. The New York publisher, Charles Scribner's Sons, has produced under the auspices of the British Council a fine series on British writers which is of particular interest to those studying literature.

If it is information on people that is required, then there are at least three lines of inquiry. If they are famous, consult *The Dictionary of National Biography*. The first 22 volumes present material on people living until 1900. Then each decade of the 20th century has a separate volume devoted to its 'great and good'. General matters are dealt with in the various dictionaries on the derivations of surnames. Here it's possible to trace the most basic of family matters. Thirdly, if it's just the name, address and telephone number that you want, it's likely to be listed in the range of **telephone directories** which are usually on display and which cover the whole country.

Reference libraries usually have current **newspapers** and **periodicals**. These rooms are therefore well equipped to provide you with facts and ideas about yesterday as well as to matters relating to, say, the earliest geological periods of time. What has happened in between is recorded in detail ... and this information is available – for us.

Work out problems: language, understanding, summary

The problems in this chapter test: vocabulary, style, usage (including grammar), understanding, summary, punctuation and spelling. Answers are provided on pages 236–38, but do not look at the answer to a problem until you have written out your own solution. Use your dictionary and revise the relevant section (or sections) of this book while you are working out each problem and studying the answer.

Problem 1 (answers on page 236)

Form the negative of each of the following words by adding a prefix: confirmed, defensible, honourable, logical, proper, rational.

Problem 2 (answers on page 236)

For each of the following words write down a homophone. Then use each of the homophones that you have supplied in a sentence (six sentences in all) to show that you understand its meaning and use: beech, birth, maize, stake, taught, vale.

Problem 3 (answers on page 236)

Part of each of the sentences in this question is underlined. The underlined part is repeated after the letter **A** (printed below the sentence). After the letters **B** and **C** two other versions of the underlined part are given. By writing down the appropriate letter (**A**, **B** or **C**), indicate which of the three versions would be the best English in the context of the sentence.

1. The north face of a wall generally suits shade-loving <u>plants, the plants may not like the cold however</u>.
    - **A** plants, the plants may not like the cold however.
    - **B** plants, however the plants may not like the cold.
    - **C** plants; the plants, however, may not like the cold.

2   An unemployed person, the report shows, is <u>spending less than half on food than the weekly sum</u> spent by those in employment.
    A spending less than half on food than the weekly sum
    B spending on food less than half the weekly sum
    C spending less than half on food as compared with the weekly sum

3   Some diesel cars are <u>as fast as petrol-engined cars</u> of the same capacity and far more economical with fuel.
    A as fast as petrol-engined cars
    B equally as fast as petrol-engined cars
    C as equally fast as petrol-engined cars

4   We are hardly surprised <u>nowadays</u> when a popular newspaper, hungry for circulation, announces that there are fortunes to be won in its latest competition.
    A nowadays
    B in this day and age
    C currently

5   The candidate assured the voters that he would spend <u>the majority</u> of his time on parliamentary business.
    A the majority
    B the maximum amount
    C most

6   Seeing my old friend again after so many years, <u>he seemed very fit</u>.
    A he seemed very fit.
    B I thought he seemed very fit.
    C he struck me as seeming very fit.

7   The promoters of this entertainment must be either lacking in all sense of artistry <u>or they are shamelessly exploiting</u> their simple-minded audiences.
    A or they are shamelessly exploiting
    B if not shamelessly exploiting
    C or shamelessly exploiting

8   Ten minutes before the final whistle, United's careful tactics <u>literally came unstuck</u>.
    A literally came unstuck.
    B came unstuck.
    C definitely came unstuck.

9   Both my son and daughter did well in the examination but his career, unlike <u>hers</u>, lay in science.
    A hers
    B hers'
    C her's

10 If the new vaccine can be perfected, <u>hopefully this disease will be conquered</u>.
    A hopefully this disease will be conquered.
    B this disease will – hopefully – be conquered.
    C it may be hoped that this disease will be conquered.

Problem 4 (answers on page 236)

Rewrite the following sentence in reported speech, using each of the given introductions in turn (three sentences in all):

Do you always go to the seaside for your holidays?

1 Jane will ask me ...
2 I have asked Jane ...
3 Jane asked her aunt ...

Problem 5 (answers on page 236)

Rewrite the following passage in reported speech:

> 'I can't understand what's wrong with my new saw,' said Mr Brown. 'It's so blunt, it wouldn't cut butter.'
> 'There's nothing wrong with it, Dad,' replied his seven-year-old son Tommy. 'I know, because I cut through a big nail with it only yesterday.'

Problem 6 (answers on page 236)

> Bodily labour is of two kinds: either that which a man submits to for his livelihood or that which he undergoes for his pleasure. The latter of them generally changes the name of labour for that of exercise, but differs only from ordinary labour as it rises from another motive.
>
> A country life abounds in both these kinds of labour and, for that reason, gives a man a greater stock of health, and consequently a fuller enjoyment of himself than any other way of life.

1 Supply a suitable short title for the passage.
2 Make clear in your own words the distinction drawn between exercise and labour.
3 Make clear in your own words the three stages of the argument in the second paragraph by which the writer seeks to prove the superiority of a country life.

Problem 7 (answers on page 237)

Fill each gap in the following sentences with a word that, in the context, is of opposite meaning to the *italicised* word.

1 Although most of the characters in this novel are *fictitious*, some ... persons are introduced.
2 The ... vegetation of the upper slopes was now replaced by the *prolific* growth of the plains.
3 The *natural* charm and simple dignity of the old king were in sharp contrast to the ... manner and foppish airs of his son.
4 In less than six months, the financier sank from the *zenith* to the ... of his fortunes.
5 The *clumsiness* of the clown, his partner in the double act, heightened our appreciation of the juggler's ... .

Problem 8 (answers on page 237)

Some of the following sentences are examples of good usage; others are faulty. Each of the faulty sentences contains an error of one of the kinds indicated by **B, C, D, E** below.

A No error.
B Wrong choice of word – i.e. mistaken use of a word for one that it resembles.
   Example: We could not except their invitation.
C Lack of agreement (subject/verb or noun/pronoun).

Example: A packet of chocolates were given to each child.
A person can only do their best.

D Incorrect punctuation.
Example: Fan belt, distributor, sparking-plugs, were carefully checked.

E Unattached or wrongly attached phrases.
Examples: They enjoyed their hot drinks, cold after a swim.
Crossing the street, the church is a fine spectacle.

If a sentence contains no error of the kind **B**, **C**, **D** or **E**, mark it **A**; otherwise mark it with the letter corresponding to the kind of error it contains.

1. He designed a remarkable engine and being air-cooled he was able to cut production costs.
2. They promised the electors less interference and fewer taxes.
3. One of Europe's most imminent scientists then addressed the meeting.
4. Red Rum was one of the finest racehorses that has ever been seen.
5. People, who are over 65, qualify for age-relief under present tax regulations.
6. An editor's decision to publish or not to publish a scandalous story depends on what his criteria are.
7. After 1900, the merit of Hardy's poetry was widely recognised, but formally he was better known for his novels.
8. Labouring in heavy seas, the trawler put out distress signals at midnight.
9. Keeping up with fashion, the old furniture was sent to auction and replaced by modern pieces.
10. With those qualifications, you could try to become a journalist; alternately, you could train as a librarian.

Problem 9 (answers on page 237)

Which of the two sentences in each of the following pairs more accurately conveys the sense intended?

1a. I had a letter from my father, who was staying in London.
1b. I had a letter from my father who was staying in London.

2a. Visitors are requested not to give the animals food, which will harm them.
2b. Visitors are requested not to give the animals food which will harm them.

3a. My experience has been that horses, which are mealy-muzzled, run well.
3b. My experience has been that horses which are mealy-muzzled run well.

Problem 10 (answers on page 237)

Bring each of these sentences into line with good English usage. Make as few changes as possible and do not alter the intended sense.

1. All students do not learn German.
2. The reason why he was not elected to the committee was because he made such a bad speech.
3. Cowering under the bridge, an enemy patrol saw the bedraggled and frightened fugitive.
4. Walking is perhaps the best form of relaxation for, unlike golf, fishing or motoring, no elaborate and expensive equipment is required.

5 In recent years, sales have proved conclusively that customers prefer automatic than twin-tub washers.

Problem 11 (answers on page 237)

Select the appropriate letter from the list below to indicate which of these sentences are grammatically correct.
1 His alibi was good.
2 The criteria was questionable.
3 The ensemble was playing at the Wigmore Hall.
4 The parenthesis was marked off with commas.
5 The phenomena was thoroughly investigated.

    A 1 and 2 only
    B 2 and 3 only
    C 3 and 5 only
    D 1, 3 and 4 only
    E 2, 4 and 5 only

Problem 12 (answers on page 237)

Select the appropriate letter to indicate the correct meaning of each of these words.
1 mortuary is:
    A brickwork
    B a keen sense of disappointment
    C a building in which dead bodies are kept for a time
    D a deadening sensation in the limbs
2 plummet is:
    A a small plum
    B a sounding-line
    C graphite
    D a nestling's feather
3 ossification is:
    A being snubbed
    B becoming stupid
    C over-eating
    D turning (or being turned) into bone
4 proselytise is:
    A to demonstrate angrily
    B to turn verse into prose
    C to make converts
    D to take precedence
5 subjugate is:
    A to strangle
    B to conquer
    C to name the inflexions of a verb
    D to delegate authority

Problem 13 (answers on page 237)

Read this passage carefully and then answer the questions.

In our time it is broadly true that political writing is bad writing. Where it is not true it will generally be found that the writer is some kind of rebel, expressing his private opinions, and not a 'party line'. Orthodoxy, of whatever colour, seems to demand a lifeless, imitative style. The political
5 dialects to be found in pamphlets, leading articles, manifestos, White Papers

and the speeches of Under-Secretaries do, of course, vary from party to party, but they are all alike in that one almost never finds in them a fresh, vivid, home-made turn of speech. When one watches some tired hack on the platform mechanically repeating the familiar phrases – *bestial atrocities,* *iron heel, blood-stained tyranny, free peoples of the world, stand shoulder to shoulder* – one often has the curious feeling that one is not watching a live human being but some kind of dummy: a feeling which suddenly becomes stronger at moments when the light catches the speaker's spectacles and turns them into blank discs which seem to have no eyes behind them. And this is not altogether fanciful. A speaker who uses that kind of phraseology has gone some distance towards turning himself into a machine. The appropriate noises are coming out of his larynx, but his brain is not involved as it would be if he were choosing his words for himself. If the speech he is making is one that he is accustomed to make over and over again, he may be almost unconscious of what he is saying, as one is when one utters the responses in church. And this reduced state of consciousness, if not indispensable, is at any rate favourable to political conformity.

1 As used in the passage, 'Orthodoxy, of whatever colour' (lines 3–4) means much the same as
 A any style of writing
 B religious belief of any kind
 C conformity with the accepted beliefs of any political party
 D emotive expressions of the right or the left

2 The writer asserts in lines 4–8 that
 A dialects hamper politicians
 B the political speeches of Under-Secretaries are more vivid than pamphlets, leading articles and manifestos
 C the various parties differ widely in their propaganda
 D the language of political speeches and writing is stale, ready-made stuff

3 The 'tired hack on the platform' (lines 8–9) is
 A a weary rebel
 B a partly defaced slogan behind the speaker
 C part of the public address system
 D a politician mouthing platitudes

4 The suggestion in lines 12–15 is that
 A the speaker's eyesight is poor
 B the speaker is dehumanised
 C the speaker lacks political insight
 D the speaker is not the centre of attention

5 The phrase 'that kind of phraseology' (lines 15–16) refers to
 A the 'private opinions' mentioned earlier
 B expressions such as those in italics
 C home-made turns of speech
 D the responses made in church services

6 The writer is highly critical of the political language 'of our time' for all but one of the following reasons; which one?
 A It is repetitive.
 B It is not the product of hard thought.
 C It increases party differences.
 D It reflects a lowered level of political awareness.

Problem 14 (answers on page 237)

Study this passage carefully and then answer the questions.

> There are many striking similarities between English and German. Some of the most commonly used words in the two languages look alike and sound similar: *Gras* = grass; *Korn* = corn; *Haus* = house; *bringen* = to bring; *hart* = hard; *gut* = good. These are but a very few of many possible examples. Philologists have proved that many English and German words which no longer look or sound similar, and which now have very different meanings, go back to a common origin. In grammar, too, the languages share certain characteristics, notably in the formation of comparatives and superlatives, the conjugation of verbs, and the genitive case. The evidence that the two tongues derive from the same source is overwhelming; but it is equally true that they have developed along very different lines, as anyone who is in a position to contrast the complications of German grammar with the simplicity of English grammar will readily agree.

1. In not more than 10 words, provide a suitable title for the passage.
2. Identify three points mentioned in the passage that are used to prove a common origin for the two languages.
3. Which of those points serves to bring out both their similarities and their differences?
4. Summarise the passage in not more than 40 of your own words.

Problem 15 (answers on page 237)

Rewrite the following sentences in plain, direct English. Do not change the meaning.

1. It is regretted that your claim, which has been under active consideration, cannot be accepted by the District Assessor.
2. In the majority of cases, it was possible for students to be found placements operative within the period of time elapsing between the conclusion of the summer term and the commencement of the September session.
3. If it is decided that your application for admission to this course has been successful, you will receive notification on or before 1 November.
4. For a period of several years after the cessation of hostilities, the availability of new cars to the consumer was adversely conditioned by the supply situation then obtaining, and a severe shortage developed in relation to the considerable demand experienced.
5. In my mind it is much to be deplored that the Council has thought fit not to give an affirmative response to the proposal to refurbish the seating accommodation in the concert hall on the grounds of self-imposed financial constraints.

Problem 16 (answers on page 238)

Write out the following, supplying the correct punctuation.

1. The students buses were unloading at 9 oclock.
2. Its necessary said the teacher to use punctuation youll confuse your readers if you dont.
3. The childrens enthusiasm increased as the conjuror performed trick after trick reaching a climax when a white rabbits head emerged from a top hat.

4 The builder said that he could paint the metalwork but stresses and strains were engineers problems he couldnt be expected to be responsible for the structures strength.

5 I very much doubt said Tom whether you fully understand the message I want you to deliver to Fred I certainly do replied Jack you want me to tell him that the practice will be on Thursday this week thats just the point exclaimed Tom Thursday next week not Thursday this week its on Wednesday as usual this week is it yes Ive said so twice already perhaps youd better give him the message yourself perhaps I had

Problem 17 (answers on page 238)

Select the correct words to fill the gaps in these sentences.

1 He was the kind of leader ... everybody admires. (who/whom)
2 I am sure he is the man ... we saw at the bus stop yesterday. (who/whom)
3 If the experienced players cannot understand the new rules, what hope is there for ... beginners? (we/us)
4 The cause underlying these recurrent disagreements, which are dangerous in present circumstances, ... for international action. (call/calls)
5 Nobody ... enter the keep ... obtaining written permission. (can/may; unless/without)
6 He would, I know, be grateful if you ... help him to raise money for this project. (would/will)
7 The plot of the play centres ... intricate personal relationships. (round/on)
8 The inquest exonerated the nurse ... any blame; congratulated her, in fact, on a ... decision (from/against; couragous/courageous)
9 Candidates must not enter the examination room more than 15 minutes before the paper is due to begin ... leave before it is due to end. (or/nor)
10 If that ... a knock at the door, it was probably the postman. (were/was)

Problem 18 (answers on page 238)

At some of the numbered points in the passage below, the usual marks of punctuation have been omitted. The punctuation marks omitted are of the following kinds: comma, semicolon, colon, full stop followed by capital letter. At some of the points numbered, on the other hand, none of those marks should be used, as to do so would be superfluous or even contrary to the sense of the passage. Indicate by one of the letters **A** to **E** which mark of punctuation, if any, you would use at each of the places numbered, as follows:

- **A** no mark of punctuation
- **B** comma
- **C** semicolon
- **D** colon
- **E** full stop followed by capital letter

Three possible explanations of the accident were put forward (**1**) a worn tyre, unnoticed at the time because of the many (**2**) radical changes in maintenance procedures at the garage (**3**) inadequate lubrication of the gearbox (**4**) and the fracture of a vacuum pipe (**5**) on which smoothly progressive braking depended (**6**) each of these theories was investigated (**7**) none provided a satisfactory explanation (**8**) in view of these findings (**9**) we may never know the cause of a most unusual accident (**10**) which cost lives and money (**11**) unless (**12**) that is (**13**) some quite remarkable (**14**) and unsuspected evidence is eventually uncovered.

Problem 19 (answers on page 238)

With one exception, each of the following sentences uses two expressions where one would suffice. Which sentence does *not*?

1. When the lights changed to green, the learner-driver reversed at a brisk pace back into the front of the car behind.
2. The government made great use of its argument that most of the electors would find it more preferable to pay less in taxes rather than to have increased pay.
3. You could use inferior materials, but the job would not last and it would be only marginally cheaper.
4. As expected, Betty won in the final, being a very strong forehand player and relatively superior to Celia at the net.
5. We called at the hotel in Birmingham at which, so the local news led us to believe, the touring team intended to stay at when they left London.

Problem 20 (answers on page 238)

Read the following passage and then answer the questions.

> The letter, which was signed by several of the disaffected soldiers, painted in gloomy colours the miseries of their condition, accused the two commanders of being the authors of this, and called on the higher authorities to intervene by sending a vessel to take them from that desolate spot while some of them might still be found surviving the horrors of their confinement. The letter concluded with a paragraph in which the two commanders were stigmatised as partners in a slaughterhouse: one being employed to drive in the cattle for the other to butcher.

1. Give the meaning of the following expressions as they are used in the passage: (a) disaffected; (b) painted in gloomy colours; (c) the authors of this; (d) be found surviving the horrors of their confinement; (e) stigmatised.
2. Without using figurative language, reword the soldiers' description of their commanders.

ANSWERS

Problem 1 (page 227)

unconfirmed; indefensible; dishonourable; illogical; improper; irrational.

Problem 2 (page 227)

beach; berth; maze; steak; taut; veil.

1 A sandy beach is a great asset to a holiday resort.
2 The yacht was at its berth near the old quay.
3 No visitor had ever succeeded in finding the way out of the maze, which was formed of high yew hedges.
4 Traditionally, large, juicy steaks have been the principal diet of boxers and rowing-men.
5 They pulled hard on the slack mooring rope until it was taut.
6 Her features were hidden by a veil of black lace.

Problem 3 (page 227)

1 C; 2 B; 3 A; 4 A; 5 C; 6 B; 7 C; 8 B; 9 A; 10 C.

Problem 4 (page 228)

1 Jane will ask me whether I always go to the seaside for my holidays.
2 I have asked Jane whether she always goes to the seaside for her holidays.
3 Jane asked her aunt whether she always went to the seaside for her holidays.

Problem 5 (page 229)

Mr Brown said that he could not understand what was wrong with his new saw, which was so blunt that it would no longer cut anything. His seven-year-old son Tommy replied that he knew that there was nothing wrong with the saw because, only the day before, he had cut through a big nail with it.

Problem 6 (page 229)

1 A Country Life: Healthiest and Best.
2 Labour is the physical work undergone for a living; whereas exercise is the physical work undertaken for pleasure.
3 The first stage of the argument states that both kinds of labour are plentiful in a country life. The second stage claims that better health follows from that. The third stage concludes that, as a result, a country life provides greater pleasure derived from enhanced self-fulfilment.

Problem 7 (page 229)

1 historical;   2 sparse;   3 artificial;   4 nadir;   5 dexterity.

Problem 8 (page 229)

1 E;   2 A;   3 B;   4 C;   5 D;   6 A;   7 B;   8 A;   9 E;   10 B.

Problem 9 (page 230)

1 a;   2 b;   3 b.

Problem 10 (page 230)

1 Not all students learn German.
2 The reason he was not elected to the committee was that he made a bad speech.
3 An enemy patrol saw the bedraggled and frightened fugitive cowering under the bridge.
4 Walking is perhaps the best form of relaxation for, unlike golf, fishing or motoring, it does not require elaborate and expensive equipment.
5 In recent years, sales have proved conclusively that customers prefer automatic to twin-tub washers.

Problem 11 (page 231)

D

Problem 12 (page 231)

1 C;   2 B;   3 D;   4 C;   5 B.

Problem 13 (page 231)

1 C;   2 D;   3 D;   4 B;   5 B;   6 C.

Problem 14 (page 233)

1 The similarities and the differences between English and German.
(9 words)
2 (a) Many of their most frequently used words look and sound alike. (b) Many other words have a common origin. (c) They have similarities of grammar.
3 The grammatical evidence.
4 The similarities between and shared origins of many English and German words, together with some grammatical affinities, prove the kinship of the two languages. Nevertheless, they have moved far apart, as their contrasting grammars show.   *(35 words)*

Problem 15 (page 233)

1 Your claim has been considered carefully, but the District Assessor is sorry to say that he cannot accept it.
2 Placements for the summer vacation were found for most students.
3 You will be told by 1 November if you have been accepted for this course.

4 For several years after the war ended, fewer cars were made than there were customers for them.
5 I deplore the Council's decision not to spend money on new seats for the concert hall.

Problem 16 (page 233)

1 The students' buses were unloading at 9 o'clock.
2 'It's necessary', said the teacher, 'to use punctuation. You'll confuse your readers if you don't.'
3 The children's enthusiasm increased as the conjuror performed trick after trick, reaching a climax when a white rabbit's head emerged from a top hat.
4 The builder said that he could paint the metalwork, but stresses and strains were engineers' problems; he couldn't be expected to be responsible for the structure's strength.
5 'I very much doubt,' said Tom, 'whether you fully understand the message I want you to deliver to Fred.'
'I certainly do,' replied Jack. 'You want me to tell him that the practice will be on Thursday this week.'
'That's just the point!' exclaimed Tom. 'Thursday next week, not Thursday this week. It's on Wednesday, as usual, this week.'
'Is it?'
'Yes. I've said so twice, already.'
'Perhaps you'd better give him the message yourself.'
'Perhaps I had!'

Problem 17 (page 234)

1	whom;	6	can;
2	whom;	7	on;
3	us;	8	from, courageous;
4	calls;	9	nor;
5	may, without;	10	was.

Problem 18 (page 234)

1 D; 2 A; 3 C; 4 C; 5 A; 6 E; 7 E; 8 E; 9 B; 10 A; 11 C; 12 B; 13 B; 14 A.

Problem 19 (page 235)

Sentence 3.

Problem 20 (page 235)

1 (a) disloyal; (b) described in depressing words; (c) responsible for their situation; (d) be still alive despite their suffering in prison; (e) singled out for blame.
2 Their commanders inflicted casualties mercilessly upon them; one driving them into the killing ground where the other slew them.

INDEX

adjectives 185–7
adverbs 189
Anglo-Saxon 21
answers 236–8
antecedent 186
antonyms 173
apostrophes 207
argumentative writing 132
article-writing 92–5
attainment targets 11–15

brackets, round 209
brackets, square 209
brainstorming 80–1

cases 198–200
circumlocution 178
clauses 194
clichés 180
colloquialisms 181
colons 206–7
commas 204–6
commas, inverted 207–9
compendious words 173
conjunctions 190
coursework 7–9

dashes 208–9
description 150–4
devices 45–6
dialects 12
dictionaries 225
differentiation 17–19
directed writing 121–9
discursive writing 154–8
dramatic writing 158–61

editing 100–19
Education Reform Act 1988 11
errors, common 195–201
examinations 2–5
exclamation mark 204
expression 131–64

fact and feeling 174

figurative language 173
finite and non-finite verbs 188
full stop 203–4

gerund 188
gestures 25
gobbledegook 180
grammar, correct 185–201

handwriting 220–4
homophones 173, 215
hyphens 209–10

idiomatic expressions 175
impressionistic writing 161–4
inflexions 185, 190
interjections 190
intransitive verbs 188
inverted commas 207–8

jargon 174

letters 84–9, 166–7
levels 17
listening 11, 28–31
literacy rates 12
literal language 173
literary analysis 43–6

malapropisms 177
Middle English 21
misusing words 177–83
mood of verbs 188

narrative 135–50
National Curriculum 3, 11
Norman French 21
nouns 186

Old English 21

participles 188
parts of speech 185–6
personal letters 166–7
phrases 191, 200–1

phrase structures 192–3
pomposity 179
précis 102
predicate 172, 191
prepositions 189–90
presentation 5, 220–4
problems 227–35
pronouns 186, 196–7, 201
proverbial expressions 175
punctuation 203–10

question mark 204

reading 12, 33–47
Received Pronunciation 12
reference material 225–6
reported speech 108–10
reports 89–92
round brackets 209

self-assessment 27
sentences 191, 193–5
slang 182
speaking and listening 11, 25–31
speech mechanisms 26
spelling 212–18
square brackets 209
Standard English 12
subject 191
suffixes 172
summary 101, 102–19
synonyms 172

tautology 178
tenses 187
transitive verbs 188

verbosity 180
verbs 187–9, 195–6, 200
vocabulary 79, 171
voice projection 26

words, using 169–75
writing 15, 78–82, 84–98

Macmillan Work Out Series

For GCSE examinations
Accounting
Biology
Business Studies
Chemistry
Computer Studies
English Key Stage 4
French (cassette and pack available)
Geography
German (cassette and pack available)
Modern World History
Human Biology
Core Maths Key Stage 4
Revise Mathematics to further level
Physics
Religious Studies
Science
Social and Economic History
Spanish (cassette and pack available)
Statistics

For A Level examinations
Accounting
Biology
Business Studies
Chemistry
Economics
English
French (cassette and pack available)
Mathematics
Physics
Psychology
Sociology
Statistics